The Urban Struggle f Environmental and Sc

This book discusses the current demographic shifts of blacks, Latinos, and other people of color out of certain strong-market cities and the growing fear of displacement among low-income urban residents. It documents these populations' efforts to remain in their communities and highlights how this leads to community organizing around economic, environmental, and social justice. The book shows how residents of once-neglected urban communities are standing up to city economic development agencies, influential real estate developers, universities, and others to remain in their neighborhoods, protect their interests, and transform their communities into sustainable, healthy communities. These communities are deploying new strategies that build off of past struggles over urban renewal. Based on seven years of research, this book draws on a wealth of material to conduct a case study analysis of eight low-/mixed-income communities in Boston, New York, San Francisco, and Washington, DC.

This timely book is aimed at researchers and postgraduate students interested in urban policy and politics, community development, urban studies, environmental justice, urban public health, sociology, community-based research methods, and urban planning theory and practice. It will also be of interest to policy makers, community activists, and the private sector.

Malo André Hutson is an Assistant Professor in the Department of City and Regional Planning at the University of California at Berkeley, USA, and Associate Director of the Institute of Urban and Regional Development. He is also a faculty affiliate of the UC Berkeley/UCSF Medical School Robert Wood Johnson Foundation Health and Society Scholars program.

Routledge Equity, Justice and the Sustainable City Series
Series editors: Julian Agyeman, Zarina Patel,
Abdou Maliq Simone, and Stephen Zavestoski

This series positions equity and justice as central elements of the transition toward sustainable cities. This series introduces critical perspectives and new approaches to the practice and theory of urban planning and policy that ask how the world's cities can become "greener" while becoming more fair, equitable and just.

The Routledge Equity, Justice and the Sustainable City series addresses sustainable city trends in the global North and South and investigates them for their potential to ensure a transition to urban sustainability that is equitable and just for all. These trends include municipal climate action plans; resource scarcity as a tipping point into a vortex of urban dysfunction; inclusive urbanization; "complete streets" as a tool for realizing more "livable cities"; and the use of information and analytics toward the creation of "smart cities".

This series welcomes submissions for high-level, cutting-edge research books that push thinking about sustainability, cities, justice, and equity in new directions by challenging current conceptualizations and developing new ones. This series offers theoretical, methodological, and empirical advances that can be used by professionals and as supplementary reading in courses in urban geography, urban sociology, urban policy, environment and sustainability, development studies, planning, and a wide range of academic disciplines.

Incomplete Streets
Processes, practices and possibilities
Edited by Stephen Zavestoski and Julian Agyeman

Planning Sustainable Cities and Regions
Towards more equitable development
Karen Chapple

The Urban Struggle for Economic, Environmental and Social Justice
Deepening their roots
Malo André Hutson

"At last, a book that looks at some of the ways in which gentrification has been reined in. The book provides a wide-ranging and largely convincing account of the alliances that have made possible some legal constraints to be placed on unrestrained gentrification."

−Tim Butler, King's College London, UK

The Urban Struggle for Economic, Environmental and Social Justice

Deepening their roots

Malo André Hutson

LONDON AND NEW YORK

First published 2016
by Routledge
2 Park Square, Milton Park, Abingdon, Oxfordshire OX14 4RN
and by Routledge
711 Third Avenue, New York, NY 10017

First issued in paperback 2016

*Routledge is an imprint of the Taylor & Francis Group, an informa
business.*

British Library Cataloguing-in-Publication Data
A catalogue record for this book is available from the British Library.

Library of Congress Cataloging-in-Publication Data
Hutson, Malo, author.
   The urban struggle for economic, environmental and social justice :
deepening their roots / Malo Andr? Hutson.
      pages cm
   Includes bibliographical references and index.
   1. Community development, Urban—United States.   2. Urban
policy—United States.   3. Sociology, Urban—United States.   I. Title.
   HN90.C6H87 2016
   307.1'4160973—dc23
   2015023453

ISBN 13: 978-0-415-78544-0 (pbk)
ISBN 13: 978-1-138-81770-8 (hbk)

Typeset in Sabon
by Apex CoVantage, LLC

Contents

Illustrations

Table

Figures

Preface
The idea and rationale for this book

The idea for researching and writing this book grew out of my personal, professional, and academic work. My interest in this research topic was first sparked by my own lived experience, and that of observing the experiences of the people closest to me. Like many African Americans of their generation, my grandparents left behind their small-town roots in Mississippi in search of more opportunity. After two decades in the army, my grandparents settled in Inglewood, California, in the 1970s. My great-uncles and great-aunts followed, along with their families, and ultimately settled in Inglewood and Compton, California. (Decades later, some of these same relatives would move back to Mississippi.)

Most of my adolescence, however, was spent in a suburb outside of Los Angeles, in the Inland Empire. By the time I was in junior high, my mother, and one of her sisters, both young, single mothers, moved their children (including me) to the Inland Empire in search of affordability, safety, and good public schools. By sixteen I understood some of the complicated choices my mother had made for my siblings and me. My mother could not afford to house us in the coastal cities in California closer to her family without living in the most dangerous neighborhoods within some of the most under-performing public school districts. My mother chose safety and better schools over staying close to her extended family network.

But with this choice came isolation. We were poor and did not own a car, *in the Inland Empire in Southern California in the 1980s and early 1990s.* Anyone who has lived or visited the area knows that public transportation was minimal at the time (so minimal it was practically nonexistent). So where we lived greatly impacted my life and my trajectory. On one hand, I lived in a community that at the time was much safer than what my mother would have been able to afford had we lived along the coast. On the other hand, I observed the challenges of keeping a job without adequate transportation. This experience shaped my own personal preference for living in the urban core.

Although I did not know that my family's choices were indicative of an urban shift occurring at the time, my own experiences laid the foundation for my interest in issues related to where people live, why they choose to live there, and why where they live matters. I did not understand this interest as a precursor for my future path into urban planning, and more specifically examining community development, poverty, and health equity issues. But this interest would shape my future academic choices.

After high school I moved to the Bay Area and attended college at the University of California at Berkeley. This was the first time in my young life that I had the opportunity to live in a densely populated area, within walking distance to everything that I needed with access to public transit that would take me anywhere I wanted to go. I saw first-hand the benefits of having this access.

While at Berkeley, I also was able to witness the neighborhood change happening in San Francisco in the mid- to late 1990s. The first dot-com boom was under way and young people from all over the world flocked to the Bay Area, especially San Francisco, to work and live. Rents quickly soared and housing prices started to reach unprecedented levels. Neighborhoods in San Francisco such as the South of Market and Mission District were transformed by housing construction and the older warehouses in the area were converted to meet Internet and software companies' growing demand for office space (Beitel, 2013). As I completed my bachelor's and master's in city planning, I personally witnessed some of the battles that took place in the Mission District over gentrification and displacement.

Still, I had no concept of how big of a phenomenon this issue was until I moved to Boston, Massachusetts, to attend graduate school. As a black man growing up in Southern California, I had heard stories about Boston and its history of racial strife. I had also heard about the majority black neighborhood of Roxbury and its rich culture and history. While a graduate student at the Massachusetts Institute of Technology in the early 2000s, I chose to live in Roxbury and in the Jamaica Plain neighborhood in Boston.

It did not take long for me to witness all the changes happening in these two neighborhoods and in other neighborhoods such as Mission Hill and the South End (which according to my neighbors was well on its way to gentrifying). Old brownstones were being completely gutted and renovated; new cafes and restaurants were popping up and replacing the older bodegas or liquor stores. The change was not necessarily rapid, but it was constant. By the mid-2000s, you did not need research to tell you what was happening; you could see the difference in these neighborhoods with respect to the investment in housing and infrastructure. The neighborhoods I lived in were still relatively diverse, so when more affluent residents bought homes (which were still a bargain relative to homes in other parts of the city), it was obvious. Moreover, the Longwood Medical and Academic Area in Boston, which I will discuss in greater detail later on in this book, was expanding and the development was noticeable. New buildings were rising and the streets and neighborhoods adjacent to the development were impacted by traffic congestion, increases in monthly rents, and the overall demand for housing.

All of these prior experiences exposed me to the changes happening in some urban neighborhoods. My interest in neighborhood change and community development peaked after I began a work assignment in Washington, DC, between the years 2002 and 2005. Before this, I had traveled rather frequently to Washington, DC for the better part of ten years, but those trips were short and my ability to explore the city was limited. This time my assignment required me to travel around Washington, DC, and I could see the changes taking place. For example, my trips to the Adams Morgan neighborhood enabled me to see how widespread the home renovations were. When I would go out to eat on U Street I was amazed to see the pace at which new restaurants and bars opened. Even more noticeable was the demographic shift. The people frequenting these establishments were in many ways like me at the time; they were relatively young, fresh out of college, and starting their careers. Many were raised in the suburbs and were determined to live "the city life." But they were diverse racially and ethnically.

Seeing these physical, economic, and demographic changes in neighborhoods that were historically majority black or people of color raised many questions for me. Why was this change "suddenly" happening? What does this change mean for the long-term residents? How will residents, especially less affluent residents, endure this change economically?

These questions laid the foundation for this book. After I returned to the Bay Area as a professor of community development at Berkeley, I saw first-hand the change that has happened and is happening in San Francisco, which has gained international attention. The level of neighborhood change and displacement is not only impacting San Francisco but also cities within the region, like Oakland. San Francisco has lost most of its black population and now Oakland has lost more than 25 percent of its black population in the past decade (Kuruvilla, 2011). Fear about gentrification grows as housing costs reach stratospheric levels and monthly rents are beyond what many low- to moderate-income households can afford. More recently, fear of "gentrification" and displacement is spreading through Richmond, California, a predominately working-class black city about eighteen miles from San Francisco.

Even with the assumption that neighborhoods change and have always changed, this change seems different than those in the past. This urban change in strong-market cities, driven by many external factors (such as the access to and abundance of cheap investment capital, rising income inequality, restructuring of the labor market, and preference for city living), appears to be more intense and has serious consequences for the middle-class, less affluent individuals, and communities of color. So how does a community "survive" this change? What community strategies and policies can keep people in place? This is what this book attempts to understand.

1 The new struggle for economic, environmental, and social justice

Introduction

Today, strong-market cities such as Boston, New York, Seattle, San Francisco, and Washington, DC, are experiencing tremendous economic growth fueled by high-skilled labor, investment capital, and entrepreneurial activity (Moretti, 2012). These cities have witnessed significant job growth in information and knowledge-based jobs in sectors such as biotechnology, engineering, medical research and services, software development, and pharmaceuticals, which require formal education and/or advanced skills (Moretti, 2012). As a result, high-skilled labor has migrated to these cities in search of economic and entrepreneurial opportunities. This growth contributes to the rising cost of land and housing, resulting in gentrification[1] (and in some cases super-gentrification) and the displacement of many less-skilled, poor, and working-class urban populations out of the city to less affluent outer-ring suburbs (Lees, 2003; Frey, 2011).

Much of the planning literature has focused on discussions regarding how to measure gentrification and its relationship to displacement (Sumka, 1979; Marcuse, 1986; Freeman and Braconi, 2004), identifying the gentrifiers (Castells, 1983; Lauria and Knopp, 1985; Ley, 1994) and the resistance to gentrification (Hartman, 1984; Newman and Wyly, 2006), and describing the process of gentrification and neighborhood change (Clay, 1979; Hackworth and Smith, 2001). In addition, previous research and theory in this area suggests that the current economic growth and growing inequality within strong market cities is a result of market forces (Sassen 1998, 2000) or direct neoliberal policies by government that make it a "consummate agent of the market" (Smith, 1979, 2002). For example, many argue that the rising cost of rents and housing prices in California are simply a direct result of low supply and high demand or that the growing income inequality found in cities such as San Francisco can partially be explained by the skills and education mismatch between low-income job seekers and the higher-skilled, higher-pay knowledge- and information-based jobs (Moretti, 2012). Some scholars also suggest that the growing income inequality and rising cost of living within strong-market cities is a direct result of city, state, and federal policies that have contributed to a bifurcated labor market of high-skilled, high-income jobs on one end and lower-skilled, lower-income jobs on the other, resulting in the hollowing out of middle-class jobs and contributing to growing income inequality (Smith, 2002; Hacker and Pierson, 2010).

While this book observes factors typically associated with gentrification and the risk of displacement, this book does not focus on its causes. Instead, this work focuses on the strategies residents, community groups, and local government officials are using to resist gentrification and includes examples of these strategies. These chapters discuss how relationships between community members and local government officials form, and can become strained, over the course of this resistance. It examines how community members use organizing, planning, and community development tools, local ballot initiatives, and the courts to resist gentrification.

Methodology

This book is based on the culmination of seven years of research in community and economic development across four cities nationwide. To examine how community members and community organizations resist neighborhood change, I conducted case studies of certain neighborhoods in four strong-market cities: Boston, New York City, San Francisco, and Washington, DC. I selected neighborhoods in strong-market cities in the United States because strong-market cities have specific characteristics that make them well-suited to case studies examining issues related to gentrification. They all have strong economies driven largely by innovation sectors (defined as advanced manufacturing, information technology, life sciences, medical devices, robotics, new materials, and nanotechnology), finance, advanced research, and a highly skilled labor force (Moretti, 2012). All four of my case study cities rank within the top six of U.S. metropolitan areas in this category. Each case study city is located in a metropolitan region that has also experienced an increase in suburban poverty over the past decade.

I selected these four case study cities based on a number of factors. First, the cities had to be strong-market cities, as discussed earlier. These cities have a high concentration of knowledge-based jobs, high levels of an educated/skilled workforce (based on those twenty-five years or older with a B.A. or higher). Second, I looked at the level of gross metropolitan product (GMP). Third, I analyzed neighborhood change using government administrative data (U.S. Census, American Community Survey, Annual Housing Survey from HUD, Home Mortgage Disclosure Act data) for the period between 1990 and 2010. I selected cities according to significant changes in the following categories of demographic data that infer displacement: income (defined as individual and household income), housing (defined as the number of affordable housing units, market-priced housing units, physical upgrading of housing stock), and educational status (including professional or managerial individuals/households, renters, educational attainment such as a B.A. for those twenty-five years and older). Finally, I looked at cities with significant community mobilization around resisting gentrification and displacement.

As part of my research, I conducted 112 in-depth interviews with elected officials, real estate developers, community and nonprofit leaders, and community residents. In addition, I was a participant observer at community meetings, public protests, and community organizing events. I was also a direct observer at public hearings and spent time either living in or visiting these neighborhoods for several weeks at a time, allowing me to interact with local residents and walk around the neighborhoods that are part of my case studies. I also, where possible, gathered documents related to development plans, community benefits agreements, and memorandums of understanding. I also read newspaper articles, Internet blogs, and other sources of media to gather background information.

Although a significant proportion of my research includes an analysis at the metropolitan and city levels, my case studies focus on specific neighborhoods within Boston, New York, San Francisco, and Washington, DC, where community activism and organizing is concentrated around large real estate development projects and neighborhood demographic and economic change is happening rapidly.

Outline of this book

Chapter 2 focuses on the demographic shift back into cities over recent decades. I also discuss how the post–World War II economic restructuring has transformed strong-market cities from industrial and manufacturing centers to centers of innovation and creativity led by knowledge-based sectors. As a consequence, strong-market cities are no longer built on an economy based on industrial and manufacturing sectors but instead are built on advanced research and development sectors, causing these cities to be increasingly in competition globally with other cities to innovate and promote entrepreneurial activity, to attract investment capital, and to recruit highly skilled labor in order to support and expand high-value sectors. This results in local governments, real estate developers, universities/research centers, and others working together to maximize the use value of land, thus causing the development of underutilized land. Ultimately, this causes social stratification between individuals and place, resulting in inequality within cities and regions (Logan and Molotch, 1987).

I also describe an awakening that has been taking hold since the 1990s within traditionally marginalized urban communities of color. These communities are concerned with displacement, the rising cost of living, high unemployment, low-performing schools, and other social ills and how this places them at a disadvantage in the new economy. In response to these economic and social pressures, these communities have formed community coalitions focused on *place-based* community development aimed at improving their economic, environmental, and social conditions. This new movement is different from previous community development efforts during the periods of urban renewal. These grassroots community efforts across the country have adopted an environmental and social justice framework that is fighting for such things as good-quality jobs, affordable housing, and sustainable development, with the goal of creating "healthy sustainable" urban communities.

Chapter 3 presents the case study of Boston, Massachusetts, and how Boston is arguably the leading center for research and innovation in the medical field. I discuss how the Longwood Medical and Academic Area (LMA) is continually expanding into the surrounding poorer neighborhoods of color. This has created a contentious relationship between LMA institutions and community residents around traffic congestion, rising land and housing costs, displacement of lower-income individuals, gentrification, and environmental pollution. I also analyze how Jamaica Plain Neighborhood Development Corporation (JPNDC) and other nonprofit community-based organization (CBOs) partners were able to form a public-private partnership with local hospitals, medical facilities, and research organizations that led to a community-focused workforce development and community benefits program in Boston. This case study demonstrates how Boston became one of the first cities to tie economic development to community-based outcomes aimed at helping some of Boston's most disadvantaged and vulnerable residents through the city's redevelopment agency.

In Chapter 4, I discuss residents' struggle to hold government and developers accountable for promises made to them in conjunction with the Atlantic Yards/Pacific Park development in Brooklyn, New York. The Atlantic Yards/Pacific Park development was originally proposed as a mixed-use commercial and residential development on approximately twenty-two acres of land in Brooklyn. The development was supposed to include the construction of sixteen high-rise buildings, including the Barclays Center, the home of the National Basketball Association's New Jersey Nets franchise. I follow how the BrooklynSpeaks community coalition organized residents to ensure that the Atlantic Yards/Pacific Park development provided local residents with the community benefits that the private developers promised to them.

Chapter 5 discusses the demographic and economic changes happening in San Francisco from the growth of the information and technology sectors. I document how San Francisco's housing and rental markets continue to rise, making it hard for low- to moderate-income residents to stay in their neighborhoods, particularly the city's Mission District neighborhood. I analyze the efforts of Calle 24, a community coalition, and how it has successfully organized local residents to advocate for affordable housing as well as work with the City of San Francisco to preserve the history and culture of the predominately Latino neighborhood.

Chapter 6 presents the case study of the economic and demographic changes in Washington, DC. Specifically, I focus on the Columbia Heights, Logan Circle, and Shaw neighborhoods of Washington, DC. I document how the city has experienced significant growth of jobs and redevelopment over the past twenty years, leading to drastic demographic shifts, a rise in housing prices, and an increase in new investments in infrastructure and local amenities (such as restaurants, parks, and bicycle lanes). I follow the efforts of ONE DC, a membership-based community organization focused on promoting equitable development for local residents and challenging local city government to provide the community with more local control over the land use and planning process.

Chapter 7 argues that previously used community development efforts and policies over the past twenty years have been ineffective in addressing poverty, inequality, and displacement given today's changes within strong-market cities. I emphasize that new place-based community development strategies, programs, and policies are needed to adequately address the growing inequality and to preserve historic neighborhoods and communities of color within these cities. Finally, I argue that the current economic crisis of home foreclosures, high unemployment, and increased income/wealth inequality and poverty ironically has strengthened community development grassroots efforts. A window of opportunity exists because big-city mayors and other "progressive" city leaders do not want to repeat mistakes made during the urban renewal period of the late 1940s–1970s when millions of poor, largely black communities were demolished or torn apart by large infrastructure, commercial, or housing developments.

I discuss how grassroots community development can lead to the design and implementation of healthy, sustainable urban communities. In order to reduce poverty, inequality, and displacement and to create healthy, sustainable, urban communities of opportunity, a comprehensive, multifaceted strategy is needed. Community development leaders, advocacy organizations, and urban residents need to form a broad-based national community coalition with deep roots in local communities that is focused on implementing place-based community development strategies, practices, and programs. Moreover, these grassroots efforts must be helmed by community leaders and residents to be effective. The multifaceted strategy also requires progressive urban policies at the national and state levels in order to succeed. Given the current economic crisis impacting states and cities, this requires policies that encourage public-private partnerships aimed at improving the economic, environmental, and social aspects of low-resourced vulnerable urban communities, going beyond the place-based initiatives currently in place with the Obama administration's Sustainable Communities, Promise Neighborhoods, and Choice Neighborhoods Initiatives.

Note

1 For the purposes of this chapter, I define gentrification as the process in which more affluent populations move into an area of less affluence that results in higher prices for goods, services, and housing. This process of neighborhood transformation or neighborhood change may lead to involuntary or voluntary displacement.

Bibliography

Beitel, K. 2013. *Local Protest, Global Movements: Capital, Community, and State in San Francisco*. Philadelphia, PA: Temple University Press.

Castells, M. 1983. *The City and the Grassroots*. University of California Press: Berkeley and Los Angeles.

Clay, P. 1979. The Mature Revitalized Neighborhood: Emerging Issues in *Gentrification in Neighborhood Renewal: Middle-Class Resettlement and Incumbent Upgrading in American Neighborhoods* edited by P. Clay. D.C. Heath Publishers, pp. 57–60.

Freeman, L. and Braconi, F. 2004. Gentrification and Displacement: New York City in the 1990s. *Journal of the American Planning Association*, 70(1): 39–52.

Frey, W.H. 2011. The new metro minority map: regional shifts in Hispanics, Asians, and Blacks from Census 2010. Washington, D.C.: The Brookings Institution. Retrieved on December 19, 2011 from http://www.brookings.edu/papers/2011/0831_census_race_frey.aspx

Hackworth, J. and Smith, N. 2001. The State of Gentrification. Tijdschrift voor Economishce en Sociale Geografie, 92(4): 464–477.

Hartman, C. 1984. The Right to Stay Put, in C. Geisler and F. Popper (eds) *Land Reform, American Style*. pp. 302–318. Totowa, NJ: Rowman & Allanheld.

Kuruvilla, M. 2011. 25% drop in African American population in Oakland. *San Francisco Chronicle*, March 11 (located at www.sfgate.com/bayarea/article/25-drop-in-African-American-population-in-Oakland-2471925.php).

Lauria, M. and Knopp, L. 1985. Towards An Analysis of the Role of Gay Communities in the Urban Renaissance. *Urban Geography*, 6(2): 152–169.

Lees, L. 2003. Super-gentrification: The Case of Brooklyn Heights, New York City. *Urban Studies*, 12: 2487–2510.

Ley, D. 1994. Gentrification and the Politics of the New Middle Class. *Environment and Planning D: Society and Space.*, 12: 53–74.

Logan, J. R. and Molotch, H. L. 1987. *Urban Fortunes: The Political Economy of Place*. Berkeley: University of California Press.

Marcuse, P. 1986. Abandonment, Gentrification, and Displacement: The Linkages in New York City. In N. Smith and P. Williams (eds) *Gentrification and the City*. pp. 153–177. Boston, MA: Allen and Unwin.

Moretti, E. 2012. *The New Geography of Jobs*. New York: Houghton Mifflin Harcourt.

Newman, K. & Wyly, E.K. 2006. The Right to Stay Put, Revisited: Gentrification and Resistance to Displacement in New York City. *Urban Studies*, 43(1): 23–57.

Sassen, S. 2000. *Cities in the World Economy*. Thousand Oaks, CA: Pine Forge Press.

Sassen, S. 1998. *Globalization and Its Discontents*. New York, NY: New Press.

Smith, N. 2002. New Globalism, New Urbanism: Gentrification as Global Urban Strategy. *Antipode*, 34(3): 427–450.

Smith, N. 1979. Toward a Theory of Gentrification: A Back to the City Movement by Capital, not People. *Journal of the American Planning Association*, 45(4): 538–548.

Sumka, H.J. 1979. Neighborhood Revitalization and Displacement: A Review of the Evidence. *Journal of the American Planning Association*, 45(4): 480–487.

2 Our changing landscape

The "rediscovery" of the city and the demand for sustainable development

The postwar disinvestment in the urban core has been followed by what some call a "rediscovery of the city" (Knox, 2005; Nolon, 2013). U.S. Environmental Protection Agency (U.S. EPA) studies of residential building permit data in the fifty largest metropolitan areas show a substantial increase in new construction in central cities and older suburbs (U.S. EPA, 2012). More Americans are demanding sustainable development (Dowling, 2000; Owen, 2010; Nolon, 2013), as sustainable development (Nolon, 2013) within cities is widely accepted as critical to combating climate change (Negron, 2013). Sustainable development includes transit-oriented development, or the creation of compact, mixed-use, pedestrian-oriented communities located around public transit stations (Reconnecting America, 2007). Transit-oriented development appeals to people who want to live, work, and play in the same area. The appeal of transit-oriented development is particularly relevant to the case studies discussed in the following chapters. The neighborhoods I examined in Boston, New York, San Francisco, and Washington, DC, already had an existing integrated physical and transportation infrastructure before the increased demand for sustainable development, despite prior decades of disinvestment. This existing infrastructure renders these neighborhoods particularly amenable to transit-oriented development.

Cities and developers are capitalizing on sustainable development's appeal. Local governments are developing sustainability plans as well as policies and programs that encourage investment in large-scale revitalization projects in the urban core, all of which speaks to this demand for urban living. Discussed in more detail later, city governments have provided private developers with subsidies, tax credits, and access to publicly owned land at low cost, which has resulted in the transformation of many older, industrial parts of cities and historically underinvested neighborhoods. New development in these areas supports higher use values such as medical centers, research and development facilities, luxury condominiums and townhouses, high-end restaurants, and cafes, as well as boutique shops (Logan and Molotch, 1987). Cities are even competing with each other to develop billion-dollar entertainment districts and sports stadiums.

Although investment in the urban core of strong-market cities has resulted in "improved amenities, an improved tax base, and an increase in public services to formerly blighted areas," this trend also applies pressure on the ability of less affluent residents to remain in place (Knox, 2005). Often developers make promises in the beginning of a proposed project to win favor from local politicians, labor unions, and community residents, but then fall short of their goals and the development simply results in gentrifying the area. Not surprisingly, some projects intended to spur economic development (discussed in more detail later) but marketed as sustainable, walkable, and public transit friendly, result primarily in luxury housing developments and amenities for the affluent (Checker, 2011).

But even local governments' efforts to promote environmentally friendly development policies intended to encourage sustainable urban revitalization can lead to what some scholars describe as environmental gentrification (Checker, 2011; Pearsall, 2012). The idea of environmental gentrification is not that environmental activism causes gentrification, but that state-sponsored sustainable urban development implements what "appears as politically neutral planning that is consensual as well as ecologically and socially sensitive, [but] in practice it subordinates equity to profit-minded development" (Checker, 2011). Put another way, these sustainability initiatives fail to meet their goals to provide adequate community benefits to residents across the socioeconomic strata because they lack an explicit social justice framework (Dooling, 2009; Pearsall, 2012). For example, planning to revitalize transit-rich, historically low-income neighborhoods to accommodate and attract high-density, market-rate, mixed-use development can potentially address blight and climate change and improve the tax base, but if the government fails to engage the community already living in the neighborhood early on in the process, or proceeds to engage the community in a superficial or perfunctory way, the planning process proceeds without critical community input. As a result, these large-scale developments and revitalization efforts can result in substantial demographic shifts (Glass, 1964; Hammel and Wyly, 1996; Smith, 1996; Newman and Wyly, 2006) because the development fails to address the "how" of keeping preexisting residents in place. Any planning approach without a social justice framework can contribute to reproducing inequalities and result in sustainable urban revitalization that burdens low-wage earners and the least educated, especially immigrants and marginalized people of color (Smith, 2002; Swyngedouw and Heynen, 2003; Pearsall, 2012). This reality becomes increasingly apparent as we explore each of these identified contributors to gentrification in more detail.

The role of economic development and urban growth coalitions

Cities have evolved from centers of trade to places of production (Judd and Swantrom, 2006). Cities in the global economy strive to grow and expand by developing knowledge- and information-based industries, attracting investment capital, and cultivating a highly skilled labor force that provides them with a competitive advantage over other metropolitan areas (Saxenian, 1994). Cities must make planning decisions to stimulate economic development and accommodate growth sectors within a metropolitan area. Critical to city growth and expansion is the availability of land and how land is developed. Many institutions within the growth sector (such as universities, media, and real estate developers) view land as a commodity to be bought, sold, and developed (Logan and Molotch, 1987). The pressure on cities to develop, expand, and generate revenue leads to the formation of growth coalitions or informal arrangements comprised of such actors as government, private real estate developers, colleges and universities, large firms, and investors to facilitate large-scale development (Logan and Molotch, 1987). Unfortunately, large-scale development often adversely affects vulnerable communities.

For example, one of the largest growth sectors within metropolitan areas in the United States is made up of educational and medical institutions (Harkavy and Zuckerman, 1999). A survey of the top ten private employers in the largest twenty U.S. cities found that nearly 550,000, or 35 percent of the 1.6 million people who worked for the top ten employers, were employed by institutions of higher learning and medical facilities (Harkavy and Zuckerman, 1999). Notably, hospitals are major employers in high-poverty cities and they are difficult to close or relocate to other areas because they are likely to face substantial resistance (Barro and Cutler, 2000; McKee, 2010).

Because large urban academic, medical, and research institutions are often adjacent to or are in proximity to vulnerable communities and/or communities of color, tension springs up between these larger institutions and their surrounding communities over land (Martin, 2004). For example, vulnerable communities and communities of color have had to deal with the expansion of academic and medical institutions such as Johns Hopkins medical campus in East Baltimore, the University of Chicago in the Southside of Chicago, and the University of Southern California in South Los Angeles (Mayfield, Hellwig, and Banks, 1998; Ong et al., 2008; Hlad, 2009). In the case of Baltimore, Johns Hopkins University is leading a $1.8 billion, eighty-eight-acre, mixed-use revitalization project in East Baltimore (East Baltimore Development, Inc., 2015). The East Baltimore neighborhood has suffered from years of disinvestment and the majority black residents have experienced persistent unemployment. According to the 2010 Census, East Baltimore was more than 87 percent black and had a median household income of $15,493. In 2010, right after the recession, it was estimated that almost 54 percent of the neighborhood's population was not in the labor force.

The public-private revitalization project headed up by Johns Hopkins, when finished, will include a park, housing, research facilities, and a middle school (East Baltimore Development, Inc., 2015). The project is already well under way. In 2011, Johns Hopkins University opened the Berman Institute of Bioethics, and, in 2012, a twenty-story residential tower opened (Rienzi, 2013). In order to assemble the eighty-eight-acre parcel, 584 families had to be relocated to other areas in the city and state of Maryland (Rienzi, 2013). Some residents were provided with rental properties while new housing was constructed and others moved permanently away from the neighborhood (Rienzi, 2013).

In Los Angeles, California, the University of Southern California (USC) is also involved in a large-scale, mixed-use revitalization project. In September 2014, USC broke ground on a 1.25-million-square-foot residential and retail center called USC Village (North-Hager, 2014). The development will be the biggest in USC history and will be one of the largest developments in the history of South Los Angeles. The development is projected to cost roughly $650 million (North-Hager, 2014). The hope is that the project will result in thousands of jobs and provide a huge economic boost to the local economy.

USC, a private university, plans to build the USC Village without any public subsidies or taxpayer funds. The university estimates that it will also provide more than $40 million in community benefits, including up to $20 million to an affordable housing fund managed by the city of Los Angeles. USC also plans to improve the infrastructure around the campus by upgrading Jefferson Boulevard, improving roadway connections around campus, building a new fire station, and even opening a law clinic. Moreover, the USC Village is expected to create thousands of permanent jobs and temporary construction jobs. This raises the question of how much this development will benefit the poorer South Los Angeles residents.

The large-scale developments that Johns Hopkins and USC initiated are definitely changing the landscapes of the neighborhoods adjacent to both universities. These changes are no doubt leading to more investment, new housing, and increased economic opportunity. The real issue with these types of developments is whether they will benefit local, long-term neighborhood residents in terms of jobs, access to affordable housing, and their overall improved quality of life. I explore this topic in more detail in the next chapter.

Focusing on the role of government

Some examining gentrification within strong-market cities look carefully at the relationship between global investment capital and pro-growth actors, particularly government actors (Smith, 1979; Logan and Molotch, 1987;

Sassen, 1992; Sassen, 1998; Wyly and Hammel, 1999; Lees, 2000; Sassen, 2000; Smith, 2002). The shifting geography of jobs and the rise of the knowledge-based economy have increased investment in the urban core by land speculators, developers, and others seeking to make a profit. But mortgage lenders, real estate agents, landlords, and government agencies have all contributed to the gentrification process as well (Hackworth and Smith, 2001).

The role of government agencies is of particular interest. As previously mentioned, cities want to increase their concentration of knowledge-based industries. To do so, cities must strive to innovate, be entrepreneurial, and attract highly skilled talent and investment capital. This pressure in turn has led government agencies (at every level of government) to form public-private partnerships to develop urban land for the maximum use value, including formerly neglected or underutilized areas (Smith, 1979; Logan and Molotch, 1987), like the John Hopkins development project discussed earlier. Because new development within the urban core supports higher use values for older, abandoned land such as research and development facilities, luxury condominiums and townhouses, expensive restaurants and specialty cafes, entertainment districts and sports stadiums (Zukin, 1982), this development results in higher land values and elevated housing costs, and increased living costs generally. This phenomenon burdens low-wage earners and the least educated, whose communities are adversely impacted by this renewed urban revitalization and investment (Hartman, 1984; Newman and Wyly, 2006). Under this theory, government agencies (intentionally or not) play a significant role in the hyper-gentrification of their cities.

Elvin Wyly and Daniel Hammel argue that, during the 1990s, several shifts took place in the housing market and housing policy that led to the resurgence of gentrification. The first shift was the increased level of private investment in central land markets across many major U.S. cities (Wyly and Hammel, 1999). The second shift was the transformation of the housing finance sector, which contributed to the economic expansion within the urban core by "direct(ing) more capital to housing generally and homeownership in particular," which in turn resulted in the "proliferation of means-tested mortgage products" that broadened access to homeownership and led to significant profits for lending institutions (Stegman et al., 1991; Wyly and Hammel, 1999; Levy, Comey, and Padilla, 2006a and 2006b). The third shift, according to Wyly and Hammel, was the result of a change to low-income housing policy that focused on the dispersal of the poor by providing them with housing vouchers and certificates, and turned publicly owned and operated housing developments into semiprivate, mixed-income housing (1999). Wyly and Hammel argue that federal programs such as HOPE VI have given local government agencies redevelopment and dispersal options previously unavailable to them, all of which has aided the gentrification process within central cities.

In addition to federal policies such as HOPE VI, a number of other federal and local place-based policies have also promoted urban sustainability and livability, focusing on three critical factors: (1) reducing the concentration of poverty; (2) leveraging private-sector investment; and (3) promoting transit-oriented and mixed-use development. These policies have merely accelerated and aided the gentrification process. For example, the U.S. Department of Housing and Urban Development's (HUD) Choice Neighborhoods Initiative's primary goal is to promote "a comprehensive approach to transforming distressed areas of concentrated poverty into viable and sustainable mixed-income neighborhoods" (HUD, 2012). HUD has also teamed up with the U.S. EPA and the U.S. Department of Transportation (DOT) to form the Partnership for Sustainable Communities, an effort, again, that at its core is focused on transit-oriented and mixed-use development, mixed-income housing, leveraging private-sector investment, and promoting walkable neighborhoods (Hutson, 2011). Because these efforts are primarily aimed at revitalizing distressed urban neighborhoods and poverty reduction, they "open the door" to developers and other investors who profit from government-initiated public-private partnerships and in the long run directly and indirectly increase the displacement of poor and working-class residents (Smith, 2002).

The widening income gap and the Great Recession

Another explanation offered for the increased gentrification of neighborhoods within strong-market cities has to do with the postindustrial restructuring of the economy and the social and spatial division of labor. For example, one theory posits that over the past several decades two factors within the U.S. economy have contributed to gentrification: 1) a restructuring of the labor market[1] causing a polarization between high-skill, high-wage jobs on one end and low-skill, low-wage jobs on the other, with a significant decline in middle-skill, middle-wage jobs; and 2) an increased demand for skilled workers despite a significant slowdown in U.S. educational attainment (Autor, 2010; Moretti, 2012). This storyline suggests that a shift over the past half-century from an industrial and physical manufacturing economy to a postindustrial economy centered around knowledge-based industries (such as the Internet, software, life sciences, and scientific research and development) has resulted in an abundance of high-paying knowledge and information-based jobs within "innovation hub" metropolitan areas (Moretti, 2012). This demand for skilled labor results in increased income inequality as higher-wage earners earn five times as much as low-wage earners (U.S. Congress). At the same time, U.S. educational attainment has not kept pace with the growing demand for skilled labor (Glaeser, Resseger, and Tobio, 2009; Autor, 2010; Brookings Institution, 2010; Moretti, 2012). For example, in his book *The New Geography of Jobs*, economist Enrico Moretti makes the argument that since 1985 the United States has lost 372,000 manufacturing jobs annually while jobs in the innovation and knowledge-based sectors have grown precipitously (2012). According to his analysis, Moretti estimates that jobs in the Internet sector have grown by 634 percent over the past decade, and within the past twenty years software jobs have grown by 562 percent and life science research jobs have increased by 300 percent (Moretti, 2012). Since the 1970s, however, U.S. educational attainment has not kept pace with the demand. As a result, wages for college graduates have outpaced those of less educated workers (Goldin and Katz, 2008, 2009; Heckman and LaFontaine, 2008; Autor, 2010). This is also the case for younger adults, especially blacks and Latinos, residing in metropolitan areas. Blacks and Latinos are not increasing their educational attainment at the same rate as whites; in fact, they trail both whites and Asians by more than twenty percentage points in earning a bachelor's degree (Brookings Institution, 2010).

In addition to the increased polarization of the labor market, there has also been a decline in middle-wage/middle-skill jobs, negatively impacting middle- and working-class urban residents (Autor, 2010). For example, economist David Autor from MIT analyzed real hourly wages relative to the median by wage percentile for all U.S. workers between two time periods: 1974–1988 and 1988–2006. He found that, during the first time period, wage growth was consistently increasing in wage percentile; during the second time period, however, wages *above* and *below* the median rose relative to the median (Autor, 2010). This decline in middle-wage, middle-income jobs has contributed to the economic challenges facing the middle- and working-class populations residing in strong-market cities.

Unfortunately, the Great Recession that began in December 2007, which was marked by persistent high unemployment, a huge drop in home values, massive numbers of home foreclosures, and the significant loss of wealth for many low-to-middle-income families, only further magnified the growing income gap that exists between more affluent, higher-skilled individuals on one end of the economic spectrum and less affluent, lower-skilled individuals on the other. This has become especially apparent within strong-market metropolitan areas. For example, a 2012 report by the Pew Research Center found economic segregation of upper- and lower-income households has risen in twenty-seven of America's thirty largest metros (Pew Research Center, 2012). In addition, a study conducted by Richard Florida and Charlotta Mellander found that over several decades Americans have been sorting themselves along class lines (Florida and Mellander, 2013). This trend is becoming especially pronounced within cities and suggests that income segregation will continue without some significant policy changes (Florida and Mellander, 2013).

Strong-market cities have certainly seen a substantial increase in income disparity. Whatever the driving force, extreme income disparity allows higher-skilled and educated workers moving into previously underinvested neighborhoods to pay a high, premium price for housing and amenities that low-wage workers simply cannot. The growing income inequality between higher-skilled, higher wage earners and less-skilled, lower wage earners is shaping the spatial landscape within metropolitan areas. In strong-market metropolitan areas, higher wage earners are choosing to live in cities, which intensifies gentrification (Lees, 2003). Many higher-skilled and higher wage earners are also looking to reside in what have historically been economically disadvantaged communities of color such as the Shaw neighborhood in Washington, DC (predominately black) or the Mission District in San Francisco (predominately Latino), in part because of these neighborhoods' transportation options and close proximity to amenities.

This influx of highly educated, mobile urban professionals into strong-market cities ultimately pushes up costs for low-wage earners, thus forcing many to seek affordable housing and a lower cost of living in the suburbs. Notably, as recently as 2000, the majority of the nation's poor resided in major cities (Brookings Institution, 2010). But the Brookings Institution reports that between 2000 and 2008–2012, "the number of suburban poor living in distressed neighborhoods grew by 139 percent – almost three times the pace of growth in the cities" (Brookings Institution, 2014). This new suburban poverty has attracted mass media attention as many suburbs that were once home to primarily middle-class families have seen their level of poverty increase dramatically in a relatively short period of time.

When being middle class in the city is still not enough

But it is not just the least affluent or low wage earners who are at risk of being pushed out of strong-market cities. Households that earn enough to be labeled as "middle class" by most definitions, particularly those with children, are impacted by the housing affordability crisis and increased cost of living. For example, in 2013, the City and County of San Francisco found that households earning more than $100,000 annually, and families with children under six, were the most likely to report wanting to leave San Francisco within three years (City and County of San Francisco, 2013). The survey did not define whether the households earning more than $100,000 were comprised of an individual or a family, although the majority of the survey respondents was made up of households of two or more persons (City and County of San Francisco, 2013).

Although the survey did not link household income to family size or household characteristics, we can observe from other data and findings that a family of four, made up of two adults and two children, with a household income of $100,000 would find it very difficult to stay in San Francisco. The Economic Policy Institute's Family Budget Calculator, which calculates the annual income necessary for a household to "live securely but modestly in a given location," calculates that a two-person, two-child household in San Francisco requires a *minimum* annual income of $82,639 to survive (Economic Policy Institute, 2014).[2] This calculator assumes, however, that the family is paying "fair market rent," which HUD defines as the fortieth percentile of housing prices in the region. In 2013, the HUD calculation for fair market rent in San

Francisco for a two-bedroom apartment was $1,795.00 (HUD, 2013). Media reports from the same period, however, document findings that median rent for a two-bedroom apartment in San Francisco was $4,000 and ranged from $2,460 (for a two-bedroom in the Outer Mission/Excelsior District – the neighborhood bordering Daly City) to $5,800 (for a two-bedroom in the Financial District) (Wier, 2013). The Economic Policy Institute's calculator also assumes modest expenses for transportation, child care, and food, the latter being defined by the Department of Agriculture's "low-cost plan," which assumes food costs of less than $800 a month (USDA, 2015).

The Insight Center for Community Economic Development Self-Sufficiency Standard calculator provides a different calculation of $92,914 for a family of four with two adults, one infant, and one child under six to live in San Francisco without public or private assistance.[3] The monthly budget used for this calculator also assumes a modest standard of living, similar to the Economic Policy Institute's calculator, but provides a *slightly* higher estimate for child care costs. Still, the calculator assumes that housing will cost only $1,896. The annual budget required for a single adult, three-child household with one preschooler and two school-aged children under twelve to be self-sufficient rises to $104,800. These calculators demonstrate why a family of four earning $100,000 would find it incredibly challenging to live in San Francisco. The pressure of escalating housing costs alone would drive many families within this income bracket out of the city.

But a household of four that earns $100,000 annually, even if it is a household with two children under six, is not low-income by definition. A household of four (of any composition) earning $100,000 annually earns slightly above what the U.S. Department of Housing and Urban Development defines as a "moderate income" household, or a household "whose income is between 81 and 95 percent of the area median income,"[4] (the area median income for San Francisco being $101,900 for 2015) (S.F. Mayor's Office of Housing, 2015). Such a household also earns substantially more than what the Pew Research Center found most Americans believe is required to live a "middle-class" lifestyle in an urban area in 2012 (Pew Research Center, 2012). Combining all of this information, we find that the cost of living in certain strong-market cities, like San Francisco, is so high that a family of four – if it were made up of one adult, two children under twelve, and one preschooler – would be *by definition middle class but unable to survive without public or private assistance*. Essentially, middle incomes are not rising fast enough to keep pace with rising costs of living, particularly the cost of housing, in strong-market cities.

More than just moving populations

Whatever the dominant factors causing neighborhood change, we can see that all of the trends discussed earlier are doing more than merely moving groups from one area within a metropolitan region to another. Gentrification's consequences are galvanizing those who care about economic, environmental, and social justice to form community coalitions for several reasons.[5] First, as strong-market cities are becoming accessible only to those with a lot of money, a good education and quality, higher-paying jobs, the lack of upward mobility for low- and moderate-income households becomes glaring. Strong-market cities are part of a global network of investment capital, labor, and information (Castells, 1996). Those cities that are able to remain part of this network continue to generate investment capital and wealth, which can create economic opportunities and a high standard of living – but increasingly these opportunities are only for the "elites." Those urban residents who are not highly skilled or highly educated find themselves becoming marginalized within these cities.

Second, as cities work to be at the forefront of promoting sustainable development, energy efficiency, and the conservation of resources, residents who are pushed outward from the core are unable to benefit from these changes, and the region as a whole is impacted. For example, major cities such as Chicago, Los Angeles, New York, Philadelphia, San Francisco, Seattle, and Washington, DC, are focused on implementing programs, policies, and practices like green building standards, urban agriculture, recycling and reuse, and the overall reduction in energy use and reducing greenhouse gas emissions. These policies are being developed at a time when gas and energy prices are high, physical infrastructure is crumbling, and weather patterns seem unpredictable.

But these policies do not always reach poor populations residing along the boundaries of a metropolitan region. So poor residents of outer suburbs can face challenges accessing better jobs in the city center as our metropolitan regional transportation systems tend to be fragmented. Moreover, the foreclosure crisis has decimated the budgets of smaller suburban cities, leaving them strapped for cash to pay for police and fire protection and infrastructure improvements as well as provide an adequate level of funding for social services and education. Some have even filed for bankruptcy.

Third, the rising spatial income inequality can also have a negative impact on the health of a population, especially for poor and moderate-income people. While cities are promoting walkability and physical activity, transit-oriented development to increase public transit use, and high-density, mixed land use development, the potential displacement of the poor and moderate-income populations to the outer suburbs of metropolitan regions has adverse health outcomes. Displacement not only increases urban sprawl but can break up social networks and reduce social capital for those who are displaced. In addition, residing in outer ring suburbs can lead to obesity and increased blood pressure, and impact mental health (Wilson, Hutson, and Mujahid, 2008). Moreover, the movement of the poor to the suburbs has not resulted in an increase in social services typically found within cities.

Finally, the growing income polarization and spatial inequality within our major metropolitan areas challenge social cohesion and undermine democracy. It is important that everyone have adequate access to economic opportunities, economic mobility, affordable housing, quality neighbor-hoods, and healthy physical and social environments. The recent protests in Ferguson, Missouri, and Baltimore, Maryland, demonstrate the importance of addressing racial and economic disparities in our society. As cities grow in political clout, it is critical that our nation's poor do not simply get shuf-fled around like pieces on a chessboard – first being concentrated in inner-city ghettos and now being relegated to the outer reaches of our metropolitan areas, diminishing their economic and social opportunities and weakening their political power.

Increased resistance to neighborhood change and displacement

The case studies that follow discuss how residents of once-neglected urban neighborhoods are standing up to local governments, influential real estate developers, universities, international investors, and others to remain in their neighborhoods. They are forming community coalitions focused on protecting their interests and transforming their communities to sustain-able healthy communities (defined as economically strong, environmen-tally clean, and socially just communities). They are not fighting to stop economic development and growth; these communities are *struggling to be a part* of the new economic and social transformation taking place in their neighborhoods. They want to be at "the table" as equal and valued partners during the planning and development process. As a result, these community coalitions are implementing creative *place-based* community development strategies to require private developers to construct afford-able housing, create quality jobs, and invest in community programs and public education.

The role of community benefits agreements in the fight for equitable development

One place-based strategy includes the use of a Community Benefits Agree-ment (CBA). For the purposes of this book, I define a CBA as *a legally binding contract (or set of related contracts), setting forth a range of com-munity benefits regarding a development project or projects, and result-ing from substantial community involvement* (Gross, 2008). CBAs were initially developed in the late 1990s to measure local benefits from devel-opment projects such as jobs and affordable housing, as well as to under-stand the exposure and risk that neighboring communities were exposed to by these projects (Salkin and Lavine, 2008; Moore and Nettles, 2010; Wolf-Powers, 2010). CBAs represent a community's effort "to change policy and bring some of the benefits of development to residents directly affected by large projects" (Saito and Troung, 2014). As the familiarity and use of CBAs increases, some argue that effective CBAs must (1) be structured around a single development project; (2) be a legally enforceable contract; (3) be broad-based and address a range of community interests; and (4) be the by-product of significant community involvement and engagement (Gross, 2008).

This means that the process of negotiating the CBA must be inclusive and accountable (Gross, LeRoy, and Janis-Aparicio, 2005; Gross, 2008). For a CBA to be inclusive, the process leading up to its development should attempt to reach out to as many community residents as possible and involve them in the process to ensure that their concerns are heard and addressed before any contract is approved. The main challenge with succeeding in this step is defining clearly who the "community" is and developing comprehensive mechanisms to ensure that its members have been included in the CBA process. Accountability is also important; it is critical that a CBA be legally binding and not just include many promises to the community that cannot be enforced (Marcello, 2007; Gross, 2008; Moore and Nettles, 2010). These issues are explored more fully in Chapter 4.

The Staples Center development in Los Angeles provides an illustrative example of an effective CBA. The L.A. Live CBA for the Staples Center involved twenty-one community groups and five labor unions agreeing to support the development of the Staples Center – backed in part by public subsidies (Salkin and Lavine, 2008). In exchange, the developers agreed to make reasonable efforts to make 70 percent of the 5,500 permanent jobs generated by the development living-wage jobs; to implement a first-source hiring program that targeted groups whose homes or jobs were displaced by the development, low-income individuals living within a three-mile radius, and low-income individuals from the city's poorest census tracts; and to provide affordable housing (Salkin and Lavine, 2008).

The L.A. Live CBA is considered the model of a comprehensive CBA. Ten years later, researchers found that the developer had met its affordable housing development obligations, worked closely with community partners "to establish an effective local hiring program, and helped fund a newly created land trust" (Saito and Troung, 2014). The researchers attributed the developer's compliance in part to the developer's need for continued support from the community coalition, the strong community organizing infrastructure in place that benefits negotiations, monitoring, and implementation (Saito and Troung, 2014).

Although CBAs are defined as private agreements between a community coalition and a developer, cities often still play a role. A city may not be a party to the agreement but be involved in the CBA negotiations – either by sitting at the bargaining table or by withholding its discretionary zoning approval on a project unless a developer has entered into a CBA with a community coalition. The case study in Chapter 3 discusses this in more detail. Also, some local governments enter into master development agreements directly with the developer, in which the developer agrees to provide a series of community benefits that may look similar to the types of benefits found in a CBA.

Many community coalitions and their leaders are also seeking better ways to monitor and to evaluate outcomes negotiated through CBAs. For example, community coalitions are advocating for the creation of independent third-party monitors, which consist of individuals from multiple sectors, to evaluate and report on the progress of developers' efforts to honor the promises made in CBAs. When community organizations have to monitor and coordinate job and housing programs, it can take substantial staff resources; "studies of the implementation of CBAs suggest that funding for staff should be part of such agreements" (Saito and Troung, 2014).

In light of the increased economic activity and growth within cities leading to gentrification and displacement, community coalitions are doing more than negotiating CBAs. A "community benefits movement" (Saito and Troung, 2014) is working to inject a social justice/equitable development framework into the land use and community development process. One of the criticisms of using CBAs to achieve more equitable development is that it is both resource intensive and often limited in scope because it is project specific (Saito and Troung, 2014). These coalitions are placing pressure on local governments to link private development supported by public resources to community outcomes through land use policies and regulations, local hiring ordinances, and project labor agreements. Community coalitions are trying to achieve community benefits by partnering with local governments to develop more progressive housing policies and plans into cities' revitalization efforts and to implement living-wage ordinances. Community coalitions are also looking to other public entities to implement local hiring ordinances and apprenticeship requirements for major construction contracts (Saito and Troung, 2014).

All of these efforts have required community coalitions to organize and educate local residents about the city-planning process, specifically around issues related to housing, land use, economic development, and public contracting. The goal of these coalitions is to require public entities to incorporate many of the same ideas enumerated in CBAs into public policies and regulations that impact large contracts and projects funded by public subsidies (Saito and Troung, 2014). Ultimately, this strategy has enabled communities to incorporate land use tools as a strategy to monitor and, if needed, slow down development and mitigate the negative effects of gentrification, neighborhood change, and displacement. Chapter 5 discusses this in more detail.

Notes

1 This refers to technological change, decline in real wages, decline in labor union membership, increase in international trade and the offshoring of goods and services, and loss of manufacturing jobs.

2 This calculation comes from using the Economic Policy Institute's Family Budget Calculator, found here: www.epi.org/resources/budget/, and selecting "Two Parent Two Child" family type, California, and San Francisco.
3 This calculation comes from using the Insight Center for Community Economic Development's Self-Sufficiency Standard for California calculator, found here: www.insightcced.org/calculator.html, selecting San Francisco County, 2 Adults, 2 Children, 1 infant, 1 preschooler.
4 HUD, *Glossary of Community Planning and Development Terms*, available at http://portal.hud.gov/hudportal/HUD?src=/program_offices/comm_planning/library/glossary/m.
5 For the purposes of this book, when I refer to *social justice* I am referring to the general definition: justice in terms of the distribution of wealth, opportunities, and privileges within society (see www.oxforddictionaries.com/definition/english/social-justice).

Bibliography

Autor, D. 2010. *The Polarization of Job Opportunities in the U.S. Labor Market: Implications for Employment and Earnings*. The Hamilton Project report. Washington, DC: Center for American Progress.

Barro, J., and Cutler, D. 2000. Consolidation in the medical care marketplace, a case study from Massachusetts. In S. N. Kaplan (Ed.), *Mergers and Productivity* (pp. 9–50). Chicago, IL: University of Chicago Press.

Brookings Institution. 2010. *The State of Metropolitan America*. Washington, DC: Brookings Institution. Retrieved from www.brookings.edu/metro/StateOfMetroAmerica.aspx.

Brookings Institution. 2014. *The Growth and Spread of Concentrated Poverty, 2000 to 2008–2012*. Washington, DC: Brookings Institution.

Castells, M. 1996. *The Rise of the Network Society*. Malden, MA: Blackwell Publishers.

Checker, M., 2011. Wiped out by the "Greenwave": Environmental gentrification and the paradoxical politics of urban sustainability. *City & Society*, 23(2), 210–229.

City and County of San Francisco. 2013. City Survey Report, Office of the Controller. Prepared by CSA City Performance Unit &FM3 Research. May 20.

Dooling, S., 2009. Ecological gentrification: A research agenda exploring justice in the city. *International Journal of Urban and Regional Research*, 33(3), 621–639.

Dowling, T. J. 2000. Reflections on urban sprawl, smart growth, and the Fifth Amendment. *University of Pennsylvania Law Review*, 148(3) (January), 873–887.

East Baltimore Development, Inc. 2015. www.ebdi.org/about.

Florida, R. and Mellander, C. 2013. *Segregated city: The geography of economic segregation in America's metros*. Martin Prosperity Institute. Rotman School of Management. University of Toronto. Toronto: Canada.

Glaeser, E. L., Resseger, M., and Tobio, K. 2009. Inequality in cities. *Journal of Regional Science*, 49, 617–646.

Glass, R. 1964. Introduction. In Centre for Urban Studies (Eds.). London: Aspects of Change/ MacGibbon & Kee [reprinted in Glass R., 1989. *Cliches of Urban Doom*. Oxford: Blackwell, 133–158].

Goldin, C. and Katz, L. 2008. *The Race between Education and Technology*. Cambridge, MA: Belknap Press for Harvard University Press.

Goldin, C. and Katz, L. 2009. *Education and Technology: Supply, Demand, and Income Inequality.* Cambridge, MA: Harvard University Press.

Gross, J. 2008. Community Benefits Agreements: Definitions, values, and legal enforceability. *Journal of Affordable Housing and Community Development Law*, 17, 35–58.

Gross, J., LeRoy, G., and Janis-Aparicio, M. 2005. Community Benefits Agreements: Making development projects accountable. Good Jobs First and the California Partnership for Working Families. May.

Hackworth, J. and Smith, N. 2001. The state of gentrification. *Tijdschrift voor Economishce en Sociale Geografie*, 92(4), 464–477.

Hammel, D. J. and Wyly, E. K. 1996. A model for identifying gentrified areas with census data. *Urban Geography*, 17(3), 248–268.

Harkavy, I. and Zuckerman, H. 1999. *Eds and Meds: Cities' Hidden Assets.* Washington, DC: Brookings Institution Center on Urban and Metropolitan Policy.

Hartman, C. 1984. The right to stay put. In C. Geisler and F. Popper (Eds.), *Land Reform, American Style* (pp. 302–318). Totowa, NJ: Rowman & Allanheld.

Heckman, J. and LaFontaine, P. 2008. Education in America: College graduates and high school dropouts, Vox column, February 13, VoxEU.org.

Hlad, J. 2009. A chilly relationship between Hopkins and its neighbors begins to thaw. University of Maryland's Phillip Merrill College of Journalism. Retrieved from www.baltimoreurbanreport.com/articles/a-chilly-relationship-between-hopkins-and-its-neighbors-begins-to-thaw.

Hutson, M. A. 2011. Urban sustainability and community development: Creating healthy sustainable urban communities. San Francisco, CA: Federal Reserve Bank of San Francisco. WP-2011–03.

Judd, D. R. and Swanstrom, T. 2006. *City Politics: The Political Economy of Urban America* (6th ed.). New York: Pearson Longman.

Knox, P. L. 2005. *Urbanization: An Introduction to Urban Geography*, 394 (2nd ed.). Upper Saddle River, NJ: Prentice Hall, Inc.

Lees, L. 2000. A reappraisal of gentrification: Towards a geography of gentrification. *Progress in Human Geography*, 24(3), 389–408.

Lees, L. 2003. Super-gentrification: The case of Brooklyn Heights, New York City. *Urban Studies*, 12, 2487–2510.

Levy, D. K., Comey, J. and Padilla, S. (2006a) *In the Face of Gentrification: Case Studies of Local Efforts to Mitigate Displacement.* Washington, DC: Urban Land Institute.

Levy, D. K., Comey, J., and Padilla, S. (2006b) *Keeping the Neighborhood Affordable: A Handbook of Housing Strategies for Gentrifying Areas.* Washington, DC: Urban Land Institute.

Logan, J. R. and Molotch, H. L. 1987. *Urban Fortunes: The Political Economy of Place.* Berkeley: University of California Press.

Marcello, D. A. 2007. Community Benefits Agreements: New vehicle for investment in America's neighborhoods. *Urban Law*, 39, 657–659.

Martin, D. 2004. Personal communication, November 15.

Mayfield, L., Hellwig, M., and Banks, B. 1998. The Chicago response to urban problems: Building university/community collaborations. Great Cities Initiative Working Paper. College of Urban Planning and Public Affairs. Chicago, IL: University of Illinois at Chicago.

McKee, G. A. 2010. Health-care policy as urban policy: Hospitals and community development in the post-industrial city. Working paper 2010–10. San Francisco, CA: Federal Reserve Bank of San Francisco.

Moore, E. and Nettles, M. 2010. Advancing health through community benefits agreements. Pacific Institute report. Oakland, CA.

Moretti, E. 2012. *The New Geography of Jobs*. New York: Houghton Mifflin Harcourt.

Negron, M. 2013. Limited authority, big impact: Chicago's sustainability policies and how cities can push an agenda amidst federal and state inaction, 7 *Harv. L. & Pol'y Rev.* 277, 278.

Newman, K. and Wyly, E. K. 2006. The right to stay put, revisited: Gentrification and resistance to displacement in New York City. *Urban Studies*, 43(1), 23–57.

Nolon, J. R. 2013. Shifting paradigms transform environmental and land use law: The emergence of the law of sustainable development, 24 *Fordham Envtl. L. Rev.*, 242, 243, 255–258.

North-Hager, E. 2014. USC kicks off construction of USC Village residential-retail hub. *USC News*. September 15. https://news.usc.edu/68490/usc-kicks-off-construction-of-usc-village-residential-retail-hub/.

Ong, P., Firestine, T., Pfeiffer, D., Poon, O., and Tran, L. 2008. *The State of South LA*. Los Angeles, CA: UCLA School of Public Affairs.

Owen, D. 2010. *Green Metropolis: Why Living Smaller, Living Closer, and Driving Less Are Keys to Sustainability*. New York, NY: Penguin Group (USA), Inc.

Pearsall, H. 2012. Moving out or moving in? Resilience to environmental gentrification in New York City. *Local Environment: The International Journal of Justice and Sustainability*, 17(9), 1013–1026.

Pew Research Center. 2012. Fewer, poorer, gloomier: The lost decade of the middle class, August 12. available at www.pewsocialtrends.org/files/2012/08/pew-social-trends-lost-decade-of-the-middle-class.pdf.

Reconnecting America, Why transit-oriented development and why now? (2007). Retrieved at http://reconnectingamerica.org/assets/Uploads/tod101full.pdf.

Rienzi, G. The changing face of East Baltimore. 2013. *The Gazette*, January. http://hub.jhu.edu/gazette/2013/january/east-baltimore-changes-development.

Saito, L. and Troung, J. 2014. The LA Live Community Benefits Agreement: Evaluating the agreement results and shifting political power within the city. *Urban Affairs Review*, 1–27.

Salkin, P. E. and Lavine, A. 2008. Understanding Community Benefits Agreements: Equitable development, social justice and other considerations for developers and community organizations. *Journal of Environmental Law & Policy*, 26, 291–332.

San Francisco Mayor's Office of Housing. 2015. 2015 Maximum Income By Household Size derived from the Unadjusted Area Median Income (AMI) for HUD Metro Fair Market Rent Area (HMFA) that contains San Francisco, available at www.sf-moh.org/modules/showdocument.aspx?documentid=7823.

Sassen, S. 1992. *The Global City*. Princeton, NJ: Princeton University Press.

Sassen, S. 1998. *Globalization and Its Discontents*. New York: New Press.

Sassen, S. 2000. *Cities in the World Economy*. Thousand Oaks, CA: Pine Forge Press.

Saxenian, A. 1994. *Regional Advantage: Culture and Competition in Silicon Valley and Route 128*. Cambridge, MA: Harvard University Press.

Smith, N. 1979. Toward a theory of gentrification: A back to the city movement by capital, not people. *Journal of the American Planning Association*, 45(4), 538–548.

Smith, N., 1996. The new urban frontier: Gentrification and the revanchist city. London: Routledge.

Smith, N. 2002. New globalism, new urbanism: Gentrification as global urban strategy. *Antipode*, 34(3), 427–450.

Stegman, M., Quercia, R., McCarthy, G., and Rohe, W. 1991. Using the Panel Survey of Income Dynamics (PSID) to evaluate the affordability characteristics of alternative mortgage instruments and homeownership assistance programs. *Journal of Housing Research*, 2(2), 161–211.

Swyngedouw, E. and Heynen, N. 2003. Urban political ecology, justice, and the politics of scale. *Antipode*, 35(5), 898–918.

U.S. Senate. Choice Neighborhoods Initiative Act of 2011. 112th Cong. 1st sess. S.624. Washington, DC: GPO. March 17, 2011.

U.S. Department of Agriculture (USDA). 2015. Official USDA food plans: Cost of food at home at four levels, U.S. average, April. available at www.cnpp.usda.gov/sites/default/files/CostofFoodApr2015.pdf.

U.S. Department of Housing and Urban Development (HUD). 2013. FY 2013 Fair market rent documentation system – calculation for San Francisco, California Metro FMR area, available at http://www.huduser.gov/datasets/fmr/fmrs/fy2013_code/2013summary.odn?inputname=METRO41860MM7360*San+Francisco,+CA+HUD+Metro+FMR+Area&selection_type=hmfa&year=2013&data=2013&area_id=&fmrtype=$fmrtype$&ne_flag=$ne_flag&path=C:\huduser\wwwdata\database&incpath=C:\HUDUSER\wwwMain\datasets\fmr\fmrs\FY2013_Code.

U.S. Department of Housing and Urban Development (HUD). 2012. HUD Awards Nearly $5 Million to Spur Next Generation of Housing, Neighborhood Transformation. Retrieved at http://portal.hud.gov/hudportal/HUD?src=/press/press_releases_media_advisories/2012/HUDNo.12-164

U.S. Environmental Protection Agency (EPA) 2012. Residential construction trends in America's metropolitan regions. 2012 Edition. Retrieved at www.epa.gov/smartgrowth/pdf/residential_construction_trends.pdf.

Wier, D. 2013. San Francisco rents vary widely by neighborhood, News Fix, KQED News, May 24.

Wilson, S., Hutson, M. A., and Mujahid, M. S. 2008. How planning and zoning contribute to inequitable development, neighborhood health, and environmental injustice. *Environmental Justice*, 1(4), 211–216.

Wolf-Powers, L. 2010. Community benefits agreements and local government: A review of recent evidence. Journal of the American Planning Association, 76(2), 1–17.

Wyly, E. K. and Hammel, D. J. 1999. Islands of decay in seas of renewal: Housing policy and the resurgence of gentrification. *Housing Policy Debate*, 10(4), 711–771.

Zukin, S. 1982. *Loft Living: Culture and Capital in Urban Change*. Baltimore, MD: Johns Hopkins University Press.

3 Boston

The fight for quality jobs

The growth of Boston's health care industry

One of the most well-known academic, medical, and research complexes is the Longwood Medical and Academic Area (LMA) in Boston, Massachusetts. The LMA is a densely built environment area comprised of twenty-four institutions ranging from Harvard Medical School to hospitals and private research centers, all built on a 213-acre site adjacent to the Fenway and Mission Hill neighborhoods of Boston and the Town of Brookline (MASCO, 2012). On any given day, more than 45,000 employees and approximately 21,000 students come into the LMA, although only a third of LMA employees are Boston residents (MASCO, 2012). Federal research grants awarded to LMA institutions have grown precipitously since the early 1990s. Between 1991 and 2005, National Institutes of Health (NIH) awards more than doubled for the LMA institutions from $302 million to $927 million. In 2012 (the most recent available data), total revenue for the Medical Academic and Scientific Community Organization (MASCO), a nonprofit member organization for LMA institutions, was $7.7 billion. In terms of land use, the LMA had developed 17.6 million square feet (MASCO, 2012).

The rapid growth of academic, biotechnology, medical, and other sectors places greater demand for land by LMA institutions (Sable, 2007). More important, as LMA institutions grow, expand, and generate revenue, they want to remain in proximity to one another to take advantage of a skilled labor force, and resources from such institutions as Harvard Medical School and its teaching hospitals and private research labs. These institutions have teamed up with private developers, investors, and research institutions to ensure the continuation of their expansion efforts. The City of Boston, which benefits financially from increased tax revenue and the creation of new businesses, and benefits from the ability to retain and generate more quality jobs for residents, also aids this growth (Sable, 2007).

Unfortunately, these types of urban growth coalitions often exclude economically disadvantaged or non-property-owning residents who want to have a role in the decision-making process of how land is developed, to what extent it is developed, for what purposes, and for whom. Frequently, urban growth coalitions dominated by business interests tend to exclude vulnerable populations (such as poor people, people of color, immigrants) and undesirable industries (Sze, 2007; Wilson, Hutson, and Mujahid, 2008; Cashin, 2009; Corburn, 2009; Powell, 2009).

In the case of Boston, Massachusetts, academic, medical, and research institutions have been seeking land in the surrounding neighborhoods adjacent to or in proximity to the LMA. This has resulted in tremendous tension between LMA institutions and local residents from neighborhoods such as Mission Hill, Roxbury, and Jamaica Plain. Residents argue that the development within and surrounding the LMA is contributing to an increase in housing costs and traffic congestion and leading to gentrification. More important, a high percentage of the residents living in the Fenway-Kenmore, Jamaica Plain, and Roxbury neighborhoods are low-skilled, economically disadvantaged, or immigrant residents with limited English language skills.

In many communities, the challenge of standing up to large, powerful institutions with money, political clout, and resources can often lead to "David versus Goliath" battles over land use, transportation, rising housing costs, and gentrification. However, in the case of Boston's LMA, the local community development corporation (CDC), Jamaica Plain Neighborhood Development Corporation (JPNDC), and its partners were able to form a public-private partnership with LMA institutions, government entities, and nonprofit institutions to create a health care workforce development program aimed specifically at increasing low-skilled, economically disadvantaged residents' human capital. In addition, this public-private partnership helped secure hundreds of thousands of dollars in investments from LMA institutions for the workforce development program and other community improvements (Griffen, 2005; Root Cause, 2011).

In the global economy, it is critical for community organizations to play an important role in local economic development (Robinson, 1995; Babacan and Gopalkrishnan, 2001; Leeming, 2002; McCall, 2003; Squazzoni, 2008). CDCs are more formal institutions with public goals focused on improving quality of life for local residents (such as improved human capital, quality housing, and bridging gaps between public systems infrastructure) and bringing together agencies from the public and private sectors (Squazzoni, 2008). This case illustrates how JPNDC and its partners were able to successfully challenge LMA institutions by developing a set of strategies focused around advocacy, organizing, entrepreneurship, and political maneuvering.

Grassroots organizing for jobs and economic opportunity

Over the past three decades, Boston has experienced a precipitous increase in ethnic minorities. In 1980, Boston's population was 68 percent white. Twenty years later, Boston had become a majority-minority city with ethnic minorities totaling 50.5 percent of the population, and by 2010 the city was 53 percent nonwhite or Hispanic. In 2010, the three largest ethnic minorities in the city were blacks/African Americans (24.4 percent), Latinos (17.5 percent), and Asians (8.9 percent) (U.S. Census, 2011). Immigration has largely been responsible for the demographic shift in the city. In 2000, one out of every four Boston residents was foreign-born with the majority of newcomers from the Americas (especially from the Caribbean and South America) (City of Boston, 2006). Today, nearly 27 percent of the population is foreign-born (American Community Survey, 2011). The top countries of origin among Boston's foreign-born population are the Dominican Republic (10.1 percent), China (10.0 percent), Haiti (8.3 percent), and Vietnam (5.0 percent) (U.S. Census Bureau, 2007–2011). A significant number of immigrants settling into Boston's neighborhoods have been non-English-speaking, low-skilled individuals. For example, in the Jamaica Plain neighborhood, immigrants from Latin America and the Caribbean have struggled to learn English and obtain the jobs skills needed to gain entry into the local labor force (Griffen, 2005).

The growth of immigrants posed new challenges for JPNDC, which is located in the heart of the diverse and immigrant-rich Boston neighborhood of Jamaica Plain. Until the mid-1990s, JPNDC, like many CDCs, was primarily a developer of affordable housing and it focused on community development and organizing. As a community development corporation, JPNDC's mission has focused on promoting equitable development and equal opportunity for local residents in Jamaica Plain and the adjacent neighborhoods. The organization tries to achieve this through affordable housing, community organizing, and developing economic opportunity initiatives that "improve the lives of low- and moderate-income people and create a better community for all" (JPNDC, 2015). Over its twenty-five-plus-year history, JPNDC has gained legitimacy and respect within the community because of its dedication to improving community residents' lives.

The rapid increase in immigrants and economic changes in the neighborhood, including large-scale developments and rising housing costs, led JPNDC to focus more attention on creating economic opportunities for local residents. One strategy was to link residents to good-quality, local jobs that provided opportunities for upward mobility. One obvious place to target was the growing number of health care jobs located within Boston's LMA.

Coincidentally, JPNDC's early strategic planning process occurred during the national debate around welfare reform. The 1996 Personal Responsibility and Work Opportunity Reconciliation Act placed an enormous amount of pressure on state and local government agencies, the business community, and nonprofit social service agencies to help Boston's most economically disadvantaged residents find adequate employment – jobs that had the potential to provide the poorest residents and their families with a livable wage and upward job mobility that could lift them out of poverty. This was critical during the late 1990s in Boston when growth in knowledge-based jobs kept unemployment relatively low, decreasing from 8.6 percent in 1991 to

3 percent by 2000 (Boston Indicators Project, 2011). JPNDC and its community partners soon found themselves strategizing on how they could play a significant role in local workforce and economic development, something they had done little of in the past (Griffen, 2005).

From welfare to work

During the mid-1990s, welfare reform became a hot-button issue that both Democrats and Republicans debated vociferously. Republicans argued that the time had come for the Aid to Families with Dependent Children (AFDC) welfare program to be reformed and place greater responsibility on the individual for increasing their economic opportunities; conversely, some in the Democratic Party argued that any significant changes in the welfare system would lead to greater numbers of children and families living in poverty. The Commonwealth of Massachusetts was at the forefront of this debate – so much so that on November 1, 1995, a year before the federal government passed sweeping welfare legislation with the 1996 Personal Responsibility and Work Opportunity Reconciliation Act, the state legislature of Massachusetts, at the insistence of then Governor William F. Weld, passed new legislation that changed the previous welfare system that resulted in the creation of the Transitional Aid to Families with Dependent Children (TAFDC) program, a time-limited welfare assistance program with stringent work requirements, operating under the state Department of Transitional Assistance (DTA). It became clear that Massachusetts' new welfare reform legislation was designed to shift individuals off the state's welfare assistance program and to put "work first" under the new Full Employment Program (FEP). As one assistant commissioner in charge of overseeing the FEP initiative stated, "The cornerstone of the reform is work. It doesn't matter how you get there. This program is just a small piece of the puzzle" (BIDMC, 2004). Under the TAFDC law, an individual receiving cash assistance is only able to receive cash benefits for twenty-four months during a sixty-month time period. TAFDC also requires all able-bodied recipients with school-age children (six years or older) to participate in the Full Employment Program (FEP). FEP was designed to provide TAFDC recipients with paid work experience and on-the-job training necessary to obtain unsubsidized employment. Recipients participating in FEP receive a subsidized wage in lieu of TAFDC cash benefits and food stamps and are subject to FEP criteria in accordance with the Commonwealth of Massachusetts regulations.

Under the initial FEP plan, the state offered employers who hired welfare recipients a one-year wage subsidy: $2.50 an hour for nine months, $1.50 for the past three months. An additional $1 an hour was placed in a trust for the employee to collect at the end of the year. In the beginning of the program, the Department of Transitional Assistance was overly ambitious and set an original goal of placing 2,000 welfare recipients across Massachusetts in jobs within just eight months. However, after eight months FEP had only placed 128 recipients in jobs across the entire state. The results in Boston were equally dismal. In the city of Boston, the goal was to create 320 new jobs for welfare recipients during the same eight-month time period, but in reality the city succeeded in placing only five individuals in jobs (Grunwald, 1996). Some argued that FEP's initial success was slow because many welfare recipients lacked the education and skills necessary to land a job. In addition, many employers were apprehensive about hiring welfare recipients (Grunwald, 1996).

TAFDC was also designed to emphasize post-employment services and other supports (i.e., childcare and short-term skills development) to make it easier for welfare recipients to transition from welfare to employment, with the goal of helping them to become economically self-sufficient (Kaye et al., 2001). This political shift at the state level was significant not only because it focused on the needs of families transitioning off welfare and low-income families in general, but it forced the state agencies in charge of implementation to consolidate and streamline responsibilities in order to encourage more formal collaboration among programs serving families, workers, and children (Kaye et al., 2001). This was a significant factor in fostering multi-sector partnerships (employers, community organizations, government agencies, educational institutions, etc.).

The emergence of WIA and the consolidation of the workforce development system

In addition to welfare reform, Massachusetts was also one of the first states to consolidate its workforce development system and one-stop career center network. In 1996, Boston opened two career centers as part of Massachusetts' participation in the U.S. Department of Labor's One Stop Implementation Project. A year later, Boston's third career center opened. Boston's career centers were built around four central principles – 1) universal access; 2) service integration; 3) customer choice; and 4) accountability. More important, Boston's career centers developed a single, unified management structure that created partnerships between the private, not-for-profit, community-based organizations and public agencies (Boston PIC, 2006).

The streamlining of Massachusetts' workforce development system was further enhanced with the passage of the 1998 federal Workforce Investment Act (WIA), which superseded the Jobs Training Partnership Act (JTPA). WIA was designed to better coordinate the nation's employment and training programs, provide state and local flexibility, and promote increased accountability in jobs programs (Skillman, Sadow-Hasenberg, and Hart, 2004). Under WIA, states and local service delivery areas were mandated to provide workforce planning in partnership with businesses, elected officials, labor, and other key partners through workforce investment boards (WIBs). WIA also required every state to be subdivided into workforce development areas and to provide workforce services such as job search assistance, assessment, and training for eligible adults, dislocated workers, and youth to be delivered through one-stop centers in each area (Skillman, Sadow-Hasenberg, and Hart, 2004).

In Massachusetts, WIA's passage resulted in state officials developing a workforce investment system that was built on and guided by a partnership between the public and private sectors as well as between state and local stakeholders (Massachusetts Department of Workforce Development, 2006). The Department of Workforce Development (DWD) (formerly named the Department of Labor and Workforce Development) was designated as the state-level agency responsible for the oversight of WIA funds received from the U.S. Department of Labor Employment and Training Administration. Workforce investment boards and one-stop career centers became the core of the state's service delivery for job development and placement, training referrals and placements, and employer outreach on workforce development services (Massachusetts Department of Workforce Development, 2006).

One distinction that separated Massachusetts from other states was the fact that the state workforce development system and cash assistance programs were highly integrated very early on. For example, in Boston, individuals seeking TAFDC assistance were required to apply through a Department of Transitional Assistance office. If an applicant qualifies for TAFDC, a caseworker reviews the applicant's educational background, skills, work history, and job references before processing the application. If TAFDC recipients are subject to the work requirement, they are referred to one of the three one-stop career centers (Boston Career Link, JobNet, and The Work Place), which have contractual agreements with the Department of Transitional Assistance to provide employment assessment, job search assistance, employment services to welfare recipients, and referrals to other employment and training programs (Kaye et al., 2001). Boston is unique in that its one-stop career centers do not actually provide any job training; instead, they contract out to local employment and training organizations. This consolidated workforce development system places greater responsibility on local government agencies, employers, and community organizations to bear a larger burden of the responsibility in helping welfare recipients transition off welfare and into work.

The new welfare legislation placed an enormous amount of pressure on state agencies and local jurisdictions across Massachusetts to come up with a comprehensive strategy to help thousands of welfare recipients who faced time limits to transition off welfare and into full employment; nonetheless, it was WIA's passage that provided flexible funding to the state and local areas (i.e., Boston) to reach this goal. WIA funding, in combination with welfare-to-work funds that were already flowing into Massachusetts, was the catalyst in creating a more integrated workforce development system focused on helping adults, dislocated workers, and youth gain access to employment services and training. In the City of Boston, it was Mayor Thomas M. Menino, the city council, elected state representatives, the

Mayor's Office of Jobs and Community Services (JCS), and the Boston Private Industry Council (the local workforce investment board) who led in helping to support these workforce development efforts, especially programs exclusively for the city's most economically disadvantaged residents.

The Boston Private Industry Council (Boston PIC) and the Mayor's Office of Jobs and Community Services (JCS) played a key role in creating partnerships among employers and community-based organizations to assist former welfare recipients with their transition off public assistance and into employment. Under WIA, the Boston PIC and JCS (a department of the Boston Redevelopment Authority that dispenses private and public funds and services to Boston residents) became responsible for overseeing the workforce development system. As Skillman, Sadow-Hasenberg, and Hart stated, "Business, labor, and community organizations must be represented on state and local WIBs. The mandated membership of the WIBs is intended to increase the likelihood of serving the two main customers of the new Workforce Investment System: local businesses and individuals seeking employment" (2004). This is precisely the role of the Boston PIC, which works in partnership with JCS to develop Boston's local WIA plan – to provide strategic direction to the publicly funded workforce system, determine funding decisions, and measure the system's effectiveness in meeting the employment and training needs of individuals and the workforce needs of employers in Boston (Boston PIC, 2006). Founded in 1979, the Boston PIC is a long-time employer-led intermediary. The PIC's mission is "to strengthen Boston's communities and its workforce by connecting youth and adults with education and employment opportunities that prepare them to meet the skills demands of employers in a changing economy" (Boston PIC, 2006). In keeping with its mission, the Boston PIC has partnered with education, labor, the community, and government agencies to provide oversight of public workforce development programs (Boston PIC, 2006). Moreover, as an intermediary, the Boston PIC strives to play four interrelated roles:

1   convenes local leadership around education and workforce priorities;
2   brokers employer partnerships;
3   connects youth and adults with education and employment opportunities; and
4   measures program impact, as well as quality and scale.

In 1998, the Boston PIC, in partnership with JCS and the Economic Development and Industrial Corporation, received a four-year, $11.3 million grant from the Department of Labor to fund welfare-to-work training programs in Boston. This was significant because it was the first substantial amount of welfare-to-work funding made available to employer-sponsored training initiatives and community service programs. The U.S. DOL welfare-to-work grant helped the Boston PIC and JCS strengthen their position and clout locally among the business community because it allowed these organizations to be more than just intermediaries and conveners of local partnerships. The Boston PIC and JCS proved they could also bring in federal dollars to support workforce development activities. As a result, it was easier to get the "buy-in" from employers who were initially skeptical about hiring former welfare recipients, let alone to get involved with workforce development programs exclusively focused on welfare recipients. Suddenly, with federal dollars to subsidize local welfare-to-work programs and WIA-related activities, it became easier for local WIBs and workforce intermediaries to bring employers to the table as partners, and, in some instances, have them take the lead in managing welfare-to-work training programs. As a long-time employee of the Boston PIC told me, "Workforce development partnerships in Boston are galvanized around funding streams, which tend to include the Boston PIC. This is why I am always paying attention to what funding is available at the federal, state, and local level."

As the fiscal agent of the U.S. DOL grant, the Boston PIC solicited proposals from both public and private organizations interested in developing, managing, and implementing welfare-to-work programs. Given the mounting political pressure from elected officials at both the state and local levels to place TAFDC recipients in jobs, the Boston PIC and JCS made it a mandate that any group receiving a grant had to commit to training and placing at least twenty welfare recipients into jobs within just four months. Among the organizations that received funding were two health care welfare-to-work employment training programs – one led by the Jamaica Plain Neighborhood Development Corporation (JPNDC) and Fenway Community Development Corporation (FCDC) and the other led by Partners Health-Care System, Inc., a nonprofit coalition of health care providers (including some of Boston's largest health care employers). Because JPNDC and FCDC were both actively involved in local workforce development efforts independent of each other, the two community organizations decided to consolidate their efforts and developed a welfare-to-work program called Steps to the Future. Steps to the Future originally focused on placing participants in frontline occupations within the hospitality and health care industries. However, JPNDC/FCDC quickly discovered that the hospitality industry employment was unstable because of fluctuations in the economy. Moreover, the industry provided few opportunities for upward job mobility, especially for under-skilled workers. Given these factors, JPNDC and FCDC switched the focus of Steps to the Future and decided to exclusively target the health care industry.

JPNDC's strategy to link the growing immigrant population in Boston to jobs was politically savvy for a number of reasons. First, the growing health care sector in Boston, and in many other cities, had increased demand for skilled health workers. Therefore, JPNDC knew that if it succeeded at developing a comprehensive workforce development strategy, which meant recruiting and training local residents for health and health care–related jobs within the LMA, and across Boston, it could be mutually beneficial for both sides. Residents could potentially help meet the growing health care sector's needs and residents could gain access to the abundance of entry-level and mid-level health care jobs that go unfilled each year.

Second, JPNDC recognized that as the cost of housing and living was increasing in Boston, a comprehensive workforce development strategy targeting jobs within the health care sector was necessary because of the potential opportunity for the development of career pathways. The health services profession has a number of occupations ranging from entry-level home health aide jobs (median hourly wage $10) that require very little education to registered nurse (median hourly wage $31.48) and dental hygienist jobs (median hourly wage $33.75) that require at least a two-year associate's degree. An individual who has a high school diploma or GED and works as a home health aide could potentially advance along a career ladder to the next position up on the pay scale as a medical assistant (median hourly wage $14.12) if he or she gained an additional six to twenty-four months[1] of training at a community college or vocational/technical training school. In another example, an individual working as a licensed vocational/practical nurse (median hourly wage $20.43) whose goal is to advance along a career ladder toward becoming a registered nurse would need to complete at least a two-year RN program leading to a diploma or associate's degree combined with clinical practice in a hospital.[2] These two examples illustrate that there is room for upward job mobility within the health services profession.

A comprehensive workforce development strategy aimed at urban residents (especially those who come from ethnically and racially diverse backgrounds) also recognizes the significant shifts in the demographics of major metropolitan regions. Metropolitan regions across the United States are increasingly becoming more ethnically and racially diverse. Immigrants represented a fourth of all labor growth during the period 1980–2000 and are likely to account for an even larger percentage of the growth over the coming years (Holzer and Waller, 2003; U.S. Bureau of Labor Statistics, 2015). For example, in 2014, almost half (48.3 percent) of the foreign-born labor force was Latino and almost one quarter (24.1 percent) was Asian, compared with about 10 percent and nearly 2 percent, respectively, of the native-born labor force (U.S. Bureau of Labor Statistics, 2015). Moreover, almost a quarter of the foreign-born labor force age twenty-five and older had not completed high school, compared with 4.6 percent of the native-born labor force (U.S. Bureau of Labor Statistics, 2015). According to the latest Bureau of Labor Statistics, "the foreign born were less likely than the native born to have some college or an associate degree – 17.5 percent versus 29.9 percent" (U.S. Bureau of Labor Statistics, 2015).

This demographic shift is posing new challenges for health care providers as the "provision of medical care to culturally diverse patients now relies more heavily on cross-cultural communication than at any other time. Medical care that addresses the cultural needs of diverse populations stands at the

Table 3.1 Median annual earnings, education, and training requirements for the largest occupations in health services, 2014

Occupation	Median Annual Earnings	Education Requirements	Training Requirements
Home Health Aides	$20,820	H.S. diploma/ GED or less	None required.
Nursing Aides, Orderlies, and Attendants	$24,400	H.S. diploma/ GED or less	None required.
Medical Assistants	$24,610	H.S. diploma/ GED or equivalent	May be required to take additional training ranging from six to twenty-four months.
Dental Assistants	$29,370	H.S. diploma or equivalent	May be required to take additional training ranging from nine to twenty-four months.
Licensed Practical/ Vocation Nurses	$41,540	H.S. diploma or equivalent	Complete a twelve- to eighteen-month state-approved vocational/ practical nursing program; state licensure required.
Radiologic Technologists and Technicians	$55,910	H.S. diploma or equivalent	Must complete a twenty-four-month program in a hospital or school.
Registered Nurses	$65,470	Two-year associate's degree; four-year college degree; master's degree	Complete at least a twenty-four-month program leading to a diploma or associate's degree combined with clinical practice in hospitals; management positions require four-year college degree; master's degree required to teach or specialize.

Source: U.S. Department of Labor. Bureau of Labor Statistics. *Occupational Outlook Handbook 2014.* www.bls.gov/ooh/healthcare/home.htm.

forefront of many discussions in the health care industry" (Chong, 2002). The demand is stronger than ever for culturally and linguistically competent health care workers who can deliver care to immigrant and minority populations that is compatible with their cultural beliefs, practices, and preferred language. In the long run, this could improve patient care and make prevention and awareness programs focused on specific ethnic groups more effective (i.e., diabetes, HIV/AIDS prevention in the African American community).

Thus, hiring workers from immigrant and minority communities could be mutually beneficial for everyone involved – health care providers, patients, and the community at large. Many states with large immigrant and diverse populations such as California, New York, and Texas have already developed programs to attract more minorities to the medical profession.

Finally, although not as obvious in the beginning, JPNDC recognized the potential health benefits of connecting poorer urban residents to quality jobs. The organization and its allies believed that health care jobs could also improve local residents' health. For example, several studies of individual and population health have shown that health burdens economically and socially deprived urban populations experience are much greater than those people from higher socioeconomic backgrounds deal with. O'Campo and Yonas (2005) argue in their article, "Health of Economically Deprived Populations in Cities" in *The Handbook of Urban Health*, that "while patterns of disparity differ for various outcomes, a consistent relationship of increased morbidity and mortality has been observed for economically disadvantaged urban populations compared to less deprived counterparts for outcomes such as cardiovascular disease, homicide, mental health, asthma, and premature mortality." Given these facts, workforce development efforts focused on helping the urban poor increase their socioeconomic status would be beneficial in two ways. It would increase their economic opportunity by providing them with wages significantly higher than the federal minimum wage, but, more important, it would provide these residents with health care and dental benefits that many lower-wage jobs do not provide. This could potentially improve the health status of economically disadvantaged urban residents, especially in single-female-headed households with young children.

However, JPNDC and its allies knew it was important to keep in mind that in order for a comprehensive health care workforce development of strategy to benefit both employers and workers, a holistic approach to workforce development must be developed that incorporates both a supply-side and demand-side strategy. A comprehensive workforce development approach on the supply side would focus on improving the skills and education of under-skilled job seekers and incumbent workers. It would also make sure that these individuals had access to supportive services such as counseling, child care, case management, career counseling/coaching, and so forth in order to help them successfully complete any pre-employment training and education programs. On the demand side of the labor market, a comprehensive workforce development strategy would identify the entry-level jobs within the health care sector with the potential for good pay and benefits as well as for upward mobility. It would also focus on changing the work environment to make sure that it supports workers by conducting activities such as mentoring, career counseling, education and training classes, and by having clearly defined career pathways.

Developing a comprehensive health care workforce system

Almost a year after Steps to the Future had begun, the Bank of Boston (which was bought by Fleet Bank and later bought by Bank of America in 2005) decided to formally sponsor an incumbent career ladders program geared toward helping individuals with limited skills and economic resources advance along a career ladder. In 1999, JPNDC and FCDC teamed up again and succeeded in obtaining funding from the Bank of Boston to launch Bridges to the Future, a career ladders pilot project targeting the growing health care sector in Boston. Unlike the Steps to the Future program, Bridges to the Future (Bridges) was a much larger program and focused exclusively on incumbent health care workers within the LMA. The Bridges to the Future partners were Beth Israel Deaconess Medical Center (BIDMC) and Children's Hospital Boston. Later, Harvard Medical School, Harvard School of Dental Medicine, and New England Baptist Hospital joined the partnership. Although health care employers had been engaged in their own internal workforce development efforts, Bridges to the Future was the first program of its kind to create a partnership between a significant number of health care employers and local community organizations (in this case, JPNDC and FCDC).

The Bridges program was a three-year, $80,000-a-year project that focused exclusively on two outcomes – the retention and career advancement of entry-level, under-skilled employees in occupations such as medical administration, food service, and environmental management services. In the early stages of the program, an advisory committee comprised of academics, policy makers, and workforce development practitioners was established to help develop workforce strategies, map career pathways, and agree on the skills that would be the foundation for training pre-employment participants. This model proved instrumental in designing a program relevant to the needs of both health care employers and local residents, especially because JPNDC and FCDC were at the table during the decision-making process. For example, Bridges staff met with employers every month for seven months from February to September 2000 in order to be sure all partners fully understood each other's perspectives and how the program was to be implemented. As one former Bridges staff member told me, "It took until September 2000 for employers to finally get it! For employers to finally understand what Bridges was all about." Employers, with the persistence of JPNDC's staff and its partners, eventually came to realize that the Bridges program was not just about training entry-level employees, but was also focused on creating career pathways and improving job quality. It was about restructuring the demand side of the labor market and creating good jobs for local residents. This was different from the previous job-training models, which focused primarily on helping residents get jobs but did very little to improve the upward mobility and quality of jobs. Instead, a clear goal of the Bridges program was to help entry-level workers improve their job and language skills so that they could move up or transition into other occupations within the hospital. The second objective of the program was to help employers fill job vacancies and reduce turnover rates. One administrator at Beth Israel Deaconess Medical Center responded in an interview:

> At the time the Bridges program was developed, Beth Israel Deaconess Medical Center had a group of front-line workers that we felt could benefit from Bridges. BIDMC was looking for people with promise; we had just [gone] through a merger and needed someone to come in and help us with thinking around workforce development issues. BIDMC liked the product of Bridges. The curriculum was well thought out, the retention strategy made sense. The whole program made sense . . . the Bridges program was seen [by BIDMC administrators] as a potential solution to BIDMC's retention and training problem with entry-level employees. Bridges was a small and the safe thing to do.

Another hospital administrator in the human resources department at Children's Hospital Boston stated, "Children's had skilled shortage issues at the time the Bridges program was launched, so Children's felt that it was important to develop career ladder, promotion, and retention opportunities." Both of these statements by hospital administrators demonstrate their commitment to being a part of the Bridges program because it met their workforce needs or at least had the potential to do so. The extensive planning and design process between JPNDC and its partners with the local hospitals also helped to break down some cultural barriers that existed between employers and community organizations. The Bridges program was Boston's first large-scale effort between community organizations and the city's health care employers to work together to establish a career ladder pipeline (BIDMC, 2005, Griffen, 2005). Prior to the passage of the 1996 Personal Responsibility and Work Opportunity Reconciliation Act and the 1998 Workforce Investment Act, few nonprofit community organizations were involved in large-scale workforce development activities. Although the Bridges program was a fairly modest pilot project, it trained roughly fifty to sixty local residents a year for three years.

JPNDC and its partners also worked diligently to garner public attention about the Bridges program. They continued organizing their constituents and residents in surrounding neighborhoods about the need for more quality health care jobs for local residents. All of this had some influence on Boston's political establishment. For example, at the official kickoff event to start the Bridges to the Future program, Mayor Menino attended the ceremony along with the CEO from every participating hospital, which raised the level of the program's profile not only around the city, but within each participating hospital.

JPNDCs efforts were also bolstered when, in 2000, the Boston Public Health Commission and the Boston PIC facilitated a series of meetings and discussions with health care employers about the mismatch between the health care industry's employment needs and the supply of workers in the Boston region (Boston PIC, 2002). This effort strengthened the relationships among Boston's health care employers, community organizations, government agencies, social service providers, institutions of higher education, and labor unions. In the fall of 2001, with funding from the U.S. Department of Labor, the Boston PIC formed the Boston Health Care Consortium, a consortium that included more than fifty members representing health care employers (from acute care, extended care, home health care, and community health centers), health care professional and trade associations, state and local workforce development agencies, organized labor, community-based organizations, community and neighborhood organizations, and postsecondary institutions that offer health sciences certificates and degrees (Boston PIC, 2002). The Consortium's goal was to identify past and current strategies aimed at alleviating the health care labor shortages within Boston's health care industry. The Consortium discussed ways to improve health-career-focused school-to-career models, pre-employment skills training programs for adults, and retention and skills-upgrading programs for incumbent health care workers. The Boston Health Care Consortium provided the first real opportunity for diverse health care–related organizations and professionals from the public, not-for-profit, and private sectors to come together to express their ideas, share information, and develop strategies to address the health care workforce employment demands and challenges. It also helped build relationships and trust among disparate organizations and professionals.

The Boston Health Care Consortium was significant for local community organizations such as JPNDC because it provided them with an opportunity to build relationships with the health care industry and it also made health care providers and state officials aware of the challenges in the community with regards to jobs, skills, and underemployment. As a consequence, by the time the Bridges program's funding was almost depleted, the Commonwealth Corporation (a nonprofit Massachusetts-based workforce consulting and research agency), along with other state education and training agencies, pooled together its resources to create the Building Essential Skills through Training (BEST) Initiative in 2001. The BEST Initiative was a statewide initiative with the following goals:

- Eliminating redundancy and combining federal and state dollars into a single effort.
- Involving local-level workforce development experts in the initiative.
- Creating career ladders in various sectors.
- Defining promising practices.
- Providing sector employers with effective ways to improve their productivity and their workers' skills.

According to the Commonwealth Corporation, "The BEST Initiative was designed to support industry-driven partnerships that address the workforce development needs of Massachusetts businesses by building workers' skills through education and training. With this initiative, the state's adult education and job training agencies joined together to support regional proposals for programs that give front-line workers a foundation of skills to achieve career mobility, while reducing persistent job vacancies in key sectors" (Commonwealth Corporation, 2005).

In April 2002, JPNDC and FCDC's joint proposal was selected as one of six regional sites to be a part of the BEST Initiative. They received a $500,000 grant to create the Boston Health Care and Research Training Institute (Training Institute). This grant allowed JPNDC and FCDC to build on their experience with the Bridges program by expanding the original number of five partners under the Bank of Boston–funded program to fifteen partners under the BEST Initiative. This was critical for several reasons. First, JPNDC and its partners succeeded in their earlier efforts in negotiating with hospital administrators around job quality and training for local residents and were at the table as an equal partner during the decision-making processes. Second, JPNDC and its partners were able to make connections with local elected officials, including the mayor, as well as with local, state, and national funders. Finally, as community-centered organizations in the partnership, JPNDC and its partners were very successful in advocating for the needs of low-income, under-skilled residents. In addition, they were also excellent at reaching out to local residents and community-based organizations (CBOs) to place pressure on local politicians and LMA institutions to hire more local residents. In the eyes of elected officials and hospital administrators, JPNDC and its partners were becoming a major "outside" political player and had a powerful constituent base of residents, community leaders, and community-centered organizations.

Addressing the health care industry's employment demands in a tight labor market

Some scholars and workforce development practitioners have argued that the 1998 Workforce Investment Act has been a catalyst for helping to alleviate health care workforce shortages by pooling additional resources from both private and public sources. Moreover, they contend that the timing of WIA legislation mandating the participation of employers on state and local WIBs provided a window of opportunity for the involvement of the health care industry in workforce planning because the industry was beginning to experience a workforce shortage crisis (Skillman, Sadow-Hasenberg, and Hart, 2004). Finding a solution to this crisis motivated many health care employers to participate in the workforce development system (Skillman, Sadow-Hasenberg, and Hart, 2004).

This argument sounds rather logical, and I am certain that in other metropolitan and rural areas around the country this may have indeed been true. However, in the City of Boston, the situation was slightly different. Boston's health care sector never experienced a severe health care workforce shortage in comparison to other regions. Instead, the health services industry experienced only a modest growth in overall employment and workforce shortages were only moderate between 1993 and 2000. According to a labor market analysis conducted by the Northeastern University Center for Labor Market Studies (CLMS), Massachusetts' health care employment levels rose from 299,200 in 1993 to 325,100 by 2000, an increase of just 25,900 jobs or 8.7 percent, a growth rate less than one-third the rate of the service sector during the same time period. In Boston between 1993 and 1997, the health care industry grew at a rate of 4.7 percent (3,279 jobs) compared to the health care industry growth in the Boston suburbs at 11.3 percent (12,898 jobs) (CLMS, 2002). Much of the health services growth in the suburbs of Boston was in non-hospital settings such as home health care, extended care facilities, and physicians' offices. Between 1997 and 2000, the City of Boston's health care employment grew at a steady, but moderate 4.4 percent (3,226 jobs), while the Boston suburbs and the state overall experienced health care declines of 6.5 percent (8,275 jobs lost) and 0.7 percent (2,139 jobs lost), respectively (Boston PIC, 2002). Much of the decline in health services employment throughout the state and within the Boston suburbs was in non-hospital settings, many of the same facilities that were responsible for the rapid growth during the mid-1990s (CLMS, 2002).

Despite the modest job growth within the health services industry, the CLMS study did find that some occupations within specific health care sectors did experience workforce shortages. The CLMS researchers were able to classify most of the 25,900 jobs created in the state of Massachusetts between 1993 and 2000 into five health care sectors: hospitals, nursing homes and personal care facilities, home health care services, medical and dental laboratories, and community health centers. This revealed the following:

- between 1993 and 2000, almost all of the City of Boston's employment gains were concentrated in the hospital sector, which added more than 5,500. Hospital employment accounted for half of the city's health services employment. The largest vacancies among hospitals were in nursing (medical surgical nurses at 22 percent, CNAs at 9 percent, and RNs at 6 percent);
- extended care facilities experienced persistent shortages in direct care workers, particularly in nursing (LPNs and RNs); and
- home care agencies, medical and dental laboratories, and community health centers did not experience any significant shortages.

Overall, Boston's health services industry experienced only a moderate job vacancy rate of 3.8 percent between 1993 and 2000 with the majority of workforce shortages concentrated in nursing (LPN and RN), psychologist/counselor, and medical and technologist occupations (CLMS, 2002).

Because the majority of workforce shortages was concentrated in mostly highly skilled occupations (requiring postsecondary education/training), other factors must explain why Boston's largest health care employers became deeply involved in workforce development intermediaries targeted at increasing the supply of the frontline, entry-level health care workforce. One factor that explains this is that, during the late 1990s and into 2000, Boston was experiencing an upswing in its economy, largely driven by the information technology sector, which resulted in a record number of jobs created. Between 1992 and 2000, Boston gained more than 120,000 new jobs and reached an all-time high of just more than 700,000 total jobs (Boston Redevelopment Authority, 2000). During the same time period, Boston's unemployment rate declined from a high of 8.6 percent during the recession year of 1991, to a record low of 2.9 percent in 2000 (Boston Redevelopment Authority, 2000). The city's average unemployment rate in 2000 was one percentage point lower than the national rate and only 0.2 percentage points higher than the state average.

Although these economic indicators were encouraging, health care employers were concerned about some startling labor force trends with regards to the future supply of the health care labor force. During the rapid expansion of Massachusetts' economy during the 1990s, the state experienced only a 0.7 percent increase in the labor force, or the equivalent of roughly 21,000 workers, which was well behind the U.S. labor force growth rate of 12.2 percent for the same period (CLMS, 2002). In addition, there was a significant decline in the labor force growth rate when compared to the previous two decades, which saw growth rates of 15.2 percent (1980s) and 17.9 percent (1970s) (CLMS, 2002). Even more startling was the fact that the number of degrees awarded below the bachelor's level in health sciences had declined 37 percent overall and the total number of health sciences degrees awarded by all postsecondary institutions between the academic school years 1994–1995 and 2000–2001 in the state declined by 12 percent, from 12,024 to 10,611. Greater Boston area postsecondary institutions awarded 41.8 percent fewer associate's-level health sciences degrees during this time. The occupations most affected by statewide declines in associate's-level health sciences degrees in both absolute and relative terms were RN (-33 percent); physical therapy (-62.5 percent); medical assistant (-60.3 percent); radiologic technologist (-58.3 percent); and psychiatric/mental health services technician (-41.3 percent) (CLMS, 2002).

These numbers, in combination with a tight labor market, help to explain another reason health care employers may have gotten involved in local welfare-to-work efforts. However, in late 2001, the economy in both Boston and the state of Massachusetts had softened quite a bit. The economy was no longer experiencing a tight labor market. However, toward the late 2000s that had changed. Health care employers stated that competition for jobs within the health services industry had grown and continued to increase. During my interviews with health care employers, they often stated that competition for jobs within the hospitals and research laboratories is strong. One Partners HealthCare System administrator summed it up best when she said, "Competition for health care jobs in Boston is fierce. Partners' jobs generally receive a high volume of applications, even for entry-level positions. It is not uncommon for some positions to receive over 100 applications." Another health care administrator explained to me that the competition for jobs is especially strong within the Longwood Medical Area (LMA) because of the fact that these institutions emphasize teaching and research. He stated, "[Institutions within the LMA] are more interested in research, so they prefer well-educated workers. Competition for federal research grants and research results [is] so strong that even the administrative assistants have master's degrees from top universities. Often times, there is tension between local residents and students with BAs who want to get work experience before applying to graduate or medical school. This is especially the case in Boston."

Overall, an analysis of the health care labor market between the early 1990s and 2000 showed that Massachusetts, and Boston in particular, never experienced a severe health care workforce shortage. The health services sector grew at a moderate rate and even declined between 1997 and 2000 in Massachusetts, except for in the City of Boston. The data did reveal that some occupations such as nursing, health technicians, and technologists, and among psychologists and counselors, experienced workforce shortages. The vast majority of these occupations requires extensive postsecondary education, training, and certification. Labor market projections suggest that the occupations with the most opportunity for growth and higher pay will be those that require at least postsecondary education, training, and certification (i.e., medical records and health information technicians, dental hygienists, cardiovascular technologists/technicians, respiratory therapists, etc.). Given all of this, there must be an additional explanation as to why the largest health care employers (mainly research and teaching hospitals) in Boston have been willing to spend so much time, money, and resources in partnering with community organizations to support workforce development programs targeted at the city's most economically disadvantaged and under-skilled residents, especially when competition for these jobs is already strong.

Jobs, politics, and economic development

The rapid growth of buildings within the LMA over the years has forced institutions to look for available land in the surrounding communities adjacent or in close proximity to the LMA, such as Mission Hill, Roxbury, and Jamaica Plain. Increased development within the LMA and into the surrounding communities has been an extremely controversial and contentious issue between community residents and LMA institutions. Residents living in neighborhoods contiguous to the LMA often complain about the increased development by LMA institutions. Residents argue that the development within and surrounding the LMA is contributing to higher housing costs, traffic congestion, and gentrification. More importantly, a high percentage of the residents living in the Fenway-Kenmore, Jamaica Plain, and Roxbury neighborhoods are under-skilled, economically disadvantaged residents. These residents have protested to city officials, local state representatives, city council members, and LMA administrators that they are being pushed out of the area because of development and say that they would be less likely to oppose most development projects if residents from their communities were getting a proportion of the newly created jobs. A veteran Mission Hill community advocate commented during an interview that a job developer at the local community center had been trying to get Mission Hill residents jobs within the LMA for several years but was unsuccessful. "Residents are already connected to the LMA area because they go there for services and health care. However, many have a difficult time getting employment in the LMA. There are roughly 10 residents employed by LMA institutions! That's why Mission Works [and other community organizations] are working so hard to place residents within the Longwood Medical Area."

Apparently, Boston residents' complaints did not fall on deaf ears. Advocacy efforts to raise awareness about deleterious effects of LMA development on the local community had some influence on local and state elected officials. This led to a state policy that began monitoring how much LMA medical institutions and other medical organizations around Boston contributed to efforts that created economic opportunities, improved the quality of life, and enhanced the overall well-being of Boston's residents, especially the most impoverished. In 2001, the Massachusetts Attorney General's Office began encouraging all health maintenance organizations (HMOs) and nonprofit acute care hospitals to prepare annual community benefit reports that document the status of their community benefits programs and initiatives (MA Office of the Attorney General, 2007a, 2007b). According to the Attorney General's Office, these sets of voluntary principles "encourage Massachusetts hospitals and HMOs to continue and build upon their commitment to addressing health and social needs within their communities" (MA Office of the Attorney General, 2011). The idea behind the Attorney General's Office is to make HMO and hospital data transparent. All of the data collected from community benefits reports are placed in a publicly searchable online "Community Benefits Program Database," allowing any Massachusetts resident to monitor the level of community involvement and investment by hospitals and HMOs.

Boston's Mayor Menino and several local state representatives also openly supported health care workforce development programs, especially the Boston Health Care and Research Training Institute and the Partners in Career and Workforce Development programs. Mayor Menino, under pressure from JPNDC and other CBOs, was particularly concerned about the lack of economic opportunity and health disparities between Boston's higher-educated, higher-income residents and those residents with very little formal education and/or skills. As one city staff member commented in an interview, "There is a lot of pressure [in Boston] on hospitals to hire residents from these training programs."

Moreover, in 2003, a period during which Boston suffered an economic downturn, residents needed employment and better economic opportunities. As a result, Mayor Menino and The Boston Foundation announced a five-year, multimillion-dollar workforce development initiative (SkillWorks). During the press conference to announce the SkillWorks initiative, Mayor Menino cleverly named the president of Brigham and Women's Hospital, Dr. Gary Gottlieb, to chair the Workforce Development Committee of the Boston Private Industry Council (Boston Redevelopment Authority, 2003a). By appointing such a powerful hospital administrator to chair the local workforce development committee for the Boston PIC, the mayor sent a message to others that connecting residents to health care jobs was a priority. Mayor Menino further made his point by telling the audience and media that were present that he believed in the people of Boston and that it was the city's responsibility to give them the tools they need to compete for good-paying jobs. Mayor Menino emphasized that if given the tools, residents could support the growth of the city. He said, "[T]hey will rebuild our economy. We have invested a lot in workforce development over the past ten years and it is our responsibility to continue to support our workforce at a time when they need it most" (Boston Redevelopment Authority, 2003a). This occasion would mark the beginning of Menino's efforts to place a greater responsibility on health care employers to do more to connect Boston residents to jobs.

The SkillsWorks initiative ended up providing a substantial amount of funding to support the Training Institute's workforce development efforts. JPNDC and its partners applied and were awarded a five-year grant from SkillWorks (formerly known as the Boston Workforce Development Initiative), which further bolstered JPNDC's clout in the local community and its efforts to advocate on behalf of low-income residents. The grant, awarded to JPNDC's Training Institute, involved a $15 million workforce development initiative focused on building the skills of low-skilled, underemployed, entry-level workers in Boston. The SkillWorks initiative was funded by a major consortium of public and private funders, known as The Boston Funders Group for Workforce Development, which included contributions from the City of Boston, the Commonwealth of Massachusetts' Governor's Discretionary Workforce Investment Act grant, and nine Boston-based and national foundations: The Boston Foundation, Bank of America Private Bank, the Annie E. Casey Foundation, The William Randolph Hearst Foundations, The Hyams Foundation, The Robert Wood Johnson Foundation, The John Merck Fund, Rockefeller Foundation, The Paul and Phyllis Fireman Foundation, the State Street Trust Community Foundation, and United Way of Massachusetts Bay. Under this new funding structure, the Training

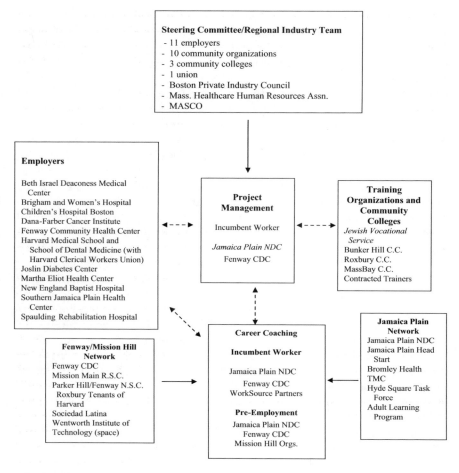

Figure 3.1 Boston Health Care and Research Training Institute organization
Source: Adapted from JPNDC.

Institute had an annual operating budget of about $650,000 and had expanded to include twenty-eight partners representing employers, social service agencies, education and training providers, community organizations, a labor union, an industry association, and the Boston Private Industry Council (see Figure 3.1). The Training Institute's primary goal was to provide local Boston neighborhood residents and current entry-level employees with skill training, education, and career support programs in the health care and research sectors. In addition, JPNDC wanted to "institutionalize" its partnership with LMA institutions to ensure that any future economic development in the LMA area would benefit local residents and include JPNDC staff and its partners in the decision-making process.

Mayor Menino took several concrete steps to make certain that his efforts to encourage health care employers to hire local residents, especially those residents in communities adjacent to the LMA, were taken seriously. The month after the press conference announcing the SkillWorks workforce development initiative, the Boston Redevelopment Authority (BRA), the Office of Jobs and Community Services (JCS), and the Boston Transportation Department, under the guidance of the mayor, announced the beginning of an eighteen-month planning process for the LMA (the "LMA Master Plan"). The development of the master plan for the LMA required the participation of city agencies, LMA institutions, and area residents. During the eighteen-month interim period preceding the completion of the LMA master plan, the BRA released a set of interim guidelines for the purposes of "governing development, preventing ad hoc growth in the LMA, and control[ing] growth in a fair and equitable manner" (Boston Redevelopment Authority, 2003b). Under the new LMA Interim Guidelines report, all institutions or developers contemplating development within the LMA would have to go through the organization's development review process.

Prior to the release of the LMA Interim Guidelines, each institution in the academic and medical area was responsible for developing its own master plan. With the creation of the LMA Interim Guidelines, the City of Boston had more influence over the development process within the LMA. More importantly, this was an opportunity for Mayor Menino to exert his political power and to increase his political support among the growing numbers of people of color and new Americans in the city by allowing him to directly influence the type of development being built within the LMA, create affordable housing and employment opportunities for local residents, and find ways to better integrate the activities and services that LMA institutions provided into the fabric of the surrounding neighborhoods. For instance, in the LMA Interim Guidelines, development was tied to workforce development, making Boston among the earliest cities in the country to tie real estate development to job development (Greenberger, 2003). The LMA Interim Guidelines clearly stated that institutions or developers contemplating development within the LMA would be required to present to BRA and JCS workforce development staff, as part of the development review process, "an assessment of current and projected workforce needs, and to work with BRA/JCS staff to formulate a workforce development plan to address those needs" (Boston Redevelopment Authority, 2003b). This required developers/institutions to provide the following:

- data on the number and percentage of current employees who are Boston residents, and the types of positions they hold;
- current and projected staffing needs; and
- a description of the institution's existing workforce development activities.

Moreover, the Workforce Development section within the LMA Interim Guidelines stated that institutions or developers may submit proposals to the BRA requesting that a portion of the development funds be placed into the Neighborhood Jobs Trust, which is used to train new workers for positions within a proposed project. The BRA/JCS workforce development staff in evaluating proposals looked for the following:

- a firm commitment for a specific number of jobs offering adequate pay and benefits;
- a high degree of institutional involvement in the design and implementation of the training program;
- a substantial commitment of in-kind resources from the institution; and
- a commitment to hiring a specific number of Boston residents.

The LMA Interim Guidelines also blatantly stated that it was expected that an LMA institution's workforce development plan would include an increased investment in the Training Institute "to ensure that this new health care career-ladder initiative continues to grow after the initial start-up grants from the City and State have expired." If LMA institutions did not make investments in the Training Institute, they had the option of making investments in the following:

- establishment of other career-ladder training models, which could, for example, build on successful school-to-work or welfare-to-work programs piloted over the past several years by Boston health care institutions and training providers (i.e., Partners in Career and Workforce Development program led by Partners HealthCare Systems, Inc.);
- establishment of intensive, on-site English as a second language (ESL) classes for current employees, preparing them for career-ladder job training programs while at the same time increasing the pool of bilingual employees (especially designed for recent immigrants to Boston); and/or
- investment in the city's English for New Bostonians initiative, or the Adult Literacy Initiative, which funds the expansion of ESL and literacy services citywide (programs targeted at increasing the language and literacy skills of immigrants in Boston, who increasingly comprise a larger percentage of Boston's population and labor force).

This had a direct influence on many LMA employers to hire local residents. For example, an administrator at Harvard Medical School stated, "This political pressure to get things going inspired [Harvard] to support programs like the Training Institute."

In addition to the workforce development guidelines, LMA institutions and developers wanting to construct buildings exceeding the BRA baselines of 75 or 150 feet (depending on location and type of building) would have to provide more benefits to the public. For instance, in early 2003, Joslin Diabetes Center had plans to build more than 1 million square feet for a research center and apartment building within the LMA. After resistance from elected officials and community residents, Joslin was forced to reduce its proposed project under the new LMA interim planning guidelines. Joslin's revised plan included only 490,000 square feet of development instead of 1 million, 150 apartment units instead of 160, a twenty-nine-floor tower instead of a thirty-seven-foot tower, and 350 parking spaces instead of 357 (Palmer, 2003). Despite Joslin's significantly reduced development plan, the organization still faced resistance from BRA staff and community groups who demanded that more affordable housing and jobs be developed for local residents. Finally, in May 2003, the BRA gave final approval for Joslin Diabetes Center to build its proposed research center and apartment complex. However, as part of the agreement with the BRA to allow Joslin to construct a building taller than the specified LMA interim guidelines, Joslin agreed to increase its current investment in workforce development in Boston from $160,000 to $330,000 between the fall of 2003 and late 2007 (Diesenhouse, 2003). Joslin also agreed to provide more affordable housing units within its proposed apartment complex. Shortly after city planners approved Joslin's development proposal, Joslin Diabetes Center president C. Ronald Kahn told *The Boston Globe*, "The city insisted on the housing" (Palmer, 2003). Apparently, this deal was worth it to Joslin because the organization's president also stated that the institution was eager to expand at its current prominent location within the LMA to be near colleagues at Harvard Medical School and sixteen other affiliated institutions. The desire for proximity to world-class research institutions and other medical facilities is a driving force that allows the BRA, other city agencies, and community organizations such as JPNDC to negotiate and demand so much from LMA institutions.

The second major step Mayor Menino took in encouraging Boston health care employers to invest and support workforce development initiatives came in the fall of 2005. The mayor announced that the City of Boston was providing $1 million in public and private funds to provide grants to help fight racial and ethnic health disparities. The Boston Health Disparities Project is a strategic plan to eliminate the health inequities that exist between Boston's white and minority residents. Among the strategies of the Health Disparities Project is an effort to improve the diversity of the health care workforce and increase job security for poorer residents.

Employment outcomes

JPNDC's workforce development efforts succeeded in reaching out to the neighborhood's most vulnerable residents. In the first few years of the program, the Training Institute trained more than 160 residents. Among those completing the program, more than 80 percent of those trained were poor women with children and the average age was just under thirty-four years.

Before participating in the Training Institute, 41 percent received housing subsidies, 50 percent received food stamps, and 38 percent were on Temporary Assistance for Needy Families. Moreover, 86 percent of the women were racial and ethnic minorities.

The average annual pre-training salary for the pre-employment participants was about $20,500 ($9.90 per hour). After completing the Training Institute program, the median starting salary was $12.00 per hour.[3] Assuming that an individual could continue working over a ten-year period, his or her earnings at the end of the period would be $26,748 (assuming a 3 percent annual raise). However, if that same individual decided to seek additional training by enrolling in the Training Institute's twelve-week Pre-Employment Training Program, he or she would make more money over the ten-year period. The initial decision to enroll in the Pre-Employment Training Program costs the average individual twelve weeks of salary ($9.90 per hour), which would equal approximately $4,750. However, after receiving training, the average Training Institute participant would earn $12.28 an hour, not including benefits. Once you factor in benefits, the average hourly salary for Training Institute participants would be $22.28 an hour. Over a ten-year period, the individual would earn $60,466 (assuming a 3 percent annual increase in salary), a difference of $23,690 between their annual salaries (taking into account the annual discounted value of 4 percent) if they had decided to forgo additional skills training.[4] Based on the total net present value of enrolling in training, it appears as though the Training Institute in the long run would help raise low-income Boston residents' annual salary the most, a total net present value for the ten-year period of $242,770. The balance of jobs that Training Institute participants obtain is not just in administrative positions, but also in laboratory technology-related positions and patient care. For example, Training Institute participants were evenly distributed across administrative (30 percent), laboratory technology (30 percent), patient care (26 percent), and other health-related occupations (14 percent). This was significant because, although some administrative and clerical jobs pay a livable wage and provide benefits, the upward mobility of these types of jobs is more limited than in nursing or direct patient care health occupations.

Conclusion

In the mid-1990s, welfare reform succeeded in placing work first, which led to the distribution of millions of federal dollars that went to support state and local efforts to help TANF recipients transition from welfare to work as well as for workforce development initiatives and programs. By the late 1990s, the Workforce Investment Act legislation helped to reorganize and streamline Massachusetts' workforce development system. Under WIA, state and local WIBs were required to include employers on their boards. This federal requirement in combination with additional government-administered

WIA funds helped get employers' "buy-in," especially in local jurisdictions such as Boston. Coincidently, by the time welfare reform and WIA legislation were implemented, Massachusetts was experiencing an economic boom driven largely by the information and technology sectors. This resulted in record low unemployment levels and a tight labor pool in Boston, which got the attention of health care employers and motivated them to be a part of state and local workforce development efforts. However, after 2001, Boston's economy experienced an economic downturn and unemployment rose. Today, competition for health care jobs remains strong and Boston's health care employers have continued to invest in health care workforce development efforts targeted at the city's most economically disadvantaged and under-skilled residents. This is, in large, part due to the political pressure from community-based organizations such as JPNDC, as well as from state and local elected officials. The City of Boston has succeeded in linking real estate development within the LMA to outcomes in the community such as jobs, investments in workforce development programs, and other public benefits.

The emergence of workforce intermediaries has raised questions about how well these intermediaries perform and what factors might help explain why some perform better than others. Robert Giloth and Richard Kazis (2004) have argued that the most successful workforce intermediaries are those that can carry out three important tasks:

1   they have an *entrepreneurial focus* on outcomes like long-term job retention, wage progression, and career mobility;
2   they *can network and partner* across supply, demand, educational, financial/funding, and spatial dimensions of regional labor markets; and
3   they have the *ability to learn and adapt* as market conditions and opportunities change.

My research findings suggest that these three factors are indeed important in determining the success of workforce intermediaries such as the Training Institute and PCWD. However, I would add two more tasks to the three Giloth and Kazis advanced. A fourth important task that helps determine the success of a workforce development intermediary is its ability to *advocate* for its participants. In the case of the Training Institute, JPNDC and their allies worked hard to advocate on behalf of their pre-employment participants. This involved contacting human resource personnel and hospital managers and supervisors on behalf of an individual. Because the volume of applications for hospital jobs has increased dramatically in recent years, it makes it that much more important for Training Institute pre-employment training program graduates to have additional help in obtaining employment.

The fifth, and perhaps one of the most important tasks for a successful intermediary to accomplish, is its ability *to build a political base of support.*

This means that workforce development intermediaries need to establish relationships with elected officials, local political leaders, community activists, and neighborhood residents to keep them informed of the intermediaries' mission, goals, and outcomes. In addition, intermediaries with a strong political base and support can better negotiate with employers when it comes to improving the workplace environment, quality of jobs, and compensation. Most employers such as those who deal directly with the public are conscientious of the way the public perceives them. Moreover, many of these employers want to be good neighbors and give back to the local community, but without strong political activism and the ability to develop partnerships, very few positive outcomes will emerge that ultimately can benefit both employers and workers.

Overall, JPNDC succeeded in promoting an equitable economic development agenda. It organized local residents to build a grassroots movement to demand good-quality jobs and started an effective jobs campaign, which brought to light the economic challenges and lack of quality jobs for some of Boston's poorest residents. JPNDC was politically savvy in reaching out and building collaborations with local community organizations, government agencies, elected officials, health care employers, and others to make the case that local residents needed better access to good-quality jobs and job support services. JPNDC knew of the changing demographics in the neighborhoods surrounding the LMA and the tension that exists over development. Thus, it could capitalize off the changing demographics in Boston and the fact that elected officials did not want to ignore the economic and social needs of such an increasingly growing segment of the voting-age population, much of which consisted of Latinos, blacks, and new Americans. JPNDC successfully got the attention of the mayor and elected officials, who in return placed political pressure on health care employers to hire local residents and also invest in community benefit programs.

Perhaps the most significant accomplishment of JPNDC and its partners was the staff's ability to be entrepreneurial. JPNDC led the way in bringing various actors together to form a public-private partnership. It formed a broad-based coalition of job training providers, community organizations, health care employers, social service providers, and labor unions, as well as educational and government agencies. This has been a key role of CDCs (Squazzoni, 2008). Moreover, JPNDC was not only successful at bringing a disparate group together, but it was a major player in the decision-making process with regard to the Training Institute. It advocated for good-quality jobs, worked with employers to define adequate career ladders, and encouraged hospitals and other health-related employers to focus on investments in community programs such as high school health care academies, community health outreach, and more.

A number of early lessons have been learned that may be relevant to other cities: (1) JPNDC and its partners' ability to gain the attention of elected officials, hospital employers, and other government agencies had a lot to do with the political ramifications of welfare reform and the need to place low-income, low-skilled Boston residents into jobs. (2) This type of public-private partnership was primarily possible because of the limited amount of valuable land within and surrounding the LMA, which was an incentive for health care employers to be at the negotiating table. (3) Community organizing is critical to address inequities and bring about positive systemic change. (4) Protest politics are sometimes necessary; in other instances, it is just as effective to try to develop an adversarial relationship that enables negotiation.

JPNDC and its partners had to overcome and in some instances still struggle to overcome a number of challenges. The first is remaining financially sustainable. There is a constant need to acquire grants and private funding. Second, there is a challenge of turnover among staff within partnership organizations, which hurts continuity and makes it more difficult for programs and practices to be institutionalized. Finally, the scale of the public-private partnership was a major challenge for JPNDC to manage logistically and required a lot of staff time and resources, sometimes at the expense of other program areas.

Overall, this case study demonstrates CDCs and CBOs' ability to have autonomy and stand up to developers and large institutions. Moreover, as the health care sector continues to be the one area of job growth within many urban areas, the strategy to link development to jobs can benefit both local residents and employers. This is particularly important given the current state of the U.S. economy and high unemployment rates within many urban communities, especially among men of color. This case study shows how public-private partnerships can at the very least lead to a discussion about inequality, poverty, and opportunity if community-oriented organizations can be equal partners at the table, and, in some instances, can lead to significant benefits for the entire community.

It is clear, based on my research in Boston, that the main reason the Training Institute has been so successful has been because of politics. Employers originally invested in these programs because it was important to Mayor Menino. The employers within the LMA are likely to continue wanting to expand both upward and outward. They understand that their ability to get building permits approved by the Boston Redevelopment Authority is tied to the workforce outcomes of neighborhood residents, especially residents living in communities contiguous to the LMA.

Government policies encouraging the business community to serve disadvantaged populations is not new. In 1977, Congress passed the Community Reinvestment Act. The Community Reinvestment Act required depository institutions to help meet the credit needs of the communities in which they operate, including low- and moderate-income neighborhoods, consistent with safe and sound banking operations (Federal Financial Institutions Examination Council, 2006). Since the CRA was enacted, tens of billions of dollars have been invested in low- to moderate-income communities. This has helped small minority- and women-owned business get started, created opportunities for homeowners in low-income communities to renovate their homes, and provided loans to small developers who have revitalized poorer, urban communities. So, in many ways, what is happening in Boston is very similar. The state of Massachusetts, the City of Boston, and elected leaders are trying to encourage Boston's largest private employers to invest in the local community's education and skills. The hope is that over time, these residents will have access to better jobs and economic opportunities that can help them move out of poverty and have enough income to become home-owners and productive tax-paying citizens. In addition, the hope is that over time, Boston's health care workforce will also better resemble its growing immigrant and minority population, resulting in increased cultural compe-tency and language proficiency, ultimately leading to better health outcomes for all of its residents. Only time will tell if this type of political strategy produces the positive outcomes that politicians and local community resi-dents desire.

Notes

1 The six to twenty-four months of additional training required to become a medi-cal assistant assumes that the individual will be attending full time. In the case of most entry-level health services workers, they do not have the resources (financial, social support, etc.) to stop working while they attend a community college or vocational/technical training program. Therefore, one can assume that in most cases where individuals need to work that it would take more time to finish these types of training programs.
2 This again assumes an individual is attending school full time.
3 This is in 2005 dollars.
4 This assumes that the Training Institute participants' pre-employment jobs did not include benefits, which, based on the pre-employment data, is an accurate assumption.

Bibliography

American Community Survey (ACS). (2011). ACS 2005–2009 estimate: Boston. Retrieved from www.bostonredevelopmentauthority.org.

Babacan, H. and Gopalkrishnan, N. 2001. Community work partnerships in a global context. *Community Development Journal*, 36(1), 3–17.

Beth Israel Deaconess Medical Center (BIDMC). 2004. Personal communication, October 29.

Boston Private Industry Council (Boston PIC) 2002. Retrieved from www.bostonpic.org/adult.

Boston Private Industry Council (Boston PIC). 2006. Retrieved from www.bostonpic.org/adult.

Boston Redevelopment Authority (BRA). 2000. www.bostonredevelopmentauthority.org.

Boston Redevelopment Authority (BRA). 2003a. Boston Redevelopment Authority. January 15. Press Release: Mayor Menino, The Boston Foundation announce workforce development plan. Retrieved from www.cityofboston.gov/bra/press.

Boston Redevelopment Authority (BRA). 2003b. Longwood medical and academic area interim guidelines report. Boston, MA: Boston Redevelopment Authority.

Cashin, S. 2009. Race, class, and real estate. In M. P. Pavel (Ed.), *Breakthrough Communities: Sustainability and Justice in the Next American Metropolis* (pp. 59–66). Cambridge, MA: MIT Press.

Center for Labor Market Studies. 2002. Northeastern University. www.northeastern. edu/clms/.

Chong, N. 2002. A model for the nation's health care industry: Kaiser Permanente's Institute for Culturally Competent Care. *The Permanente Journal*, 6(3), Summer 2002.

City of Boston, Mayor's Office of New Bostonians. 2006. New Bostonians' demographic report. Retrieved from www.cityofboston.gov/newbostonians/pdfs/dem_ report.pdf.

Commonwealth Corporation. 2005. Retrieved from www.commcorp.org/cwi/pro-grams/best/projects.html.

Corburn, J. 2009. *Toward the Healthy City: People, Places, and the Politics of Urban Planning*. Cambridge, MA: MIT Press.

Diesenhouse, S. 2003. City's RX for medical area: More housing. Joslin's $225m complex to have apartments, labs. *The Boston Globe*, July 26. [Section: Real Estate], p. D12.

Federal Financial Institutions Examination Council. 2006. www.ffiec.gov/cra/history. htm.

Giloth, R. and Kazis, R. 2004. What do workforce intermediaries do? In R. P. Giloth (Ed.), *Workforce Intermediaries for the Twenty-first Century*. Published in association with the American Assembly, Columbia University. Philadelphia, PA: Temple University Press.

Greenberger, S. 2003. City pushes local jobs at Longwood. *The Boston Globe*, March 14. [Section: Metro/Region], p. B1.

Griffen, S. 2005. Personal communication, March 22.

Grunwald, M. 1996. Welfare job plan unfulfilled as deadline nears. *The Boston Globe*, June 14. City Edition. [Section: Metro/Region], p. 1.

Holzer, H. and Waller, M. 2003. *The Workforce Investment Act: Reauthorization to Address the "Skills Gap."* Washington, DC: Brookings Institution Center on Urban and Metropolitan Policy.

Jamaica Plain Neighborhood Development Corporation. 2015. Retrieved from www.jpndc.org.

Kaye, L., et al. 2001. *Changes in Massachusetts Welfare and Work, Child Care, and Child Welfare Systems*. Washington, DC: The Urban Institute. New Federalism National Survey of America's Families.

Leeming, K. 2002. Community businesses – lessons from Liverpool, UK. *Community Development Journal*, 37, 260–267.

Massachusetts Department of Workforce Development. 2006. www.mass.gov/ lwd/.

Massachusetts Office of the Attorney General. 2007a. *Community Benefits Guidelines for Non-profit Acute Care Hospitals*. Boston, MA: Office of Attorney General Martha Coakley. Retrieved from www.cbsys.ago.state.ma.us/cbpublic/public/ hccbguides.aspx.

Massachusetts Office of the Attorney General. 2007b. *Community Benefits Guidelines for Health Maintenance Organizations*. Boston, MA: Office of Attorney

General Martha Coakley. Retrieved from www.cbsys.ago.state.ma.us/cbpublic/public/hccbguides.aspx.

Massachusetts Office of the Attorney General. 2011. Retrieved from www.cbsys.ago.state.ma.us/cbpublic/public/hccbguides.aspx.

McCall, T. 2003. Institutional design for community economic development models: Issues of opportunity and capacity. *Community Development Journal*, 38, 96–108.

Medical Academic and Scientific Community Organization. 2012. Longwood Medical and Academic Area fact sheet. Retrieved from www.masco.org/thelma/about-lma.

O'Campo, P. and Yonas, M. 2005. Health of economically deprived populations in cities. In S. Galea and D. Vlahov (Eds.), *Handbook of Urban Health: Populations, Methods, and Practice*. New York: Springer.

Palmer, Jr., T. C. 2003. BRA postpones Longwood project vote, traffic issues at diabetes center's complex are cited. *The Boston Globe*, April 11. [Section: Business], p. D3.

Powell, J. A. 2009. Reinterpreting metropolitan space as a strategy for social justice. In M. P. Pavel (Ed.), *Breakthrough Communities: Sustainability and Justice in the Next American Metropolis* (pp. 23–32). Cambridge, MA: MIT Press.

Robinson, M. 1995. Towards a new paradigm of community development. *Community Development Journal*, 30(1), 21–30.

Root Cause. 2011. Boston Health Care and Research Training Institute budget. Retrieved from www.rootcause.org/performance-measurement/profiles/boston-health-care- and-research-training-institute.

Sable, M. 2007. The impact of the biotechnology industry on local economic development in the Boston and San Diego metropolitan areas. *Technological Forecasting and Social Change*, 74(1), 36–60.

Skillman, S., Sadow-Hasenberg, J., and Hart, L. G. 2004. *Effects of the Workforce Investment Act of 1998 on Health Workforce Development in the States*. U.S. Department of Health and Human Services, Health Resources and Services Administration, Bureau of Health Professions, Office of Workforce Evaluation and Quality Assurance by the Center for Health Workforce Distribution Studies, University of Washington, Seattle, under Grant#1-U79-HP-00011–01.

Squazzoni, F. 2008. Local economic development initiatives from the bottom-up: The role of community development corporations. *Community Development Journal*, 44, 500–514.

Sze, J. 2007. *Noxious New York: The Racial Politics of Urban Health and Environmental Justice*. Cambridge, MA: MIT Press.

The Boston Indicators Project. 2011. Retrieved from www.tbf.org/indicators2006/economy/content.aspx?id1/4686.

U.S. Bureau of Labor Statistics. 2015. Retrieved at www.census.gov.

U.S. Census Bureau. 2007–2011. American Community Survey, BRA Research Division Analysis.

U.S. Census Bureau. 2011. City of Boston population. Retrieved from www.bostonredevelopmentauthoritynews.org/2011/03/23/boston-census-facts-figures/.

Wilson, S., Hutson, M., and Mujahid, M. 2008. How planning and zoning contribute to inequitable development, neighborhood health, and environmental (in)justice. *Environmental Justice*, 1, 211–216.

4   Brooklyn

The struggle for inclusive governance and transparency

"The New Jim Crowism is housing policies."
(New York Assemblymember Charles Barron)

In recent years, Brooklyn has been at the center of a national debate around gentrification, neighborhood change, and displacement. Countless articles have been written about the new hipsters moving into Brooklyn or about the professional thirtysomething parents with their Bugaboo strollers "invading" traditionally working-class neighborhoods and the neighborhood transformations that follow. In 2014, Spike Lee drew national and international attention to the gentrification debate during a lecture he gave at a Black History Month event at the Pratt Institute in Brooklyn. An audience member asked the filmmaker about the "other side of gentrification," but before he could complete his question, Mr. Lee gave an impassioned, profanity-laced response (Coscarelli, 2015). Commenting on the improved infrastructure in changing neighborhoods, Mr. Lee pointedly said, "[W]hy does it take an influx of white New Yorkers in the south Bronx, in Harlem, in Bed Stuy, in Crown Heights for the facilities to get better?" He then proceeded to describe how newcomers to the neighborhood impacted local cultural norms. He discussed how African drummers who had played music in the Mount Morris park for forty years no longer could, and how new neighbors called the police on his own father, a jazz musician who bought his home in 1968, for playing an acoustic bass.

Mr. Lee's response contributed to the national debate about the positive and negative impacts of gentrification on neighborhoods, especially traditionally black neighborhoods. Some highlighted the disruption of gentrification on a neighborhood and people's lives as rising rents have caused people to move and lose their social networks while others questioned the full negative impact of gentrification on established black communities in places like New York and Washington, DC. Some accused Spike Lee of being a gentrifier and contributing to the problem that he was ranting about while others questioned if gentrification was bad at all for a neighborhood (Davidson, 2015).

Mr. Lee's response echoed the thoughts and feelings of many local residents from San Francisco to Washington, DC, who have or are experiencing gentrification. In my interviews, several residents have commented on the "lack of respect" that the new upwardly mobile, higher-income residents show toward the people, culture, and institutions that previously existed in the neighborhood before they arrived. Others accuse newcomers of having what is commonly called the "Christopher Columbus Syndrome," characterizing new arrivals as acting as though they have suddenly discovered the neighborhood and demanding the cultural norms in place give way to their own preferences and sets of rules. Perhaps one of the most common themes emerging from my interviews with residents is similar to what Mr. Lee said regarding city services and infrastructure. Many residents said it's like they did not exist before more affluent whites and others moved into their neighborhoods because basic services, such as street lights getting fixed, sidewalks being repaired, or the city cracking down on illegal dumping in their neighborhood, were lacking. They also did not experience as much police presence or the construction of dog parks and bike lanes until after the new arrivals.

Mr. Lee's comments and the national attention they garnered, the proliferation of articles about gentrification, and even a *Saturday Night Live* Brooklyn gentrification skit all highlight the precipitous demographic and economic changes impacting Brooklyn. At a community meeting in Brooklyn, New York, hosted by Movement to Protect the People (a community group comprised of local residents, business owners, and activists), New York Assemblymember Charles Barron was speaking to the energetic crowd of organized community residents who had come out to discuss the economic changes happening in Brooklyn. Mr. Barron stood before the crowd and described what he called the "New Jim Crow."

The "New Jim Crow," according to Assemblymember Barron, is found in the politics of housing. He discussed the development of luxury housing in Brooklyn and how it was changing the community's character. He explained that not enough affordable housing was being constructed for the people who currently lived in the neighborhood. In addition, he said that the rising cost of housing and living has many residents desperate for jobs, and community residents are in a "survival mentality." He contended that people could no longer live in the communities that they grew up in and argued that the city needed housing for working-class residents. "Developers [are] maximizing their profits at the expense of residents who grow up in the community. Power starts with the city planning commission. [We] [n]eed to fight for permanently affordable housing." Assemblymember Barron went on to discuss how there has been a noticeable and measurable drop in the black population, while the white population has increased in Brooklyn.

Brooklyn demographic and economic change

Since 2000, Brooklyn has experienced a boom in housing costs and overall cost of living. According to a report from the Office of the New York

City Comptroller, *The Growing Gap: New York City's Housing Affordability Challenge*, between 2000 and 2012, median apartment rents in New York City rose by 75 percent and during this same period, real incomes for New York residents declined (Braconi and Corson, 2014). In addition, housing affordability became more difficult for *every* income group, with those earning less than $40,000 a year hit hard by the economic changes (Braconi and Corson, 2014). The affordability crisis was even more dramatic in Brooklyn. Between the same twelve-year period, rents grew highest in Brooklyn, where the average monthly rent increased by 70 percent (Braconi and Corson, 2014).

The Growing Gap report explained that part of the housing affordability crisis in New York City was a result of three major possible explanations. The first is gentrification (Braconi and Corson, 2014). Between 2000 and 2012, Brooklyn gained the most mid- and high-income households (those making $100,000 or more annually) by roughly 28,000, while Manhattan was second with an increase of about 21,500 households (Braconi and Corson, 2014). More important, the New York City comptroller's analysis suggests "there is a positive correlation between the increase in the number of middle- and high-income households residing in a neighborhood and the rate of increase in real average rents" (Braconi and Corson, 2014).

The second possible factor for the housing affordability crisis in New York City, and especially Brooklyn, may relate to rent regulation. New York City lost a net 152,751 affordable housing units in New York City's rent stabilization system between 1994 and 2012 (Braconi and Corson, 2014). Finally, New York City has experienced a population increase and housing supply has not kept pace with the demand, a very similar situation to that seen in San Francisco.

In a recent analysis of gentrification in fifty of the United States' most populous cities, the analysis found that nearly 30 percent of New York City's census tracts had gentrified since 2000.[1] In Brooklyn, several tracts within the neighborhoods of Fort Greene, Prospect Heights, and Crown Heights had gentrified.[2] These census tracts experienced a significant growth in both home values and educational attainment. All of these economic and demographic changes have mobilized community residents in these neighborhoods to advocate for affordable housing and good-quality jobs, and to address large-scale development, which they perceive as a threat to maintaining neighborhood cohesion and preserving a sense of place. Perhaps no development has gathered as much negative attention and activism in Brooklyn than the Atlantic Yards/Pacific Park project.

"Hoops without housing": the Atlantic Yards/Pacific Park development

Over the past two decades, tension around development, gentrification, and neighborhood change in Brooklyn has intensified, especially since the controversial Atlantic Yards development (now renamed Pacific Park) by

Forest City Ratner Companies and the Empire State Development Corporation (ESDC) was announced in December 2003.[3] The Atlantic Yards development has symbolized the problem with large-scale developments that ignore the community's history and fail to engage residents through a meaningful community engagement process. For many low-income and middle-class residents of Brooklyn, the Atlantic Yards project and its lack of transparency and public participation in the planning process has served as a lightning rod to galvanize local residents against development that does not take into consideration the local community's social, economic, and environmental needs.

This project began when the private development company approached the city to develop the project (Fainstein, 2009). The initial plans for the $2.5 billion Atlantic Yards/Pacific Park development included mixed-use commercial and residential development on approximately twenty-two acres of land over the Atlantic Rail Yards, adjacent to the Atlantic Center and Atlantic Terminal. The proposal included the development of sixteen high-rise buildings, including the Barclays Center, home of the Brooklyn Nets National Basketball Association franchise. Many of the buildings (three office buildings and thirteen apartment buildings) were supposed to range in height from 110 to 452 feet and one of the buildings was supposed to rise 108 feet higher than the nearby Williamsburgh Savings Bank Building (Morrone, 2005).[4] New York Governor George Pataki, New York City Mayor Michael R. Bloomberg, the Reverend Al Sharpton, and rap mogul Jay-Z all publicly supported the project (Confessore, 2005). The Regional Plan Association (RPA), an independent regional planning association operating in the thirty-one-county region of Connecticut, New Jersey, and New York, officially endorsed the Atlantic Rail Yards development, but recommended changes in the second phase of the development (RPA, 2006). The RPA's support of the Atlantic Yards development was based on its belief that "large scale development belongs near transit hubs like Atlantic Terminal" is good for the city (RPA, 2006). This focus on transit-oriented development is not unlike the San Francisco case, where the state and the regional planning association are advocating for development along major transit stations and along transit corridors.

Many Brooklyn residents living within the area of the proposed Atlantic Yards development, however, felt that this development did not fit the historic character of the brownstone homes in the neighborhood or blend in well with the low- and mid-rise development. In addition, the neighborhood's long-term residents and small business owners were concerned about such a large-scale development and what negative impact it would have on them economically and environmentally. Coalitions such as Develop Don't Destroy Brooklyn (DDDB), a volunteer-run coalition of roughly twenty-one community organizations, stood in opposition to the Atlantic Yards project and fought hard to stop it (DDDB, 2015). In addition to DDDB, more than fifty organizations opposed the Forest City Ratner Companies–ESDC

Figure 4.1 Barclays Arena from Atlantic Avenue
Source: Malo André Hutson, June 2012.

public-private development and waged countless protests and lawsuits to
stop the development from moving forward. For example, DDDB filed two
lawsuits challenging the State of New York's environmental review process
and use of eminent domain to condemn privately owned properties
(Del Signore, 2008).

Figure 4.2 Barclays Arena being built
Source: Malo, André Hutson, June 2012.

During the bidding process to develop the 8.4-acre Atlantic Yards property (formerly Vanderbilt Yards) owned by the Metropolitan Transportation Authority, Extell Development Company bid $150 million in cash, while Forest City Ratner Companies bid only $50 million, a difference of $100 million. Both bids were well below the Metropolitan Transportation Authority's appraisal of the site at $214.5 million (DDDB, 2005). At the time, DDDB's spokesperson Daniel Goldstein stated that the community preferred the Extell proposal over the Forest City Ratner Companies proposal "by a large margin as it fulfills the key principles we have been fighting for over the past two years" (DDDB, 2005; Essex Development Company, 2005).

In an attempt to gain support for the project and overcome the growing negative publicity claiming the development was a blatant example of the misuse of public funds and government power to support a wealthy, well-connected developer, Forest City Ratner Companies rolled out a strategy that many large developers do in low-income and working-class communities: it promised residents desperate for economic opportunity good-paying jobs and affordable housing. Forest City Ratner Companies and its supporters launched the marketing campaign "jobs, housing and hoops" (Oder, 2004). Earlier meetings regarding job opportunities with the Atlantic Yards project drew thousands of people, especially underemployed or unemployed black men (Oder, 2004). Advocates of the project promised local residents that the project would generate at least 1,500 construction jobs; an additional 1,500–6,400 permanent jobs would be created as well as 2,250 units of affordable housing (Fainstein, 2009). Forest City Ratner Companies estimated that the entire development would generate $5.6 billion in tax revenue over thirty years (Fainstein, 2009).

Forest City Ratner Companies also entered into a community benefits agreement with a group of community, nonprofit, and government entities in order to solidify their support among Brooklyn residents. The newly formed and highly controversial coalition negotiated a community benefits agreement with the Atlantic Yards Development Co., LLC and Brooklyn Arena, LLC (Confessore, 2005). Some of the key players in the community coalition included the All-Faith Council of Brooklyn, Brooklyn United for Innovative Local Development, Downtown Brooklyn Neighborhood Alliance, First Atlantic Terminal Housing Committee, New York State Association of Minority Contractors, and Public Housing Communities (New York City Housing Authority). As part of the contractual agreement, the project developers of Atlantic Yards agreed to provide a number of benefits for community residents such as workforce development and job placement, first-source hiring, affordable housing, educational initiatives, small business development, and contracting, as well as community amenities and facilities – health care center, parks, and open space if development plans moved forward (Brooklyn Atlantic Yards Community Benefits Agreement, 2005). Specifically, the CBA promised it would create numerous benefits to Brooklyn residents affected by the development, including:

- the creation of at least 50 percent affordable housing units (out of 4,500) and 10 percent senior housing;
- the development of a comprehensive job training program that would create 8,500 permanent jobs;
- the hiring of 35 percent minority and 10 percent woman construction contractors during the development of the project;
- a new health care center for residents;
- a set-aside of six acres of open space available for public use; and
- an effort to integrate the arena into the community by providing community-related activities and facilities.

(Markey, 2009)

Residents and community organizations alleged that the Atlantic Yards CBA was a sham soon after it was formed. For example, the Atlantic Yards CBA was supposed to be modeled after the Staples Center CBA in Los Angeles, which included more than thirty community organizations, many of which did not support the project. In contrast, the Atlantic Yards CBA included only eight organizations, all of which supported the project. In addition, many Brooklyn residents accused Forest City Ratner Companies of buying the support of community organizations such as BUILD. Press reports claimed that BUILD did not incorporate until after Forest City Ratner Companies announced the plans for the Atlantic Yards development. Forest City Ratner Companies denied providing financial support to launch BUILD, but according to press reports, a spokesman said that, as part of the Community Benefits Agreement, the company gave BUILD a $100,000 grant and covered its overhead costs (Confessore, 2005).[5]

Although the CBA agreement's legitimacy has been questioned, some of the most contentious issues around the Atlantic Yards development involve the level of public-sector financial support, the ESDC's use of eminent domain to acquire property, and the exclusion of the public and overall lack of transparency in the planning process (Fainstein, 2009). For instance, the ESDC exercised its authority to seize land surrounding the proposed development project through the use of eminent domain, and it also had the authority to override local land use laws (Fainstein, 2009). Local residents criticized the ESDC as arbitrarily designating properties within the development site as blighted (Garnard et al., 2014). The ESDC did not deem the project footprint as blighted until more than two and a half years after the project was publicly announced and seventeen months after the City and State of New York signed a memorandum of understanding with Forest City Ratner Companies (Garnard et al., 2014). Adding to the controversy and accusations of public corruption surrounding the Atlantic Yards development was the fact the ESDC was the lead state agency reviewing the Atlantic Yards proposal, whose members are appointed by the governor. Community members criticized the city as allowing the ESDC to circumvent the local land use process, bypassing all local oversight processes such as those required by the Uniform Land Use Review Procedure (ULURP), which mandates the involvement of elected legislative bodies such as neighborhood councils, borough presidents, and the city council (Fainstein, 2009; Garnard et al., 2014).

The controversy around the use of eminent domain led Daniel Goldstein and some of his neighbors to sue the ESDC in January 2007, claiming that the agency's use of eminent domain was a violation of the State of New York's constitution. Goldstein and other residents argued the circumstances did not support the ESDC's designation of their properties as blighted and that the use of eminent domain was not a legitimate "public use" within the meaning of the state's constitution (Goldstein, 2009). The court disagreed, and, two years later, in a deferential opinion, held that the blight designations were for the legislative agencies to make, and, unless there could be "no room for reasonable difference of opinion as to whether an area is blighted," judges would not interfere with an agency's determination (Goldstein, 2009).

While this lawsuit challenging the use of eminent domain to take private property did not succeed at challenging the use of eminent domain, it slowed the project down. In addition, in the fall of 2008, the U.S. stock market crashed, sending the financial markets into a tailspin. The real estate industry was hit hard, and the home foreclosure crisis was in full swing. In December 2008, Forest City Enterprises President Charles Ratner announced to investors shortly after the company's stock price dropped 15 percent that there would be an abrupt halt to all work within the Atlantic Yards site because of financial challenges (Durkin and Sederstrom, 2008). Ratner was reported as saying, "I think we can successfully delay until we are prepared to start [the project]. . . . I can't tell you in this market when that can be. How long? I don't know." A few days later, *The Wall Street Journal* reported that Frank Gehry had laid off more than a dozen staff members assigned to work on the Atlantic Yards project (Frangos and Karp, 2008). In addition, it was reported that Forest City Enterprises, Inc. was facing serious financial challenges as a result of the recession. The harsh economic realities began to dog the company, and in 2010 the National Basketball Association Board of Governors approved the sale of the New Jersey Nets to Russian billionaire Mikhail Prokhorov (which made him the first non-American owner of an NBA franchise) (Albergotti, 2010). In the deal, Prokhorov agreed to pay $260 million to current owner Bruce Ratner for an 80 percent stake in the franchise and a 45 percent stake in the Barclays Arena. He was also provided with an option to purchase 20 percent of the surrounding real estate development Ratner plans to build (Albergotti, 2010). This deal provided Bruce Ratner with much-needed financial capital to keep his dream of the Atlantic Yards project moving. After all, according to *The Wall Street Journal* journalist Matthew Futterman, although Bruce Ratner bought the basketball team for $300 million, "Mr. Ratner admittedly wasn't a basketball fan. The only reason he made the deal was so he could build an arena and a massive development in downtown Brooklyn across the street from two very profitable shopping centers he began building there a decade ago" (Futterman, 2010).

The impact of the Atlantic Yards project on surrounding neighborhoods

Ratner's public comments about his determination to see the Atlantic Yards project completed and the negative publicity surrounding the Atlantic Yards project reverberated throughout Brooklyn, especially in the neighborhoods in close proximity to the project. Residents were fearful that commercial and historical residential buildings could be deemed "blighted" and taken through eminent domain the same way they were taken within the Atlantic Yards project site. As a result, many neighbors and community groups within the Prospect Heights and Crown Heights neighborhoods organized to try and prevent this from happening. One of the major concerns in both neighborhoods was that the Atlantic Yards development would be the catalyst for other larger buildings encroaching into their neighborhoods, which would threaten the neighborhoods' scale and character if historic buildings were lost to demolition or were altered. Many residents have called for the city, and especially the Department of City Planning, to work with the communities in these two neighborhoods to protect the neighborhoods' character by "preserving a sense of place." Residents acknowledge the importance of striking a balance between growth and protecting the history and character of Prospect Heights and Crown Heights.

As a result of this concern, especially after seeing the negative impact of the Atlantic Yards project, leaders and organizations from both Crown Heights North and Prospect Heights organized successfully in establishing parts of their neighborhoods as historic districts through the New York City Landmarks Preservation Commission. To be designated a historic district is a time-consuming process that requires significant documentation. The Landmarks Preservation Commission identifies potential landmarks and historic districts through surveys and other Commission-initiated research as well as through an evaluation process from members of the public, elected or civic officials, or other parties. After the initial Commission review, the following must occur:

1   an additional evaluation of properties;
2   Commissioner review and Chair determination;
3   vote to calendar a public hearing;
4   public hearing is held;
5   discussion and designation of report;
6   Commission vote;
7   City Planning Commission review of report;
8   City Council vote.

Once all of these documents are submitted, the final designation can take several years.

In the case of Crown Heights, residents have succeeded in getting a large swath of their neighborhood designated a historic district. For example, the Crown Heights North Association started its process in 2005, and in 2007, the city approved Phase 1 of the multiphase historic district process (Caratzas and Danza, 2007). Phase 1 included 472 buildings; the city approved Phase 2 in 2011, and that included an additional 600 plus buildings (Caratzas, 2011); and Phase 3 was completed in 2015 and also included more than 600 additional buildings (Caratzas, 2015).

Soon after residents in Crown Heights initiated their process to become a historic district, Prospect Heights did the same. The Prospect Heights Neighborhood Development Council as well as the Municipal Art Society (MAS) and others began exploring the ways that a significant portion of the Prospect Heights neighborhood could be designated a historic district. As the discussions for the historic district gained steamed, supporters of Prospect Heights becoming a historic district included key politicians and community groups such as Brooklyn Borough President Marty Markowitz, Councilmember Letitia James, and Congresswoman Yvette Clarke, as well as representatives from Community Board 8, the Prospect Heights Neighborhood District Council, DDDC, and others (Kamping-Carder, 2008). At the time of the historic designation process, the Municipal Art Society Director of

Advocacy and Policy said that, "MAS applauds the Landmarks Preservation Commission for moving to protect this very special and threatened neighborhood. This is a historic district of exceptionally fine architecture and without the protection of historic district designation this neighborhood is at risk because of increasing development pressures caused by the Atlantic Yards development" (The Municipal Art Society of New York, 2008).

The Landmarks Preservation Commission designated the Prospect Heights Historic District in 2009, creating the largest historic district in NYC since the 1990s. It includes 850 row houses and several institutional and commercial buildings (Danza, 2009). The designation prevents development that does not fit the neighborhood's historic character, but the designation does not cover the entire Prospect Heights neighborhood. It also does not prevent new development in the area, just development perceived as "out of context."

A community's fight for government accountability and transparency

Despite all the promises made to the community through the CBA, a decade later, Forest City Ratner Companies had not delivered on most of the promises it made in the CBA. In September 2012, the Barclays Arena opened and as of 2015, not one apartment building has been completed. Affordable housing and jobs were the big selling points to the local community, but Forest City Ratner Companies' failure to deliver on those initial promises added to residents' anger – many of whom had, along with community leaders and some elected officials, been against the Atlantic Yards project from the beginning. Residents expressed that they felt that their voices had not been heard and their repeated calls to be a part of the planning process were not respected. Consequently, residents began organizing themselves and educating themselves about land use laws and the planning process in general. They felt that the only way to take on "big developers" was to hold them accountable for their actions, but, more important, they needed to hold the elected government officials at the state and local levels accountable to "the people."

BrooklynSpeaks is one initiative that has attempted to do just that. Brooklyn Speaks is an initiative sponsored by civic associations, community-based organizations, and advocacy groups founded in 2006. The initiative's primary mission is to advocate for transparency by state and city government officials, especially around governance, and to involve the public in the decision-making process (BrooklynSpeaks, 2015). In addition, BrooklynSpeaks is focused on the current and potential environmental concerns surrounding the Atlantic Yards project. According to BrooklynSpeaks, its primary mission is as follows:

> The sponsors continue to work to create a dialog among residents, Community Boards, elected officials and State and City agencies around responsible development at the Atlantic Yards site that meets Brooklyn's

needs and addresses the concerns of surrounding neighborhoods, while maintaining accountability to the taxpayers of the City and the State.

(BrooklynSpeaks, 2015)

The list of members ranges from neighborhood associations and councils from the surrounding neighborhoods such as Boreum Hill and Brooklyn Heights, Park Slope, and Prospect Heights to progressive community organizations such as the Atlantic Avenue Local Development Corporation, Brown Community Development Corporation, Diaspora Community Services, and the Fifth Avenue Committee. Since it was founded, BrooklynSpeaks has signed up more than 5,700 supporters and has created a set of four development principles for the Atlantic Yards development: (1) Respect and integrate with surrounding neighborhoods; (2) include a transportation plan that works; (3) create affordable housing that meets the community's needs; and (4) be truly accountable to the public (BrooklynSpeaks, 2009a and 2009b).

The first principle (respect and integrate with surrounding neighborhoods) came out of BrooklynSpeaks' position that Forest City Ratner's original proposal was too large in scale, had too many high-rise buildings that would dwarf the rest of the neighborhood, and in general lacked a true integration with the surrounding neighborhood because it did not have enough street connections running through the development site. In addition, the sponsors of the initiative have been concerned that the Atlantic Yards site has produced only an arena and no affordable housing as promised.

The second principle (include a transportation plan that works) was a response to the original Atlantic Yards plan: according to BrooklynSpeaks, the original plan would generate roughly 20,000 new vehicular trips daily. There were major concerns about the negative impact that this would have on air quality and overall quality of life for local residents. In the modified Atlantic Yards plan, BrooklynSpeaks is still concerned about the amount of surface parking in the area and has called for the city and state governments to (BrooklynSpeaks, 2015):

- Adopt mass transit incentives and demand management strategies to reduce by 50 percent the number of parking spaces programmed for the Arena under the revised plan.
- Limit interim surface parking to no more than this reduced number of spaces allocated for the Arena, and define a specific timeline for their replacement by open space or non-parking uses at grade.
- Provide adequate state and city funding for the MTA to ensure that transit service to the development is preserved and enhanced.
- Implement residential permit parking in surrounding neighborhoods to ensure that they are not overwhelmed with cars searching for free parking on game and event days.
- Design and implement traffic-calming measures on the streets in surrounding neighborhoods to ensure pedestrian and cyclist safety.

The third principle (create affordable housing that meets the community's needs) was the consequence of BrooklynSpeaks' general dissatisfaction with Forest City Ratner Companies' ability to produce the 2,250 affordable housing units promised in the original development plan. Moreover, sponsors of the initiative felt like the affordability standards were too high for the average Brooklyn resident. As a result, they worked with their allies to turn up the political pressure on local and state government officials to ensure that the Atlantic Yards development site delivers on its affordable housing promises. For example, BrooklynSpeaks demanded that affordable housing be calculated according to Brooklyn Area Median Incomes (AMI) and require that two-thirds of the promised affordable units be completed within ten years of project start and not within twenty years when many of the residents who were displaced for the project to be built will likely not benefit from the new housing. Finally, BrooklynSpeaks demanded that the Atlantic Yards project prioritize low- and moderate-income families who were displaced from the development site footprint area for new affordable units (Brooklyn-Speaks, 2009b).

Finally, the fourth principle (be truly accountable to the public) was in direct response to the lack of initial community engagement. Brooklyn-Speaks, as well as many other organizations, residents, and elected officials, has pointed out that the ESDC did not engage the public in the planning and development process. In addition, "the agency has promised to hold regular meetings with local elected officials but failed to do so. Finally, when approving the modified plan in June 2009, [the] ESDC made crucial determinations about the environmental impact of the project without having the new arena proposal, but merely relied on the developer's assertion that future changes would comply with the previous project's design guidelines" (Brooklyn-Speaks, 2015). As a result, the BrooklynSpeaks sponsors believe Atlantic Yards must (1) include oversight by a dedicated LDC, subsidiary, or public benefit corporation that includes board members appointed in consultation with local legislators; and (2) actively involve a formal advisory board made up of representatives from civic associations, community-based organizations, and community boards from affected neighborhoods.

Growing tired of waiting for the state and local governments to address their major concerns surrounding the Atlantic Yards development, BrooklynSpeaks and local residents began preparing to file a legal challenge against Forest City Ratner Companies and the ESDC under the Federal Fair Housing Act, which permits a claim for a violation if there are discriminatory effects, even absent discriminatory intent. The sponsors were prepared to claim that the 2009 agreements between Forest City Ratner Companies and the ESDC's delays around building affordable housing that it promised until 2035 would result in fewer African Americans in Brooklyn community districts 2, 3, 6, and 8 having access to Atlantic Yards' affordable apartments (BrooklynSpeaks, 2014). As part of their legal case, the Fifth Avenue Committee commissioned a study that found that in 2000, African Americans comprised 52 percent of the population of the combined area of community districts 2, 3, 6, and 8, which surrounds the Atlantic Yards development, but by 2010 had declined to 40 percent. The study estimated that African Americans will represent only 15 percent of the districts' population by 2035 (BrooklynSpeaks, 2014). In preparation for their lawsuit, BrooklynSpeaks retained the legal services of the law firm WilmerHale, who provided assistance to the initiative pro bono.

As the pressure and criticism by community groups and local residents mounted against Forest City Ratner Companies, the ESDC, and elected officials, all parties announced they had reached a settlement agreement on June 27, 2014, ironically nine years to the day after the controversial Atlantic Yards CBA was signed.[6] The ESDC, working with Forest City Ratner Companies, and New York City made five significant changes to the Atlantic Yards project. The key changes include (Adams, 2014):

- completion of all 2,250 affordable apartments by May 2025 (with penalties of up to $5 million if they do not meet their affordable housing requirement);
- start of construction of at least 590 affordable apartments within twelve months (with penalties for not meeting this requirement); and
- creation of an ESDC subsidiary, the Atlantic Yards Community Development Corporation (AYCDC), which will be responsible for monitoring the delivery of public commitments related to the Atlantic Yards project by making policy recommendations to the ESDC Board of Directors. The AYCDC will be governed by a board of fourteen directors appointed by the governor of New York State, the mayor of New York City, the Brooklyn Borough president, the speaker of the New York State Assembly, president pro tem of the New York State Senate, and the speaker of the New York City Council.

According to a letter dated June 25, 2014, to Michelle de la Uz, executive director of the Fifth Avenue Committee, and Gib Veconi, treasurer of the Prospect Heights Neighborhood Development Council and a key leader in helping the neighborhood gain historic district designation, the ESDC promised to do the following:

First, ESD will require that all affordable housing units embodied in the existing agreements be built by 2025, ten years earlier than currently required. Project Site Affordable Housing Units (i.e., 2,250 Affordable Housing Units) will be required to have a temporary certificate of occupancy ("TCO") or certificate of occupancy ("C of O") by May 2025, subject to extensions set forth in the Development Agreement and the General Project Plan. To the extent this requirement is not met, FCRC and/or the project sponsors (hereinafter "FCRC") will pay Liquidated Damages of $2,000/month/unit for every Affordable Housing Unit that does not have a TCO or C of O.

Second, ESD will require that two affordable buildings, totaling not less than 590 units of affordable housing, be built in the next phase of development at the Project, with the first of the two buildings to commence this year. In particular, Building 14 (B14) will be commenced by December 31, 2014 and Building 3 (B3) by June 30, 2015, each in accordance with the subsidy letters for each such building from the New York City Housing Development Corporation dated May 16, 2014, subject to Unavoidable Delay and assuming no Affordable Housing Subsidy Unavailability or Market Financing Unavailability, as these terms are defined in the Atlantic Yards General Project Plan and Development Agreement. . . .

Third, ESD will require FCRC to build affordable housing as it constructs market rate housing. In particular, ESD will amend the Development Agreement to require that a minimum of 35% of all units for which construction has commenced at any time will be Affordable Housing Units until construction of 1,050 Affordable Housing Units has commenced. Thereafter, this percentage requirement may drop to a minimum of 25. However, by 2025, FCRC must complete 2,250 Affordable Units (which comprises 35% of the anticipated residential units to be built at the Project site as specified in its Modified General Project Plan). If at any time FCRC falls below the 35%/25% threshold, it will not be able to complete a single market rate unit until the threshold is again met.

Fourth, ESD will direct all Liquidated Damages to the New York City Housing Trust Fund, a fund administered by the NYC Department of Housing Preservation & Development, to fund preservation or development of affordable housing with preference given to projects in Brooklyn Community Districts 2, 3, 6 and 8.

Fifth, ESD agrees, subject to and following approval by its Board of Directors ("the directors"), to create a new subsidiary, the Atlantic Yards Community Development Corporation ("AYCDC"), to improve the oversight and monitoring of the Project.

The letter also stated that as part of this agreement, BrooklynSpeaks' coalition members will sign a "Covenant not to Sue" the ESDC, Forest City Ratner Companies, and other Covered Parties for any claims or causes of action existing as of June 27, 2014.[7]

In addition to the five specific changes the ESDC outlined, Forest City Ratner Companies agreed to a one-time contribution of $250,000 to establish the Atlantic Yards Tenant Protection Fund. As part of this contribution, Forest City Ratner Companies required that the Mutual Housing Association of New York (one of the original eight signatories of the Atlantic Yards CBA) be included in "an on-going dialogue with the community to develop a strategy which would address issues such as tenant assistance and economic integration" (Gilmartin, 2014). The Atlantic Yards Tenant Protection

Fund was established with the Brooklyn Community Foundation to provide eviction prevention services to low- and moderate-income residents vulnerable to displacement in the jurisdiction of Community Boards 2, 3, 6, and 8 in Brooklyn (BrooklynSpeaks, 2014). As a condition of receiving any funds from the Tenant Protection Fund, a grant recipient is required to commit in writing that no funds from the Tenant Protection Fund will support any lobbying or litigation efforts where Forest City Ratner Companies or its subsidiary Atlantic Yards Development Company, LLC or affiliates is an adverse party.

A few days before the settlement agreement was signed, the City of New York's deputy mayor for housing and economic development, Alicia Glen, wrote a letter to Executive Director Michelle de la Uz on June 24, 2014, in response to the community's concerns regarding community displacement as a result of large scale re-zonings and projects, including the Atlantic Yards (Glen, 2014). In the letter, Deputy Mayor Glen promised that the city, consistent with fair housing law, would review the affordable housing lottery preferences and take into account the surrounding community residents' ties to the neighborhood, including ties of those displaced since 2006, when the General Project Plan was first approved. She stated that "any liquidated damages from the Atlantic Yards project that are deposited into the New York City Affordable Housing Trust Fund will go to fund preservation or development of affordable housing with preference given to projects in Community Boards 2, 3, 6, and 8 in Brooklyn (Glen, 2014).

At the announcement of the settlement, New York Governor Andrew Cuomo focused on the importance of building affordable housing in a timely manner as well as including the public in the planning and development process going forward. The governor stated that the state was putting the development of Atlantic Yards on the "fast track" to expedite the construction of thousands of affordable housing units in Brooklyn, and promised that the state's plan would "ensure this vital housing is built quickly and efficiently and that the community is engaged in every step of the project. This agreement is a win for the State and most importantly for Brooklyn residents who will finally begin to see affordable buildings being constructed in their neighborhoods" (Cuomo, 2014). Mayor de Blasio tried to put a positive spin on this agreement; after all, he was not mayor at the time the Atlantic Yards project plans were approved in 2006 and again in 2009. Mayor de Blasio celebrated the city's work with the state and the neighborhood coalition. "The agreement means two 100-percent affordable buildings will go in the ground starting next year, with units serving a more diverse range of families. And what's remarkable is that compared to the project's first building, we've secured nearly twice as many affordable units for our City investment."

However, two of the leading advocates for the community organizations trying to hold Forest City Ratner Companies, the state, and New York City accountable for their actions took a very different tone than the governor and mayor. Executive Director Michelle de la Uz said after the settlement was announced, "This agreement between the BrooklynSpeaks community groups, local residents, New York State and Forest City is an important step at a crucial phase in Atlantic Yards development. It will help ensure that inclusion, transparency, and public accountability are part of the project moving forward." Treasurer Gib Veconi said, "The economic realities of solving the city's affordable housing crisis will increasingly call for public/private partnerships similar to the Atlantic Yards project. Today's agreement shows that communities can work with the State to hold developers accountable for their commitments to the public. The BrooklynSpeaks sponsors are gratified to have been able to play a role in accelerating the delivery of affordable housing at Atlantic Yards, and will continue to constructively engage the State, the City and the developers as we advocate for the residents of the communities surrounding the project in the months and years ahead." Both de la Uz and Veconi stressed the importance of holding government accountable and keeping it transparent. Both also acknowledged that local residents are facing economic challenges and that the lack of affordable housing is a serious challenge that will require the city and state to play a role in addressing this issue.

Although the Atlantic Yards project managed to move forward with very little transparency and no real public participation in the planning and development processes, the settlement agreement is a big step in addressing some of the most salient issues and potential legal challenges brought by BrooklynSpeaks and its allies – government accountability and transparency. The settlement agreement put into place some mechanisms and processes for monitoring the promises Forest City Ratner Companies first laid out with regards to affordable housing, community engagement, and ways of dealing with environmental concerns. For example, under the current agreement, at least 770 affordable apartments are expected to be available by October 2016, if you include the 180 affordable apartments currently under construction with the B2 BKLYN development. As of now, the first apartment building being built, B2 BKLYN, a thirty-two-story modular tower, specifies that a portion of affordable units would be for low-income families of four who make $48,000 a year or less, moderate-income families earning up to $88,000, and middle-income families earning up to $104,000 (Bagli, 2014).

According to the original 2009 project agreement between Forest City Ratner and the ESDC, it would have resulted in only 300 affordable apartments by 2022 (Alberts, 2014; Bagli, 2014). More important, the settlement agreement holds the state and local governments (the ESDC and New York City) accountable for their actions with regards to the Atlantic Yards development, especially given that the government has provided the developer millions of dollars in subsidies for the Atlantic Yards project.

Key factors contributing to settlement deal

The settlement agreement among the state, the city, Forest City Ratner Companies, and community groups partly came about after eleven years of struggle on behalf of community organizations, which included countless protests, litigation and the threat of litigation, and calls for government accountability and transparency. Other reasons leading to settlement have to do with political timing and Chinese investors. All of these factors combined proved to pave the way for a settlement deal and perhaps a new chapter in the development of the Atlantic Yards site.

In February 2014, Mayor Bill de Blasio announced an ambitious plan to build 80,000 new affordable housing units and to preserve an additional 120,000 units of housing over ten years at a cost of $41 billion from a combination of city, state, and private funds (de Blasio, 2014). The affordable housing units will target a range of incomes, from extremely low (under $25,150 for a family of four) to middle class (Dailey, 2014). Part of Mayor de Blasio's plan is to be achieved through incentives for developers, the use of vacant city lands, and the re-zoning of areas across boroughs to allow for increased density and taller buildings. Mayor de Blasio also stressed the importance of the city developing a place-based approach to the planning and land use processes that is guided by early and regular input from the communities themselves, advice the Atlantic Yards project and planning process did not follow (de Blasio, 2014).

Governor Cuomo had an incentive to try and broker a deal among the state, New York City, Forest City Ratner Companies, and the Brooklyn community because the government has provided millions of dollars in subsidies to the Atlantic Yards project, used eminent domain to tear down housing, and had not built one affordable housing unit at the site eleven years after the development plans were approved. Cuomo himself campaigned on "cleaning up Albany" and even created the Moreland Commission, a supposedly independent commission charged with investigating corruption in state government. However, as multiple news agencies reported, Governor Cuomo's staff put up roadblocks to investigations with close ties to the governor. For example, during an attempt to subpoena the Real Estate Board of New York, whose leaders have supported Governor Cuomo financially, the commission met with resistance (Craig, Rashbaum, and Kaplan, 2014). In another example, *The New York Times* reported that the Moreland Commission served a subpoena to Buying Time, a media-buying firm that has placed television advertisements for Governor Cuomo's campaigns. As the word of the subpoena reached Governor Cuomo's top aide, the commission was told to "pull it back" (Craig, Rashbaum, and Kaplan, 2014). The governor eventually disbanded the commission just a short time after it was formed. It was clear that the scandals plaguing Albany and the governor's repeated claims to want to "clean up Albany" influenced him in making sure that the settlement agreement deal was reached.

Finally, a critical factor in getting the settlement deal done had to do with Chinese investors. By 2014, the Atlantic Yards development site had only constructed the Barclays Arena and the costs of developing the project were only increasing. The Atlantic Yards project had already been scaled down from its initial plans and over the years since the Great Recession, Forest City Ratner Companies was in search of investment capital to jumpstart the project. In 2010, it was revealed that Forest City Ratner Companies was seeking millions of dollars to support the Atlantic Yards project from Chinese investors under the federal EB-5 immigration program (Oder, 2015).[8] The EB-5 program provides green cards to investors in return for a $500,000 investment. Forest City Ratner Companies has secured hundreds of millions of dollars utilizing the EB-5 program and has continued to seek additional funding sources to keep the Atlantic Yards project on schedule (Oder, 2015). As a result, Forest City Ratner Companies signed a joint venture on July 1, 2014, with Greenland USA, just a few days after the settlement agreement was signed. Under the development partnership agreement with Greenland USA, a subsidiary of a Chinese development firm based in Shanghai Greenland Holding Group, the company will acquire 70 percent of the project and will co-develop the project with Forest City Ratner Companies, sharing in all future project costs (Forest City Enterprises, 2014).[9] More significant, the two firms also announced that they were going to speed up the development process. Zhang Yuliang, chairman and president of Greenland Group, said in a company press release after the deal was completed, "As a company, we believe in a shared sense of community. We're very excited to join Forest City in Brooklyn. Together, we're confident we can expedite the construction of Atlantic Yards and build a new community within this extraordinary borough. New York City, like many great urban areas, is working diligently to create housing for a diverse group of people. This is something that we are excited to be part of. We are confident that Atlantic Yards will become a world-class example of how to build housing for a wide range of people, building on the history of New York as a place of promise for all" (Forest City Enterprises, 2014). Ifei Chang, president and CEO of Greenland USA, said, "We fully anticipate that Atlantic Yards will shine a light on how to build a wide range of housing for people of many different economic backgrounds. New York City, like other great urban areas, was always able to thrive because it was a magnet for young and old, native and foreign born, and a place where all could pursue their dreams" (Forest City Enterprises, 2014).

The motivation to get the Atlantic Yards project moving forward and the sudden, newfound commitment to prioritizing building housing for a wide range of "people of many different economic backgrounds" had everything to do with money. Almost since the Atlantic Yards project was announced, Forest City Ratner Companies and its partners faced criticism and were challenged in court with lawsuits. This has significantly delayed the project, resulting in hundreds of millions of dollars in project delay costs. The settlement agreement and commitment to building affordable housing first was a way for Forest City Ratner Companies and its partners to attempt to avoid any more delays as a result of lawsuits. Forest City Ratner Companies and Greenland USA needed to adjust and respond to the political realities at the state and city levels, which had new political leadership that was no longer willing to stand by and watch year after year go by without any affordable housing being built at the Atlantic Yards site. Mayor de Blasio had campaigned on government transparency and public participation, and after he had announced his 200,000 housing plan for New York City he needed every unit of affordable housing he could muster. In addition, the rising cost of housing and overall cost of living in the city has intensified the complaints about gentrification and neighborhood displacement of long-term low- and moderate-income residents. Given all of these political and social realities, the developers saw the settlement agreement as a chance to make a fresh start by distancing themselves from the messy development process surrounding the Atlantic Yards project by creating a "new community" in Brooklyn (despite a community having already existed before the project came along). As a result, the developers renamed and rebranded the Atlantic Yards project as Pacific Park. Eleven years after the Atlantic Yards project was announced with world-renowned architect Frank Gehry leading the design, the new phase of Atlantic Yards was now willing to shift gears and move into a new phase of the project with a new name and new architects, COOKFOX, who claim to focus on integrated, environmentally responsive design (COOKFOX Architects, 2015). The Atlantic Yards/Pacific Park project has since highlighted the eight acres of public open space, which will have play areas for children, lawns, a basketball court, dog runs, public art, and activities. In addition, the Atlantic Yards/Pacific Park project will include a health care center, a senior facility, a daycare center, and a New York City public school. On May 16, 2015, the School Construction Authority announced that a 616-seat elementary and middle school will go under construction in the summer of 2016 and fulfill another promise made by the developers when the original Atlantic Yards project was designed (New York 1 News, 2015).

It remains to be seen how transparent and responsive Forest City Ratner Companies and Greenland USA will be in the future with regards to the Atlantic Yards/Pacific Park development. It is likely that without community pressure and government oversight to hold the developers accountable, similar issues such as missed targets for building affordable housing and broken promises to fulfill agreed-upon community benefits (such as jobs) or addressing residents' environmental concerns are likely to occur. The first meeting of the Atlantic Yards Community Development Corporation, the agency charged with the project oversight, was held on February 6, 2015, at the Long Island University's Brooklyn Campus. As the Atlantic Yards/Pacific Park Development enters a new phase, with a new name, and with a new set of development partners, New York journalist Norman Oder, who has followed the project from the beginning, observes that "Whether Atlantic Yards or Pacific Park, the name distracts from the fact that the Chinese government is now the beneficiary of significant public assistance, including a zoning override, eminent domain, low-cost land, special tax breaks and even low-cost financing via immigrant investors" (Oder, 2014).

Lessons learned and the path forward

The case of the Atlantic Yards/Pacific Park project symbolizes many of the challenges so many urban communities are dealing with across the United States: large-scale development, too little government accountability, and developers making promises of lots of jobs and affordable housing that very rarely come to fruition. Low- and moderate-income families within urban communities are experiencing unprecedented increases in the cost of housing, resulting in a housing affordability crisis. This housing affordability crisis is the result of the "perfect storm" mentioned in the introduction of this book. Across the country, many strong-market cities are not building housing to meet the growing demand from the in-migration of people (domestic and foreign) who would prefer to reside in a city. In addition, the growth of knowledge-based and information jobs has led to a bifurcation of the labor market with higher-skilled, higher-paying jobs on one end and lower-skilled, lower-paying jobs on the other. Finally, these high-income individuals and wealthy foreign investors have the disposable capital to pay a premium for housing, either as their primary residence, as a second home, or as an investment property to "park" their money.

The case of New York City is no different. The city has experienced an inadequate supply of housing to meet the increased demand. It has also failed to maintain a supply of affordable housing to meet the needs of the city's most vulnerable residents such as the elderly and low- to moderate-income individuals. Adding to the housing affordability crisis has been the influx of global investment capital that is creating a market for luxury housing. Finally, the economic restructuring of the economy with the shift to knowledge- and information-based jobs coupled with stagnate wage growth has disproportionately impacted working- and middle-class families.

Inadequate housing supply

New York City continues to face greater demand for housing than it can supply. More than two-thirds of New York City residents are renters and the rental vacancy rate in 2014 was 3.45 percent. The vacancy rate in Brooklyn was even lower at just more than 3 percent (New York City Council, 2015). Data shows that rent increases have far outpaced income growth for almost ten straight years (NYU Furman Center, 2014). Rent prices in the city grew at nearly twice the rate of income between 2000 and 2013 (Lightfeldt, 2015). As of April 2015, the median price for rents in New York City is moving toward more than $2,700, amounting to 58 percent of the city's median income (Lightfeldt, 2015). In Brooklyn, median rents are above $2,900 and show no sign of slowing down (Curbed NY, 2015).

As mentioned earlier in this chapter, the rising rents place tremendous burdens on the most vulnerable New Yorkers. Unfortunately, the housing affordability crisis is likely to continue. The Furman Center for Real Estate and Urban Policy at New York University (NYU Furman Center) estimates that roughly 250,000 privately owned and subsidized housing units have been built in New York City over the past fifty years as a result of the four largest government subsidy programs – U.S. Housing and Urban Development (HUD) financing and insurance, HUD project-based rental assistance, New York City and New York State Mitchell-Lama, and the federal Low Income Housing Tax Credit (LIHTC) (NYU Furman Center, 2015). But the affordability requirement is for only a set number of years and as a result, about 25 percent of the total subsidized units in the city no longer exist under these programs (NYU Furman Center, 2015). In December 2014, the New York City Housing Authority (NYCHA) faced an $18 million shortfall of what it needed for repairs and renovations, so it agreed to sell a 5 percent stake in 900 subsidized apartments to private developers, L+M Development Partners Inc. and BFC Partner (Kusisto, 2014). NYCHA will receive $150 million from the developers and an additional $100 million over the next two years and another $100 million in revenue over the next fifteen years (Kusisto, 2014). The real concern is that after tax-exempt bonds and federal tax credits end in thirty years, the apartments could be eligible to be converted to market rate. Although this would still need NYCHA's approval, this brings New York closer to privatizing public housing.

Global capital investment

New York City continues to attract billions of dollars of global capital into its real estate market. Unfortunately, most of this investment money is for "market-rate" luxury housing, which is way beyond the reach of most everyday New Yorkers. Roughly $8 billion is spent on luxury housing annually in New York City, costing more than $5 million for each unit (Story and Saul, 2015). This amount has tripled over the past decade, and more than half of those sales in 2014 were to shell companies where the identity of the buyer is hidden (Story and Saul, 2015). Perhaps one of the best examples of this is the Time Warner Center in Manhattan, where recent sales for condominiums have been well above $15 million and 64 percent of the condominiums are owned by shell companies (Story and Saul, 2015).

In 2014, Canadian investors put $3.4 billion into New York City real estate followed by Chinese investors at $3.35 billion, a 43 percent increase over 2013 (Solomont, 2015). Recently, Chinese-owned companies have spent billions purchasing New York City commercial and residential properties, even the historic Waldorf-Astoria Hotel for nearly $2 billion (Dulaney, 2015). This investment appears to be elevating real estate prices and makes it possible for only institutional investors such as banks and private equity firms to participate. Moreover, the foreclosure crisis has transferred wealth from many working- and middle-class homeowners to large institutional investors.

Stagnate wages and income inequality

The final major factor contributing to the housing affordability crisis for New York's working- and middle-class families is the fact the income gap has widened and real wages have remained stagnant. Real wages have skyrocketed for those at the top of the income ladder (top 1 percent) and remained relatively flat for those at the bottom (lower 20 percent). According to a study from the City University of New York's Graduate Center (CUNY), between 1990 and 2010, the top 1 percent of median-income earners went from $452,415 to $716,625 (an increase of nearly 34 percent) and controlled roughly 54 percent of total household income (Bergad, 2014). However, the story was very different for those with median incomes in the lower 20 percent. They went from $13,140 to $14,168 and went from controlling 3.3 percent of total household income to controlling 3 percent. CUNY also found that the income gap was pronounced by race and ethnicity. It found that New York City's non-Hispanic white population was the wealthiest out of all major race/ethnic groups in the city, and "had the largest share of their households in high income-earning categories than the rest of the City's population."[10] It also found that 42 percent of non-Hispanic white households earned more than $100,000 yearly, whereas only 30 percent of Asian, 23 percent of non-Hispanic black, and 19 percent of Latino households earned more than $100,000 in 2010.

Stagnant wages have only exacerbated the problem of less affluent residents being able to afford to live in New York City. For example, the Fiscal Policy Institute analysis showed that, between 2009–2013, average annual real wage changes were -0.1 percent for the first wage decile, -2.0 percent for the second decile, 0.8 percent for the median (or the fifth decile), and -0.2 percent for the ninth decile (City of New York, 2015). However, the most recent analysis suggests real wages for New Yorkers has inched up a bit, but not nearly enough (New York City, 2015). Moreover, 42 percent of New York City families (2.7 million people) have incomes below the level necessary to provide basic family needs (Pearce, 2014). It is unlikely that New York City's most vulnerable populations will improve their financial situations unless some aggressive policy changes are made.

Communities' struggles continue

For the average New Yorker, the battle to stay in their neighborhoods requires a comprehensive strategy. At the core of this strategy is community organizing. Across New York City, and especially in Brooklyn, residents are trying to resist displacement by large-scale development projects and rising housing costs. Residents are not necessarily opposed to commercial and residential development that creates local jobs, economic opportunities, and affordable housing, but they tend to oppose development and planning processes that do not include deep community engagement and do not have a comprehensive and transparent public participatory process. From many residents' perspective, it is entirely undemocratic to completely bypass the public participatory processes that can accompany development.

But as a consequence of the larger exogenous economic, political, and social factors contributing to the housing affordability crisis and growing income gap, residents are working to insert themselves in the planning and development processes, to hold government accountable and transparent, and to continually demand community benefits. In Brooklyn, residents and community organizations' struggles around the Atlantic Yards/Pacific Park project have been ongoing for more than a decade, and finally the state and city are holding the developers accountable for their promises. More important, the state and city have taken the first step at creating a public participatory process and an organization that can potentially monitor the Atlantic Yards/Pacific Park project's negative impacts on the community, as well as measure, evaluate, and report on the benefits to the community.

Nearby, residents in Prospect Heights and Crown Heights are fighting landlords attempting to end rent regulation or evict tenants so they can capitalize on rising rents and housing prices. The Crown Heights Tenants Union is one of the organizations at the forefront of this struggle. It has worked hard to organize hundreds of tenants across buildings, has staged protests, and is trying to get property owners to sign a collective bargaining agreement (Crown Heights Tenant Union, 2015). It has also issued a list of demands such as a five-year rent freeze; right to repairs; right to organize; and a list of rights for current residents regarding repairs, renovations, and buyouts (Crown Heights Tenant Union, 2015). It is too early to determine whether these efforts will successfully keep residents in their homes and neighborhoods, but these efforts signal that the movement to demand more affordable housing and equitable economic development, and to address the factors that contribute to racial and ethnic inequalities, is only growing. Organized residents are demanding a more transparent and accountable government and trying to create a fair and just city and city government is responding.

Mayor de Blasio's plan to spend roughly $41 billion to build and preserve 200,000 units of housing over the next decade is the most ambitious housing plan of any city in the United States (de Blasio, 2014). Just to put this into perspective, San Francisco Mayor Ed Lee has proposed to build or rehabilitate 30,000 units of housing in the city by 2020 (City and County of San Francisco, 2014). Mayor de Blasio's plan aims to create neighborhoods that are diverse, that are affordable across a range of incomes, and that promote homeless, senior, supportive, and accessible housing. The plan calls for refining city financing tools and expanding funding sources for affordable housing. Some of the key specific elements of the plan call for implementing a mandatory Inclusionary Housing Program that will require a portion of the new housing to be permanently affordable to low- or moderate-income households in parts of the city that have experienced re-zonings. In addition, the mayor plans to develop affordable housing on underused public and private sites, similar to an initiative in San Francisco. The city will create two new programs – the Neighborhood Construction Program (NCP) and the New Infill Homeownership Opportunities Program (NIHOP). According to the mayor's housing plan, these programs "will aggregate sites to develop affordable housing, including one- to four-family homeownership opportunities and up to 20 unit rental buildings. These programs will focus on developing capacity among smaller developers with a particular focus on local not-for-profits and [community development corporations (CDCs]" (de Blasio, 2014). If these efforts are implemented effectively, they could have a significant positive impact on New Yorkers struggling to make ends meet.

Perhaps one of the most innovative and potentially effective programs the mayor introduced is the new mixed-income housing program. The traditional affordable/market-rate housing split is "80/20." However, the mayor's mixed-income program calls for a pilot program that will target 20 percent of a housing project's units to low-income households, 30 percent to moderate-income households, and 50 percent to middle-income households (de Blasio, 2014). This addresses an issue residents and policy makers raised in all four of the case studies examined in this book. The traditional "80/20" affordable/market-rate housing split is not effective in promoting true mixed-income developments and neighborhoods. It is crucial for cities to have a diverse pool of people that includes workers, diverse family structures, different age groups, and people with disabilities, requiring a more progressive and creative solution to mixed-income housing.

Another potentially effective policy Mayor de Blasio introduced is the need to reform zoning, building, and housing codes, and other regulations that are likely to lower costs and encourage development opportunities. There is an urgent need to build more housing in New York City that can meet the growing demand and keep housing costs down. Some regulation and bureaucratic processes miss the mark – they do nothing to support participatory planning and democratic processes and only slow down the development process and increase costs. State and city governments must look at ways to fast-track where appropriate and create incentives for private and nonprofit developers to construct affordable housing.

The city has also proposed developing more supportive housing for the most vulnerable populations within New York City as well. Homelessness is a serious challenge for the city and addressing the root causes can be daunting. However, a city can take some tangible steps to address the homelessness problem. Mayor de Blasio has proposed making a larger investment in housing that also provides supportive services for people with mental health and substance abuse issues.

Finally the mayor plans to address the income gap and the need for many residents to have access to good-quality jobs by working with local communities and "stakeholders" to ensure that quality jobs exist for residents. It is estimated that the construction and preservation of 200,000 units of housing will create about 194,000 jobs and about 7,100 of them will be permanent (de Blasio, 2014). Therefore the mayor is proposing that these jobs be a part of a targeted local hiring program and that they are "integrated with the City's broader workforce development initiatives."

Notes

1 For a complete description of the methodology, see www.governing.com/gov-data/gentrification-report-methodology.html.
2 New York City gentrification maps and data. *Governing*. www.governing.com/gov-data/new-york-gentrification-maps-demographic-data.html.
3 Forest City Ratner is a subsidiary of Forest City Enterprises, one of the largest publicly traded real estate firms in the United States. The ESDC is a semi-public redevelopment agency in New York State.
4 The current Atlantic Yards project proposal consists of a twenty-two-acre, $4.9 billion development that features the 18,000-seat Barclays Arena, which has hosted more than 300 events since opening in September 2012, including the Brooklyn Nets, concerts, and other events; the development of a reconfigured LIRR train yard and subway facility improvements; the development of sixteen buildings for residential, office, and retail uses and potentially a hotel, including up to 6,430 apartments, which will include 4,500 rental units of which 2,250 units (50 percent) will be affordable to low, moderate-, and middle-income households; and the creation of eight acres of publicly accessible open space (ESDC, 2015).
5 BUILD closed its offices and dissolved in 2012.
6 The agreement was signed between New York State, Fifth Avenue Committee, Pratt Area Community Council, Brown Community Development Corporation, Boerum Hill Association, Diaspora Community Services, Park Slope Civic Council, Prospect Heights Neighborhood Development Council, Benita Clark, Hermelinda Gumbs, Daron Hudson, and Renee Mintz.
7 Covered Parties means the State of New York, New York State Urban Development Corporation d/b/a Empire State Development, City of New York, New York City Economic Development Corporation, Forest City Ratner Companies, LLC, and Greenland Holding Group Co Ltd. and any parent company, affiliate, subsidiary, department, or agency of any of these entities and all past, present, and future officials, directors, officers, employees, attorneys, consultants, and agents and the successors and assigns of each of them.
8 U.S. Citizenship and Immigration Service (USCIS) administers the Immigrant Investor Program, also known as "EB-5," created by Congress in 1990 to stimulate the U.S. economy through job creation and capital investment by foreign investors. Under a pilot immigration program first enacted in 1992 and regularly reauthorized since, certain EB-5 visas also are set aside for investors in Regional Centers designated by USCIS based on proposals for promoting economic growth (see www.uscis.gov/eb-5).
9 In 2012, Greenland Group ranked 359th on *Fortune Magazine*'s list of the top 500 global enterprises, 73rd among the top 500 Chinese companies, and first among Chinese real estate enterprises. It achieved revenues of $36.6 billion and a total profit of approximately $2 billion in 2012.

10 Their median household income was $80,500 compared with $61,200 for Asians, $55,386 for non-Hispanic blacks, and $42,840 for Latinos. See Bergad (2011).

Bibliography

Adams, K. 2014. Re: Atlantic Yards Project. Kenneth G. Adams to Michelle de la Uz, Gib Veconi. June 25. www.brooklynspeaks.net/sites/default/files/esdc_letter_0.pdf.

Albergotti, R. 2010. Russian billionaire takes control of the New Jersey Nets. *Metropolis* (blog), May 11. http://blogs.wsj.com/metropolis/2010/05/11/russian-billionaire-takes-control-of-the-new-jersey-nets/.

Alberts, H. R. 2014. Atlantic Yards to build more affordable housing much sooner. *Curbed NY* (blog), June 27. http://ny.curbed.com/archives/2014/06/27/atlantic_yards_to_build_more_affordable_housing_much_sooner.php.

Bagli, C. V. 2014. Plan expedited for affordable housing near Barclays Center in Brooklyn. *The New York Times*, June 26. www.nytimes.com/2014/06/27/nyregion/plan-expedited-for-affordable-units-at-atlantic-yards-near-downtown-brooklyn.html?partner=rss&emc=rss&_r=1.

Bergad, L. W. 2011. Trends in median household income among New York City Latinos in comparative perspective, 1990–2011. Latino Data Project Report 54, table 2, p. 10, at http://clacls.gc.cuny.edu/.

Bergad, L. W. 2014. *The Concentration of Wealth in New York City: Changes in the Structure of Household Income by Race/Ethnic Groups and Latino Nationalities 1990–2010.* Report. January. http://clacls.gc.cuny.edu/files/2014/01/Household-Income-Concentration-in-NYC-1990–2010.pdf.

Braconi, F. and Corson, S. 2014. *The Growing Gap: New York City's Housing Affordability Challenge.* Report. April. http://comptroller.nyc.gov/wp-content/uploads/documents/Growing_Gap.pdf.

Brooklyn Atlantic Yards Community Benefits Agreement. 2005.

BrooklynSpeaks. 2009a. BrooklynSpeaks Principles: Be truly accountable to the public. Brooklyn Speaks. December 11. www.brooklynspeaks.net/node/8.

BrooklynSpeaks. 2009b. BrooklynSpeaks Principles: Create affordable housing that meets the community's needs. Brooklyn Speaks. December 11. www.brooklynspeaks.net/node/7.

BrooklynSpeaks. 2014. Community groups and local residents reach historic accord with New York State and developers of Brooklyn's Atlantic Yards Project. Brooklyn Speaks. June 27. www.brooklynspeaks.net/groups-reach-historic-agreement-atlantic-yards.

BrooklynSpeaks. 2015. About BrooklynSpeaks. BrooklynSpeaks. www.brooklynspeaks.net/about.

Caratzas, M. 2011. *Crown Heights North Historic District II Designation Report.* Report. June 28. http://s-media.nyc.gov/agencies/lpc/lp/2361.pdf.

Caratzas, M. 2015. *Crown Heights North III Historic District Designation Report.* Report. March 24. http://s-media.nyc.gov/agencies/lpc/lp/2489.pdf.

Caratzas, M. D. and Danza, C. 2007. *Crown Heights North Historic District Designation Report.* Report. April 24. http://s-media.nyc.gov/agencies/lpc/lp/2204.pdf.

City and County of San Francisco. Office of the Mayor. 2014. Mayor Lee outlines bold 2014 agenda in State of the City Address. News release, January 17. www.sfmayor.org/index.aspx?recordid=507&page=846.

Confessore, N. 2005. To build arena in Brooklyn, developer first builds bridges. *The New York Times*, October 14. www.nytimes.com/2005/10/14/nyregion/14yards. html?pagewanted=all&_r=1&.

COOKFOX. 2015. Mission. COOKFOX Architects. www.cookfox.com/mission. html.

Coscarelli, J. 2015. Spike Lee's amazing rant against gentrification: "We Been Here!" *New York Magazine*, February 25. http://nymag.com/daily/intelligencer/2014/02/ spike-lee-amazing-rant-against-gentrification.html.

Craig, S., Rashbaum, W. K., and Kaplan. T. 2014. The short life of an anticorruption commission. *The New York Times*, July 23. www.nytimes.com/interactive/ 2014/07/23/nyregion/timeline-of-the-moreland-commission.html?_r=0#/# time336_8833.

Crown Heights Tenant Union. 2015. Our demands. Crown Heights Tenant Union. http://crownheightstenantunion.org/our-demands/.

Cuomo, A. 2014. Governor Cuomo announces comprehensive plan to accelerate the development of Atlantic Yards project and ensure timely delivery of public benefits. Governor Andrew M. Cuomo. June 27. www.governor.ny.gov/news/ governor-cuomo-announces-comprehensive-plan-accelerate-development-atlantic- yards-project-and.

Curbed NY. 2015. Rental market reports. *Curbed NY*. http://ny.curbed.com/tags/ rental-market-reports.

Dailey, J. 2014. De Blasio unveils 10-year, $41B affordable housing plan. *Curbed NY* (blog), May 5. http://ny.curbed.com/archives/2014/05/05/de_blasio_unveils_ 10year_41b_affordable_housing_plan.php.

Danza, C. 2009. Prospect Heights Historic District: Designation Report. www.nyc. gov/html/lpc/downloads/pdf/reports/prospecthts.pdf.

Davidson, J. 2015. Is gentrification all bad? *New York Magazine*, February 2. http:// nymag.com/news/features/gentrification-2014-2/.

de Blasio, Bill. 2014. Housing New York: A Five-Borough, Ten-Year Plan. The City of New York. www.nyc.gov/html/housing/assets/downloads/pdf/housing_ plan.pdf.

Del Signore, J. 2008. Lawsuits and recession hobbling Atlantic Yards project. *Gothamist*. January 28. http://gothamist.com/2008/01/28/lawsuits_and_re.php.

Develop Don't Destroy Brooklyn (DDDB). 2005. Extell bids $150 million vs. Rat- ner's $50 million for the MTA's rail yards in Brooklyn. News release, July 25. www.developdontdestroy.org/bids/release.php.

Develop Don't Destroy Brooklyn (DDDB). 2015. The opposition. Develop Don't Destroy Brooklyn. http://dddb.net/php/opposition.php.

Dulaney, C. 2015. Waldorf Astoria hotel sale completed. *The Wall Street Journal*, February 11. www.wsj.com/articles/waldorf-astoria-hotel-sale-completed- 1423705536.

Durkin, E. and Sederstrom, J. 2008. Atlantic Yards will go up . . . when economy does. *New York Daily News*, December 11. www.nydailynews.com/new-york/ brooklyn/atlantic-yards-economy-article-1.356934.

Empire State Development Corporation. 2015. www.esd.ny.gov/.

Essex Development Company. 2005. Vanderbilt yard proposal. July 6. http://dddb. net/documents/extell/Extell_MTAproposal.pdf.

Fainstein, S. S. 2009. Mega-projects in New York, London and Amsterdam. *International Journal of Urban and Regional Research*, 32(4), 768–785.

Forest City Enterprises. 2014. Forest City and Greenland Group close on joint venture at Atlantic Yards in Brooklyn. News release, July 1. http://ir.forestcity.net/phoenix.zhtml?c=88464&p=irol-newsArticle&id=1944055.

Frangos, A. and Karp, J. 2008. Gehry lays off staff. *The Wall Street Journal*, December 17. www.wsj.com/articles/SB122946954327912109.

Furman Center for Real Estate and Urban Policy at New York University (NYU Furman Center). 2013. *10 ISSUES FOR NYC'S NEXT MAYOR: How should the next mayor prioritize the preservation of existing affordable housing units?* Report. http://furmancenter.org/files/publications/NYChousing_Preservation.pdf.

Furman Center for Real Estate and Urban Policy at New York University (NYU Furman Center). 2014. *State of New York City's housing and neighborhoods in 2014.* Report. NYU Furman Center. http://furmancenter.org/files/sotc/SOC2013_HighRes.pdf.

Futterman, M. 2010. Bruce Ratner's NBA Waterloo. *The Wall Street Journal*, May 11. www.wsj.com/articles/SB10001424052748703880304575236621848424814.

Garnard, J., et al. 2014. Brooklyn case study: Atlantic Yards. Department of City and Regional Planning. University of California at Berkeley. Unpublished.

Gilmartin, M. 2014. Re: Atlantic Yards Redevelopment Project. MaryAnne Gilmartin to Michelle de la Uz, Gib Veconi. June 25. www.brooklynspeaks.net/sites/default/files/fcrc_letter_0.pdf.

Glen, A. 2014. Alicia K. Glen to Michelle de la Uz. June 24. www.brooklynspeaks.net/sites/default/files/nyc_letter_0.pdf.

Goldstein, V. 2009. New York State Urban Development Corporation, 13 N.Y.3d. 511 (2009).

Kamping-Carder, L. 2008. Everyone loves Prospect Heights historic designation. *Observer.* October 28. http://observer.com/2008/10/everyone-loves-prospect-heights-historic-designation/.

Kusisto, L. 2014. New York City to sell public housing stake. *The Wall Street Journal*, December 7. www.wsj.com/articles/new-york-city-to-sell-public-housing-stake-to-developers-1418004966?cb=logged0.17592483619228005.

Lightfeldt, A. 2015. Bright lights, big rent burden: Understanding New York City's rent affordability problem. *Street Easy* (blog), March 1. http://streeteasy.com/blog/new-york-city-rent-affordability/.

Markey, N. 2009. Atlantic Yards Community Benefit Agreement: A case study of organizing community support for development, 27 *Pace Envtl. L. Rev.* 377 (2009).

Morrone, F. 2005. Vanishing vistas: Will the "borough of churches" become a "borough of skyscrapers?" *No Land Grab* (blog), March.

Municipal Art Society of New York. 2008. Show the love at tomorrow's LPC Prospect Heights hearing. Municipal Art Society of New York. October 27. www.mas.org/show-the-love-at-lpc%E2%80%99s-prospect-heights-hearing-on-tuesday/.

New York 1 News. 2015. Home of future school at Pacific Park development revealed. Online posting. May 16. NY 1 News. www.ny1.com/nyc/brooklyn/news/2015/05/16/home-of-future-school-at-pacific-park-development-revealed.html.

New York City. 2015. *New York City's Recovery Finally Starts Generating Wage Gains.* Report. April 13. http://fiscalpolicy.org/wp-content/uploads/2015/04/NYCs-recovery-generating-wage-gains.pdf.

New York City Council. 2015. Submitting letter from the United States Bureau of the Census containing results of the 2014 New York City Housing and Vacancy

Survey. The New York City Council. February 12. http://legistar.council.nyc.gov/LegislationDetail.aspx?ID=2170491&GUID=28488EB2–5C81–49EF-AAA9–8A09F5A7F0B1&Options=&Search=.

Oder, N. 2004. The culture of cheating: The failed promise of union apprenticeships. *Atlantic Yards/Pacific Park Report* (blog), July 10. http://atlanticyardsreport.blogspot.com/p/the-atlantic-yards-cba-promised-path-to.html.

Oder, N. 2014. After 11 years of controversy, Atlantic Yards becomes Pacific Park Brooklyn. *Next City*, August 26. http://nextcity.org/daily/entry/brooklyn-development-atlantic-yards-name-change-pacific-park-brooklyn.

Oder, N. 2015. After report charging favoritism in EB-5, industry advocates nervous of reforms; why shouldn't immigrant investment do more for the public? *Atlantic Yards/Pacific Park Report* (blog), April 23. http://atlanticyardsreport.blogspot.com/2015/04/after-report-charging-favoritism-in-eb.html.

Pearce, D. 2014. *Overlooked and Undercounted, The Struggle to Make Ends Meet in New York City*, Prepared for the Women's Center for Education and Career Advancement with support from The United Way of New York City, The New York Community Trust, and City Harvest, December. Seventy-eight percent of households with inadequate incomes are headed by a person of color.

Regional Plan Association. (RPA). 2006. RPA supports Atlantic Yards' arena block, wants changes in second phase of development. News release, August 22. www.rpa.org/pdf/RPAAYpressrelease082206.pdf.

Solomont, E. B. 2015. The year of the Chinese investor. *The Real Deal: New York RealEstateNews*,March1.http://therealdeal.com/issues_articles/the-year-of-the-chinese-investor/.

Story, L. and Saul, S. 2015. New York Real Estate. *The New York Times*, February 7. www.nytimes.com/2015/02/08/nyregion/stream-of-foreign-wealth-flows-to-time-warner-condos.html?_r=0.

5 San Francisco
The fight to preserve the Mission District

> "It's great that we have so many [financial] resources because we are San Francisco, but being San Francisco is also our greatest challenge!"
>
> (San Francisco Mission District Resident)

It was a sunny and warm spring Saturday afternoon on March 28, 2015, in San Francisco's Mission District, when more than 100 angry residents, community activists, and nonprofit organizations joined San Francisco Board of Supervisor David Campos at a community meeting at the Brava Theater for an affordable housing town hall discussion. Many of the people in attendance were local residents who had faced eviction, were concerned about it, or knew of people who had been displaced out of the Mission District neighborhood. A grandmother stood up and told her story of how her landlord had recently evicted her because he wanted to sell his building to a big developer. You could hear the stress and worry in this grandmother's voice as she told the crowd how she takes care of her five-year-old granddaughter and could not afford to find another adequate place to live in San Francisco. A man in his thirties stood up and told the audience that his landlord had just alerted him and his neighbors that they, too, would be evicted because the landlord was going to sell their apartment building to a real estate investment company. Many long-term Mission residents told story after story about how the "new tech money" and "greedy real estate developers" are driving up housing prices, rents, and the overall cost of living in San Francisco. Others told stories about how the "ruthless" and "callous" landlords were evicting and intimidating them and their immigrant neighbors to move. Finally, others mentioned that San Francisco was in danger of losing its soul, its uniqueness, and its culture of political activism to the influx of young techies who had not yet experienced life. They feared that San Francisco and especially the Mission, with its art, culture, and murals, would become a boring and bland place.

San Francisco has long enjoyed a reputation as America's most liberal and progressive big city. After World War II, the city experienced the "San Francisco Renaissance," and was home to activist writers and artists in the San

Francisco Bay Area like Kenneth Rexroth and Robert Duncan. These writers and artists were later joined by the Beat Generation of poets and writers in the 1950s who challenged and rejected conventional standards. One of those poets was Lawrence Ferlinghetti, who founded the well-known City Lights Bookstore in San Francisco (The Literature Network, 2015). In the 1960s, the city experienced the influx of hippies and the 1967 Summer of Love. In the 1970s, San Francisco's gay rights movement led to the creation of one of the first gay neighborhoods, the Castro District, and the election of Harvey Milk, the first openly gay official elected to public office in California, to the San Francisco Board of Supervisors. More recently, the city became the first municipality in the United States to issue same-sex marriage licenses.

Lately, however, the City by the Bay has gained national and international attention, not for its progressive politics, but because of its laissez-faire economics and growing income inequality. The city working-class residents once dominated has become well known for its $1 million median home prices, artisan cafes, and expensive trendy restaurants, and the recent uproar over $4 toast (Knight and Tucker, 2013). The growth and expansion of companies in the city such as Amazon.com, Twitter, LinkedIn, Lyft, Uber, Salesforce.com, Airbnb, and Pinterest have attracted an influx of technology workers who spend their disposable income all over the city. Many in San Francisco see the rise of technology workers, and the payroll tax exemption that some companies received to stay in San Francisco, as part of the problem contributing to rising housing prices, rents, and the overall cost of living that is responsible for displacing middle- and working-class residents (City and County of San Francisco, 2014).

There is no question that the technology industry generates tremendous wealth for some. Twitter's initial public offering (IPO) in November 2013 created 1,600 millionaires (Bort, 2013). It is also apparent that the new rich in San Francisco are willing to pay a premium for the limited supply of rental and for-sale housing, take private car services, and ride private technology shuttle buses equipped with lounge seating, Wi-Fi, coffee, and pressed juices (Cantor, 2015). It is not surprising, then, that the increased cost of rents, housing prices, and overall cost of living in San Francisco has resulted in a tremendous amount of anti-technology backlash. Protesters have held rallies and demonstrations outside of technology companies and tried to block Google buses and other technology shuttle buses from transporting workers from San Francisco to Silicon Valley.

These protests, and the broader social movements for economic, environmental, and social justice, are in direct response to an economy stagnant for middle- and lower-class workers over the past two decades as well as the inadequate supply of housing construction (especially affordable housing) within San Francisco and the greater Northern California Bay Area. The growth of higher-skilled, higher-paid jobs and the influx of global capital investment into the city are driving up the cost of rents and housing prices, pushing homeownership beyond the reach of most hard-working San

Franciscans. These conditions have also led to coordinated efforts by residents within San Francisco's Mission District to utilize land use planning tools to protect, preserve, and maintain the history, culture, and fabric of the community.

San Francisco's technology boom 2.0 and growing income inequality

Over the past twenty years, San Francisco has experienced two relatively large economic booms. The first, marked by the dot-com boom, gained momentum in the mid-1990s and burst in the early 2000s. During this first period, the unemployment rate in San Francisco reached a record low of 3 percent. The demand for housing spiked and the overall cost of living increased. Multimedia companies and other technology start-ups expanded throughout the city, especially in the older, industrial neighborhoods on the east side of San Francisco. This first boom resulted in cries of gentrification and displacement from local working-class and poor residents.

Now the city is experiencing a second economic boom, and it too is largely driven by the growth of the technology sector. Billion-dollar technology firms such as Twitter, Google, and Facebook have opened new offices in the city. These firms have directly created thousands of jobs and the growth of the technology sector has resulted in the indirect creation of thousands of jobs that support the technology sector and its employees (Moretti, 2012). According to a recent economic study of San Francisco's economy, since the start of the Great Recession in December 2007, San Francisco has added more private-sector jobs than forty-seven of the fifty states (Mandel, 2014). Over the past four years, the city has added more than 67,000 private-sector jobs (a 15 percent gain), with the tech sector accounting for almost a third of those jobs (Mandel, 2014). In addition, it is estimated that the technology sector has been responsible for the creation of nearly 50,000 private-sector, non-tech jobs over the same period (Mandel, 2014). These jobs consist of construction, manufacturing, health and education, arts and recreation, and restaurants and bars (Mandel, 2014). In 2012, the technology sector contributed $9.2 billion in wages to the local economy (22 percent of the total) (Mandel, 2014). All of this technology growth has helped reduce San Francisco's unemployment rate from a high of 9.4 percent in January 2011 to 3.8 percent as of the end of 2014 – much lower than the state of California's unemployment rate of 7 percent (December 2014).

San Francisco also has a decent jobs mix; however, the labor market over the years has become more bifurcated with higher-wage, higher-skilled jobs at the top of the salary scale and lower-wage, lower-skilled jobs being created at the bottom and middle-class jobs declining. In 2015, according to the City of San Francisco, the leading private-sector industries with the highest average annual wage were: *financial activities* $170,404; *information* $123,968;

professional and building services $115,284; *manufacturing* $81,380; and construction $79,820 (S.F. Planning Department, 2015). However, very few of these private-sector jobs account for a large percentage of the overall average number of total jobs within the private sector with the exception of *professional and business services* at 28 percent. The rest of the top five higher-wage, private-industry-sector jobs accounted for only 20 percent of the total number of private-sector jobs – (#1) financial activities (10 percent); (#2) information (5 percent); (#5) construction (3 percent); and (#4) manufacturing (2 percent) (S.F. Planning Department, 2015). Unfortunately, most of the growth within the private sector is expected to be in low- to medium-skilled jobs such as waitpersons, retail salespersons, personal care aides, janitors and cleaners, and food preparation workers, with approximate annual pay scales ranging from $22,006 to $26,291 (S.F. Planning Department, 2015).

Unfortunately, not all residents have benefited from the growth of technology-related jobs or from the overall economic boom happening in San Francisco. The bifurcation in the labor market between higher-skilled, higher-wage jobs and lower-skilled, lower-wage jobs undoubtedly contributes to the growing income inequality in San Francisco. The median household income in the city is $75,604, much higher than the national median at $52,250 (U.S. Census, 2013). The contrast is stark when looking at median household income in San Francisco according to race and ethnicity. Whites' median household income is $96,582; median household income for Latinos is at $56,408; then median household income for Native Hawaiian and Pacific Islanders is at $45,585; and median household income for blacks is at $31,050. The city has the highest proportion of very wealthy persons (high net worth $30 million+) than any other city in the nation (ACS, 2012). Moreover, a study by the Brookings Institution, a think tank in Washington, DC, underscored the high levels of income inequality in San Francisco. According to the this study, San Francisco experienced the largest increase in its ratio between the ninety-fifth percentile household income compared to the twentieth percentile of household income from 2007 to 2012. Income for its typical twentieth-percentile household dropped $4,000 during that period to $21,313, while income for its typical ninety-fifth-percentile household increased by $28,000 to $353,576 (Berube, 2014).

The growing income inequality has especially impacted San Francisco's middle-class households. The middle class finds itself too wealthy to qualify for many of the city's social benefits programs and too poor to afford to purchase or rent a home and to pay for amenities and services such as childcare, transportation, medical care, and education. Since 1990, San Francisco's middle-class households have shrunk from 45 percent to 34 percent in 2012, while the city's high-income population has grown modestly from 30 percent to 32 percent during the same time period.

California and San Francisco's affordable housing crisis

Adding to the squeeze of the middle and working classes is the housing crisis. California, and especially San Francisco, has some of the highest housing costs in the United States. A significant reason for California and San Francisco's affordable housing crisis has to do with the very low supply and high demand. Since the 1970s, the state's construction of market-rate and affordable housing has not kept up with housing demand. Currently the state is in the process of building roughly 100,000 to 140,000 units of housing, but, in reality, in order to begin to address the high demand for housing, researchers estimate that housing developers would need to build upward of 230,000 units of housing annually (Taylor, 2015). The lack of market-rate and affordable housing is especially challenging in cities like San Francisco where land values are high, resistance to large-scale housing developments is fierce, environmental policies are more stringent, and the cost of construction is higher compared to other places (Taylor, 2015). For example, the California Legislative Analyst's Office (LAO) conducted a study on California's housing crisis and found that a number of factors prevent housing developers from increasing the supply of housing, especially dense housing

Figure 5.1 Victorians in the Mission District
Source: Malo André Hutson.

within coastal cities. A major factor is that in coastal cities, communities' resistance to new housing can be strong and residents often use local land use authority to slow or stop housing from being built. This has been the case in San Francisco.

Barriers to developing new housing

In addition to community resistance to housing developments, experts have observed that the California Environmental Quality Act (CEQA) process, a statute that requires state and local agencies to identify the significant environmental impacts of proposed projects and to avoid or mitigate those impacts, if feasible, can slow a project housing project down or reduce its size (CA Department of Justice, 2011). For example, under CEQA, a project cannot move forward until all concerns are addressed, either through mitigation or with a determination by elected officials that the benefits of the project outweigh the costs (CA Department of Justice, 2011). Even if a local governing board approves a project, residents can challenge a CEQA review, resulting in a lengthy legal battle (Taylor, 2015). In a study the California Legislative Analyst's Office conducted, which analyzed CEQA documents that the ten largest cities in California submitted to the state between 2004 and 2013, the LAO found that it "took local agencies about two and a half years to approve housing projects that required an [environmental impact report]" (Taylor, 2015). In a state where the housing demand outstrips supply enormously, any delays to the construction of market-rate and affordable housing are likely to result in higher housing costs and rents, disproportionately negatively impacting low-income residents.

Another challenge to the increased construction of new housing has to do with limited incentives by local governments to approve housing developments. Given a choice between approving commercial development versus housing developments, many are likely to choose commercial developments (such as retail, hotels, or businesses) because of the higher fiscal benefits (Taylor, 2015). Housing, on the other hand, may not always provide the same fiscal benefits to cities and can result in higher demands for local governments to provide local services. This again is a significant barrier to building more housing in coastal cities such as San Francisco.

Finally, another impediment to the increased construction of housing has to do with the limited amount of available land and the cost of land, which can push up the cost of housing construction, especially in a city like San Francisco. Because San Francisco is only forty-nine square miles and surrounded by water, there is not a lot of available land to build large-scale housing developments. In addition, high land, construction, and labor costs result in housing developers focusing on building luxury housing to make bigger profits as opposed to moderate- and low-income-priced housing. Researchers estimate that it costs between $350,000 and $700,000 to build a unit of housing in San Francisco. Much of the new housing developments in San Francisco have been high-rise luxury housing and limited affordable housing. San Francisco recently approved a $500 million condominium tower in the South of Market neighborhood, making it the most expensive condominium development in the city's history (Dineen, 2015). The fifty-three-story, 190-unit building is likely to sell the 2,000-plus square foot units for an average of $5.4 million (Dineen, 2015).

Unfortunately, all of the barriers contributing to the inadequate supply of housing construction around the Bay Area and within San Francisco make most housing virtually unaffordable for working-class and low-income households and only marginally affordable to those families who consider themselves middle class. As of July 2014, news media reported that the median home price of a single-family dwelling or condominium in San Francisco was $1 million (Pender, 2014). And San Francisco also has the highest rents in the nine-county Bay Area, with the average rent of market-rate apartments and townhomes (ranging from studios to three bedrooms) being $3,229 (Pender, 2014). According to real estate data, just 15 percent of for-sale homes in the city are affordable to middle-class San Franciscans, making it the least affordable market in the nation (Meronek, 2015).

Figure 5.2 Condominiums being built in the Mission District
Source: Malo André Hutson.

Lack of inclusionary housing

Housing development also does not adequately address the needs of low- and moderate-income families. And while San Francisco has attempted to address the inadequate supply of affordable housing through rent subsidies, rent stabilization, housing assistance, and affordable housing requirements, historically the demand has outstripped supply by a factor of five to one (City of San Francisco Housing Element, 2015). The growing cost of living due to the construction of affordable housing and rising income inequality in San Francisco has also hit the poorest households and individuals hard. Estimates suggest that California households with incomes in the bottom quartile spend 67 percent of their income on housing, about 11 percent more than low-income households elsewhere (Taylor, 2015). This trend is consistent across income groups, but decreases as household income rises (Taylor, 2015). The increased costs of rent and housing have left many of the most vulnerable populations with very few alternatives but to live in crowded conditions. In 2010, according to data analyzed by the City of San Francisco Human Services Agency, roughly 42.4 percent of San Francisco's Latino households were doubled up, which is defined by "households that include an adult who is not the householder, spouse, or cohabitating part-ner of the householder." Just slightly more than 37 percent of Asian/Pacific Islander households are doubled up, followed by 25 percent of black house-holds and 18 percent of white households (Kelly, 2014).

A reason for this has to do with the lack of inclusionary housing provided to meet the needs of San Francisco's most vulnerable populations. In 1992, San Francisco passed the citywide Inclusionary Affordable Housing Pro-gram, which required housing developers who build five units or more to sell or rent 15–20 percent of units in new residential developments at a below market rate (BMR) that is affordable to low- or middle-income households (Temkin, Theodos, and Price, 2010). The city's Inclusionary Housing Pro-gram has since been amended to require housing developers who build ten units or more of new housing to pay an affordable housing fee. Project spon-sors also have other options if they choose not to pay the fee; this includes providing 12 percent of their units on site or 20 percent of their units off site as affordable to low- to moderate-income households (S.F. Mayor's Office of Housing, 2015b).[1] In an effort to manage the regional growth and accom-modate projected housing needs throughout the Bay Area, the Association of Bay Area Governments (ABAG) (the comprehensive regional planning agency and Council of Governments for the nine counties and 101 cities and towns of the San Francisco Bay region) allocates a number of housing units at various income levels to each community in the region based on projected job growth. ABAG has allocated nearly 29,000 new units of housing in San Francisco through the year 2022, with almost 57 percent of those units required to be affordable to households of moderate income (defined as 120 percent of Area Median Income, AMI) or below (ABAG, 2015). Despite the call for an average of more than 3,600 units of housing to be built annually, the City of San Francisco has not kept pace. In 2013 (most recent data available), San Francisco built 2,499 units of housing; however, 537 separate units were lost because of demolition, mergers, or removal of illegal units, resulting in a net of only 1,960 units of additional housing, far below what is necessary to meet demand (S.F. Planning Department Housing Inventory, 2013). Moreover, this amount of housing was consistent with the ten-year annual average of 1,932 units of housing constructed within the city (S.F. Planning Department Housing Inventory, 2013). To make matters worse for those in need of low- to moderate-income housing, only 712 of the 1,932 housing units built in 2013 were affordable.

The California Housing Partnership Corporation (CHPC) 2014 report concludes that the city lacks 40,845 homes to house very-low-income (VLI) and extremely low-income (ELI) households. Because of increasing rents and declining median incomes, 59 percent of VLI households spend more than half their income on rent and 81 percent of VLI households spend more than 30 percent of their income on rent in the city, the majority of low-income households are severely cost-burdened. Numerous cuts to affordable housing funding (including the elimination of redevelopment agencies and a loss of CDBG funds) prevent many families from achieving a reasonable standard of living in San Francisco (CA Housing Partnership Corporation, 2014).

Overall, housing assistance and other critical services are out of reach for families still too poor to meet the Self-Sufficiency Standard discussed in Chapter 2. Affordable housing needs of both low-income *and* moderate-income families with children have not been met. The U.S. Department of Health and Human Services issues the Federal Poverty Guidelines as a standard to both measure poverty and define eligibility thresholds for public benefits programs, such as Medicaid and CHIP (Families USA, 2014). A household of three people is considered below the federal poverty threshold if it earns less than $19,790 and at a 150 percent of the poverty threshold at $35,775. The U.S. Department of Housing and Urban Development (HUD) issues calculations for median family incomes (MFI) by county to assist in defining household income levels and determining eligibility for various affordable and public housing assistance programs (HUD, 2014b). Extremely low-income households earn a maximum of 30 percent of the MFI, very low-income households earn a maximum of 50 percent of the MFI, and low-income households earn a maximum of 80 percent of the MFI. For the purposes of obtaining Section 8 housing, household income must not exceed 50 percent of the area's median income (HUD, 2014a). For the County of San Francisco, the AMI for a family of four is $101,900; the threshold for four people is therefore $50,950 (CA Housing and Community Development, 2014). A family of four who fails to meet the Self-Sufficiency Standard (discussed in Chapter 2) may still make well over the threshold to qualify for Section 8 housing.

Reducing greenhouse gas emissions and promoting transit-oriented development

Adding to the fears of gentrification and displacement among the middle class, the working class, and the poor in San Francisco, as well as in the surrounding cities of Oakland and San Jose, is the state of California's focus on promoting transit-oriented development (TOD) in order to reduce greenhouse gas emissions. In 2008, California lawmakers passed Senate Bill 375 (SB 375), the California Sustainable Communities and Climate Protection Act of 2008, which established a new framework for how metropolitan regions across the state would address their regional housing need allocation (RHNA). SB 375 requires each of the state's eighteen metropolitan areas to develop a Sustainable Communities Strategy (SCS) with the goals of reducing greenhouse gas (GHG) emissions from cars and light trucks and accommodating all needed housing growth within the region (ABAG, 2014). SB 375 seeks to ensure that future land uses (through RHNA and other plans) are coordinated with long-term transportation investments (ABAG, 2014).

The focus on building housing near transportation stations or along heavily traveled transportation routes can certainly be beneficial to reducing suburban sprawl, creating walkable communities, and increasing ridership, but data from studies that have analyzed TOD have found that investments around transit stops often drive up housing prices and result in the displacement of less affluent residents (Pollack, Bluestone, and Billingham, 2010). For example, Northeastern University's "Maintaining Diversity in America's Transit-Rich Neighborhoods" study found that

> transit investment frequently changes the surrounding neighborhood. While patterns of neighborhood change vary, the most predominant pattern is one in which housing becomes more expensive, neighborhood residents become wealthier and vehicle ownership becomes more common. And in some of the newly transit-rich neighborhoods . . . a new transit station can set in motion a cycle of unintended consequences in which core transit users – such as renters and low income households – are priced out in favor of higher-income, car-owning residents who are less likely to use public transit for commuting.
>
> (Pollack et al., 2010)

TOD works best if there is a focus on equitable economic development that attempts to minimize displacement by incorporating development of affordable housing, preserving rental property, and establishing funding for land acquisition around transit stations and routes. Examples include the successful Fruitvale Village in Oakland, California, or the efforts by the city of San Leandro, California, which developed a TOD strategy to increase affordable housing by using in-lieu fees from developers under the city's inclusionary zoning ordinance to subsidize affordable housing adjacent to the Bay Area Rapid Transit (BART) rail station. The TOD housing projects that are making their way into San Francisco's Mission District neighborhood, however, are located where rents are increasing and residents are at risk of being displaced like they were in the late 1990s and early 2000 when more than 1,000 Latino families had been displaced (does not include undocumented immigrants) and rental evictions nearly tripled from 965 in 1993 to 2,730 in 2000 (Mirabal, 2009). Along Valencia Street, 50 percent of businesses that existed in 1990 had disappeared by 1998 (Mirabal, 2009). San Francisco's high housing costs have also contributed to increasing commutes: San Francisco is now the city with the longest average commutes in the state of California at seventy-two minutes per day, which is roughly 30 percent longer than the U.S. average (Taylor, 2015). As of 2010, 27 percent of San Francisco workers commuted into the city; by 2020, it is estimated that commuters will account for about 43 percent of jobs.

Demographic and neighborhood change within the Mission District

Perhaps no neighborhood in San Francisco has experienced as much change as the Mission District. Between 2000 and 2010, the Latino population in the Mission District declined from 50 percent to 39 percent (Weinberg, 2015b). Moreover, housing prices and rents have soared during the past two decades. For example, the median home price in the Mission District has seen an increase of more than 75 percent since 2001 rising from $508,567 to $892,217 in 2014 (Weinberg, 2015c). In the first part of 2015, the median rent for a one-bedroom apartment cost $3,410 a month, much higher than other affluent neighborhoods in San Francisco (O'Brien, 2015). A number of factors have contributed to this increase, primarily a low number of housing units being built and very few BMR housing units being constructed. According to a recent analysis, since 2009, 777 new units have been built or entitled in the Mission District, 13 percent of which (99 units) are BMR inclusionary units. The neighborhood also had the second highest number of no-fault evictions (popularly known as Ellis Act evictions) in the entire city at 233 between 2009 and 2013, behind the South of Market neighborhood at 384 (Weinberg, 2015c). The Ellis Act is a provision in California law that provides landlords with a legal way to "go out of business." As rent and housing prices have increased, landlords have used the Ellis Act to evict tenants and then sell their properties to real estate developers. This practice has been increasing across San Francisco and limits the supply of affordable housing. A 2013 memorandum to San Francisco Board of Supervisor David Campos from the San Francisco Budget and Legislative Analyst found that while all evictions had increased 38.2 percent between 2010 and 2013, Ellis Act evictions standing alone had increased by 169 percent during the same period (from 43 to 116) (S.F. Budget Legislative Analyst, 2013). This same report also found that the citywide rental vacancy rate had gone from 6.4 percent in 2009 to 2.8 percent in 2012.

Neighborhood resistance against neighborhood change and displacement

All of these changes over the past twenty years have motivated organizations, residents, and other concerned citizens to organize around neighborhood change that creates a risk of displacement (voluntary or involuntary) because of the lack of affordable housing and the overall increase in the cost of living. Concern over gentrification and neighborhood change prompted different strategies in three key neighborhoods undergoing neighborhood change in San Francisco – Bayview Hunters Point, Central Market/ Tenderloin, and the Mission District (Lower 24th Street). Residents, non-profits, and businesses within the Mission District neighborhood who have succeeded at organizing and working with the City of San Francisco to protect and preserve the Latino identity, culture, and history in the neighborhood as well as to keep families and mom-and-pop businesses from being displaced. They have reframed the discussion around sustainability to include equity and justice using land use tools to try to prevent inequitable development and displacement.

Early activism, community planning, and land use controls

The community sentiments expressed at the spring 2015 community meeting I described at the outset of this chapter are the product of decades of neighborhood change. Likewise, many of the community strategies I have observed residents employ within the Mission over the past two years are likely the consequence of decades of community activism against gentrification. Analyzing the strategies Mission residents are using today to fight gentrification requires looking backward to understand both how the Mission came to be the culturally rich neighborhood that it is and how residents have worked to substantially increase citizen participation in the city-planning process.

After World War II, there was an increase in immigration within the Mission District of people coming from Mexico and Central and South America. This helped make the Mission District a thriving Latino/a neighborhood. As various economic booms have impacted San Francisco, the Mission District's lower half section, or Lower 24th Street as the locals say, has become the "heart" of the neighborhood's Latino/a community. The area represents a culturally diverse group of residents who have built thriving Latino/a cultural and community institutions and served as a center of organizing for social justice issues not only domestically, but abroad as well.

The first dot-com boom in the 1990s brought physical and economic changes to the Mission District. The information technology sector grew at a rapid pace and the demand for commercial space approached unprecedented levels. In response to this demand and the growing technology sector, the City of San Francisco engaged in efforts to change land use controls and to "rezone large portions of the City's industrial land for multi-media use," especially within the Mission District. The demand for housing and commercial space put tremendous pressure on artists, nonprofits, and the most vulnerable residents with limited incomes (Beitel, 2013). Fear of gentrification and displacement was widespread and many in the community were looking for city leaders to step up and address the rising rents, displacement, and growing inequality.

In 2001, the San Francisco Planning Department commenced an Eastern Neighborhoods community-planning process to address the growing information technology sector and increased demand for housing. Specifically, the Eastern Neighborhoods community-planning process included the heavily industrial neighborhoods of the Mission District, Central Waterfront, East South of Market, and Showplace Square/Potrero Hill, with the explicit goal of developing new zoning controls for the industrial portions of these neighborhoods. The Eastern Neighborhoods Plan called for rezoning of roughly half of the existing industrial areas in these four neighborhoods to mixed-use zones that would encourage new housing – with the goal of reducing the housing demand pressure.

Four years after the initial engagement of the Eastern Neighborhoods community-planning process, the San Francisco Planning Department finally expanded the community-planning process to address other issues critical to these four communities, such as affordable housing, transportation, parks and open space, urban design, and community facilities. The Planning Department began working with the neighborhood stakeholders to create Area Plans for each neighborhood to articulate a vision for the future. For example, the Mission District Area Plan called for preserving the neighborhood's diversity and vitality, minimizing displacement, and increasing affordable housing, while also persevering and enhancing the unique character of the Mission District's commercial areas (S.F. Planning Department, 2008).

Perhaps the most significant part of the Mission District Area Plan called for the elimination of density limits and for limited parking controls in some areas near Mission Street transit (S.F. Planning Department, 2008). This plan conforms to the strategy ABAG outlined to direct future housing development within the Northern California region along transit lines with a focus on transit-oriented development (ABAG, 2014). In 2008, the state of California passed the Sustainable Communities and Climate Protection Act of 2008 (Sustainable Communities Act, SB 375, Chapter 728, Statutes of 2008), which supports the state's climate action goals to reduce GHG emissions through coordinated transportation and land use planning with the goal of more sustainable communities (CA Air Resources Board, 2015). As a result, each metropolitan planning organization across the state must develop a sustainable communities strategy (SCS). The "SCS contains land use, housing, and transportation strategies that, if implemented, would allow the region to meet its GHG emission reduction targets. Once adopted by the MPO, the RTP/SCS guides the transportation policies and investments for the region" (ABAG, 2014). The focus on large-scale, transit-oriented development, in many cases high-end condominium development along the Mission District's 16th Street and 24th Street Bay Area Rapid Transit (BART) stations, has residents fearful of gentrification and displacement.

Many residents were dissatisfied with the city's planning process and did not trust the city's efforts to address the growing levels of displacement and gentrification in the Mission District neighborhood. As a result, local residents and several community-based organizations began organizing at the grassroots level to fight against gentrification and displacement within the Mission District neighborhood. A leading coalition that emerged out of these efforts was the Mission Anti-Displacement Coalition (MAC), a group of organizations such as People Organized to Demand Environmental and Employment Rights (PODER), Mission Housing, St. Peter's Catholic Church, and Mission Agenda (Beitel, 2013). MAC's primary goal was to (Beitel, 2013):

1) Stop the displacement of working peoples from the Mission District and San Francisco.
2) Establish a vision and organize for affordable, healthy, culturally vibrant, and politically engaged communities.
3) Advocate for a set of urban reform demands created by the people who live, work, pray, and play in the community.

In 1999, MAC began a seven-year intensive community engagement and community organizing effort during which it conducted focus groups, surveys, and workshops and held countless small- and large-scale community meetings (People's Plan, 2006). MAC and local residents organized to challenge the San Francisco Planning Department and the San Francisco Planning Commission. MAC and its allies educated themselves about city planning, planning codes, and regulations, especially with regards to land use controls. MAC's organizing efforts resulted in a parallel, and an alternative, community-planning process to the city's. MAC compiled all the information gathered from its community-organizing efforts and produced *The People's Plan for Housing, Jobs, and Community* and presented it to the San Francisco Planning Department on November 15, 2006. The plan was the community's effort to provide an alternative to the city's Eastern Neighborhoods community-planning efforts and an effort to control the market forces driving up land prices and housing costs. *The People's Plan* called for land use controls to promote the preservation and development of affordable housing, promote and retain light industrial and artisan businesses, and provide living-wage employment opportunities.

At the very least, this activism educated neighborhood residents, local business owners, and community leaders about the planning process. For many, this was their first lesson in city planning. The effects of the first technology boom galvanized key grassroots organizations to not just fight San

Francisco's city-planning efforts, but instead to try to use planning and zoning to their own ends. Residents' fear of gentrification and displacement was so widespread that they worried that the Latino/a community and identity of the Mission District neighborhood would be drastically changed, if not eliminated. Community leaders began discussing ways to celebrate Latino/a culture and history and document the contribution that Latino/as have made to San Francisco, and the neighborhood's international ties to human rights struggles. For example, former Mission District Supervisor Jim Gonzalez promoted a program called "Flags of the Americas Program," in which Mission artists created flags that were attached to light poles along lower 24th Street as a way of recognizing the neighborhood's Latino heritage (S.F. Board of Supervisors, 2014). Later, San Francisco Supervisor Susan Leal held an economic summit and worked with local nonprofit organizations to purchase properties along 24th Street (S.F. Board of Supervisors, 2014). It was during this economic summit that the idea for a Latino Cultural District was first introduced. However, it failed to gain the traction and support it needed to reach fruition. Calle 24 SF reports that Mission District leaders came together in the late 1990s to seek resources for neighborhood services and preservation through the federal Enterprise Zone program. The first meeting of this event brought together leaders from across the Mission District neighborhood to discuss important issues such as affordable housing and economic opportunities for residents.

> The first meeting to discuss (the Enterprise Zone proposal) was held at the Mission Educational Projects, Inc. office on 24th Street, in which over 40 community leaders convened to develop a plan to curb violence, establish home ownership and affordable housing programs, spur business development, and support Latino arts and culture.
>
> (S.F. Heritage, 2014)

All of this earlier community organizing and activism during the first dot-com boom provided the infrastructure supporting the current efforts to fight against gentrification and displacement.

The emergence of the Latino Cultural District

Perhaps the loudest voices in recent years to organize against gentrification and displacement within the Mission District have been those found in Calle 24 SF. Calle 24 SF is a grassroots organization formed in 1999 by community members of 24th Street in the Mission District. Calle 24 SF is an all-volunteer organization that includes community council members representing merchants, residents, landlords, service nonprofits, arts organizations, youth, renters, homeowners, families, and artists (Calle 24 SF, 2015). Several of the organization's members have deep roots in the Mission District going back many generations. The organization's goal was to make the area safer, cleaner, and an overall healthier environment for residents, merchants, and visitors (Calle 24 SF, 2015). The area encompasses fourteen city blocks stretching from Mission Street to the west and Potrero Avenue to the east and 22nd Street to the north and Cesar Chavez Street to the south. Local residents and businesses refer to the area as the "El Corazon de la Misión" or "the Heart of the Mission."

Since its inception, Calle 24 SF has been involved in raising money for neighborhood improvements such as streetlights, sidewalk upgrades, planter boxes, and hired youth street cleanup. In addition, the organization has raised money to support local nonprofit organizations on 24th Street serving children from low-income families. In collaboration with Precita Eyes, merchants, residents, and local independent artists, Calle 24 SF created a night-time gallery walk by painting murals on merchant roll downs and lighting them on 24th Street to preserve, promote, and celebrate 24th Street murals, culture, and businesses (Calle 24 SF, 2015). Key events sponsored by Calle 24 SF include the Cesar Chavez Parade, Dia de los Muertos, and Carnival.

Recently Calle 24 SF has taken on bigger issues. The continued growth of the technology economy and the increase in technology workers moving into the community has raised fears about increased costs for housing, the diminishment of Latino culture and history, and the overall "Googlization" of the neighborhood with Google buses transporting workers to and from San Francisco to Google's Mountain View campus in Silicon Valley. Early on, leaders from Calle 24 SF have been in close communication with San Francisco Supervisor David Campos and Mayor Edwin Lee's Office of Economic and Workforce Development (OEWD). For example in 2010, Supervisor David Campos' office, OEWD, and the Local Initiative Support Corporation organized a serious of workshops with local merchants, community leaders, and residents about ways to stabilize and revitalize the low-to-moderate income area of 24th Street. This effort led by the city's Neighborhood Marketplace Initiative helped to get more people involved in addressing the social, economic, and political issues impacting the Mission District neighborhood. The Initiative also helped to increase communication among the City of San Francisco, elected officials, community leaders, nonprofit organizations, and local residents who still remembered the frustrations they felt over the Eastern Neighborhoods community-planning process.

In 2012, Mayor Edwin Lee selected 24th Street for its economic development program called the Invest in Neighborhoods Initiative, an effort to provide focused, customized assistance to meet the specific needs of San Francisco's neighborhood commercial corridors. In addition, the Invest in Neighborhoods Initiative attempts to leverage city resources from other departments such as the Planning Department, the Department of Public Works, and the Municipal Transportation Agency in order to help small businesses succeed, increase quality of life, improve physical conditions, and build community capacity (S.F. Mayor's Office of Housing, 2015a). This initiative was just another effort to stabilize the displacement of Latino businesses and residents, preserve 24th Street as the center for Latino culture and commerce, and enhance 24th Street's unique nature as a special place for San Francisco's residents and tourists (S.F. Mayor's Office of Housing, 2014a).

All of these city-planning efforts along with the technology boom and housing affordability crisis got the key leaders from Calle 24 SF to think critically about the best way to preserve the Mission District for low-income families. They were asking themselves and others, "how do you preserve the majority Latino culture, history, institutions, and businesses within the neighborhood? What is the best strategy or strategies to make this happen?" (Day, 2014). One of the ideas that gained traction was an idea that had been discussed years before, designating the lower 24th Street area of the Mission District as a Latino Cultural District. In order to do this, many Latino leaders knew they would have to document the historical, cultural, economic, and political contributions Latinos have made to San Francisco. As a result, leaders from Calle 24 SF, the San Francisco Latino Historical Society, and San Francisco Heritage, with support from Mayor Ed Lee and Supervisor David Campos, began documenting Latinos' contributions to San Francisco and to California. One example was the "Nuestra Historia" project launched in 2012 by the San Francisco Latino Historical Society in partnership with San Francisco Heritage, which focused on documenting San Francisco Latino history. The project will culminate in a written report called a "Historic Context Statement" that will chronicle Latino history as it pertains to San Francisco's physical and cultural landscape. This was the first project to be funded for the documentation of "Nuestra Historia: Documenting the Contributions of the Chicano, Latino and Indigena to the development of San Francisco" (S.F. Latino Historical Society, 2015). One of the key purposes of such documents is to be used "as guidelines for the planning department to use in the future in making decisions for the properties studied."

To further support the efforts to designate lower 24th Street a Latino Cultural District, Calle 24 SF, the San Francisco Latino Historical Society, and San Francisco Heritage produced a nine-page historical report documenting the Latino presence in San Francisco and the formation of a Latino neighborhood in the Mission District. The document was extremely thorough in recording the presence of Latinos in San Francisco and their contributions to the city and to California. For example, the document begins like this:

> The area that would later become the City of San Francisco had historically been a part of the Mexican Republic from 1821–1848. Beginning in 1833, the newly-established Mexican government began to secularize Mission lands that had been founded a half-century earlier by the Spanish, and distributed over 500 land grants to prominent families throughout California in an effort to encourage agricultural development.
>
> (S.F. Latino Historical Society, 2015)

The historic document also chronicled the immigration of people from Latin America, who settled in San Francisco in the mid-nineteenth century, and the arrival of newcomers from Central and South America as well as Cuba, the Dominican Republic, and Puerto Rico, who came after World War II. It discussed major Latino cultural and community institutions' role in providing opportunities for Latino artists to exhibit their work when mainstream galleries, museums, and spaces would not; and it highlighted how 24th Street has been a center of organizing for social justice, including the Chicano civil rights movement of the 1960s and 1970s and the Nicaraguan and Salvadoran Solidarity Movements of the 1980s and 1990s (S.F. Latino Historical Society, 2015).

This effort to document Latinos' contributions to San Francisco and community organizing on the ground helped Calle 24 SF and its allies make the case for the importance of creating lower 24th Street as a Latino Cultural District. More importantly, they were able to establish the political capital necessary among the city's elected officials to pass the Latino Cultural District resolution. Finally, in May 2014, Calle 24 SF, in collaboration with the San Francisco Latino Historical Society, San Francisco Heritage, Mayor Lee, and Supervisor Campos, had the lower 24th Street Mission District area designated as a Latino Cultural District (S.F. Mayor's Office of Housing, 2014a). The City of San Francisco Board of Supervisors unanimously passed (11–0) a resolution establishing the Calle 24 "Veinticuatro" a Latino Cultural District (S.F. Board of Supervisors, 2014).[2] The resolution is nine pages long and was based on the historical document produced by Calle 24 SF, the San Francisco Latino Historical Society, and San Francisco Heritage where it describes the history and cultural contributions of Latinos to San Francisco and California. For example, the resolution states:

> WHEREAS, The Calle 24 ("Veinticuatro") Latino Cultural District plays a significant role in the history of San Francisco; and WHEREAS, San Francisco has for centuries attracted people seeking refuge from war, upheaval and poverty in their home countries; and WHEREAS, The immigrant experience remains an integral part of California and San Francisco's history, cultural richness and economic vibrancy; . . . and WHEREAS, Throughout the 1970s and 1980s, Central American countries experienced major political conflict and families fleeing from conflict immigrated to San Francisco, greatly contributing to the Latino Identity of the Mission District and Calle 24 ("Veinticuatro") Latino Cultural District.

The resolution also includes key places of cultural significance such as La Raza Park (also known as Potrero del Sol Park), Precita Park, and the Mission Cultural Center (S.F. Mayor's Office of Housing, 2014a). The Latino Cultural District's boundaries were created based on the greatest concentration of Latino cultural landmarks, businesses, institutions, festivals, and festival routes (S.F. Latino Historical Society, 2014). The Latino Cultural District is defined as "a cultural corridor is a linear region linked together by similar cultural or heritage resources, and offering a visitor experiences that showcase those resources." The vision for Calle 24 SF's Latino Cultural District is the following:

> 24th Street as a Latino Cultural District will be an economically vibrant community that is inclusive of diverse income households and businesses that together embrace the unique Latino heritage and culture of 24th Street and celebrate Latino cultural events, activities and art while supporting a singular enclave of Latino owned/themed businesses.
>
> (S.F. Board of Supervisors, 2014)

The Calle 24 Latino Cultural District also received support from the Commission on the Environment and San Francisco Department of Environment, which passed its own resolution in "support of the creation and sustainable community impact of the Calle 24 Latino Cultural District." The resolution made a statement that the Commission on the Environment and San Francisco Department of Environment seeks to promote environmental justice across all program areas by identifying opportunities to promote putting an end to disproportionate pollution in vulnerable communities as an integral part of its environmental stewardship mission. The resolution was significant because it supported the argument that the Latino Cultural District was about sustaining the Mission District's culture, history, residents, businesses, and jobs, which in and of itself was friendly to the environment. The Commission on the Environment and the San Francisco Department of Environment used the environmental sustainability argument to protect and preserve the Mission District. Lately, the sustainability argument has been used to redevelop and transform traditional low-income communities and communities of color, resulting in what many scholars call environmental gentrification (Checker, 2011; Pearsall, 2012).

For many, the designation of lower 24th Street as a Latino Cultural District was one step in a larger strategy for merchants, nonprofit organizations, and local residents concerned about gentrification and displacement to have more control over the planning process and land use. For these individuals, the designation of the area as a Latino Cultural District paved the way for the area to eventually become a special-use district – adding a level of interim land use controls in order to slow down the construction of market-rate housing and the development of new higher-end restaurants and businesses. One San Francisco city planner told me, "residents within the Latino Cultural District are trying to use the 'land use policy toolkit' as a way of having control over land use, even if it is only a temporary fix [protecting the area from market-rate housing development and new businesses and restaurants]. Being designated a special use district allows for interim controls for up to 18 months" (S.F. Planning Department, 2015). In response to the proposed special-use district, Planning Director John Rahaim was publicly quoted as saying that the interim controls would add "an extra piece of review" to new housing proposals (Weinberg, 2015b).

The desire to transform the Latino Cultural District to a special-use district was best illustrated by Supervisor David Campos' speech at the public ribbon-cutting ceremony a few days after the Board of Supervisors had passed the resolution. He was quoted as saying the following to the enthusiastic crowd who had gathered at the corner of 24th and Harrison Streets:

> The resolution that the Board of Supervisors passed unanimously this Tuesday is historic in that it recognizes and understands the contribution of the Latino community [not only] to the Mission, but to all of San Francisco. . . . Calle 24 is the heart of the La Misión, recognizing Calle 24 as a Latino Cultural District is the first step in a longer process to preserve the integrity of [not only] Calle 24, but the entire neighborhood. We are about to begin an open transparent public community process where we as a community are going to decide and tell the powers that be at City Hall what our priorities are in terms of the institutions that we want to preserve in our neighborhood. It is going to be the people of La Misión telling City Hall this is what we want to prioritize. And then it's going to be the powers that will be listening to the people of La Misión and codifying changes to the planning code so that we can protect the culture and other institutions that we have in our neighborhood. We are all aware of the changes that are happening in our neighborhood, the Mission has become ground zero of the displacement that is happening.
> (Latino Cultural District Ribbon-Cutting Ceremony, 2014)

Supervisor Campos went on to note that San Francisco is one of the wealthiest cities in the country, but has the highest income inequality. He stated that "everyone has a *right and a place* in the City." Another community leader, Ann Cervantes from the San Francisco Latino Historical Society, stated that it was a twenty-five-year struggle to pass the Latino Cultural District resolution. She passionately stated that in the 1960s, the urban core of the city was abandoned and it was San Francisco's ethnic communities who turned these neighborhoods around and turned them into unique neighborhoods. These neighborhoods are *now* communities that are valued (Latino Cultural District Ribbon Cutting Ceremony, 2014). Other community leaders stated that the Mission District and its residents must resist cultural tourism and maintain its rich history, culture, and institutions.

Calle 24, after having its resolution passed unanimously by the San Francisco Board of Supervisors, released the following statement on its Web site:

> We are proud of our community-driven process to determine the future of our community.

But we are saddened and disturbed that the ability to determine our future is disrespected by real estate and investment interests that do not understand or care about the issues of our community, especially at a time when many families, residents, artist, non-profits and small businesses are being displaced by unchecked development and skyrocketing rents.

We ask the city family to hear the voices of our community, those who have been negatively impacted, and those who bring a vision to the table to help stop the displacement and create housing that is truly for all.

(http://calle24sf.org/latino-cultural-district-planning/)

The Latino Cultural District

After the passage of the Latino Cultural District resolution, Calle 24 SF engaged in a six-month community-planning process to find out what community residents' priorities were. These meetings were supported by the Mayor's Office of Economic and Workforce Development and often included several city staff members from the San Francisco Planning Department as well. As part of its process, Calle 24 SF analyzed the needs of the community. It found out that displacement was happening and was a big issue. Residents were concerned about land uses in the neighborhood and how the community could work with the city to better serve local residents. Finally, it was clear that there was also a lack of market-rate housing in the neighborhood. This encouraged Calle 24 SF to look for other models elsewhere that might help it succeed at mitigating the negative effects of gentrification and displacement. One such place was the efforts of Little Tokyo in Los Angeles and another was the Fruitvale District in Oakland, California. For example, in one meeting that I attended, members of Calle 24 SF met with community leaders from the Unity Council and the Local Initiative Support Corporation (LISC) in the Fruitvale District. In the 1990s, the Unity Council had formed a transit-oriented development in partnership with the Bay Area Rapid Transit (BART) agency. The Unity Council has been able to create and develop a Latino-oriented commercial and residential area with shops, restaurants, and a large number of affordable housing units. Leaders of Calle 24 SF wanted to learn about how the Unity Council has been able to create and sustain a strong Latino community and commercial area.

At this particular meeting, Calle 24 SF and its allies also had invited an urban planner from Los Angeles' Little Tokyo Service Center Community Development Corporation (LTSC) to discuss the organization's efforts at preserving the majority Japanese community. In recent years, the Little Tokyo neighborhood of Los Angeles has faced development pressures and the community was successful in resisting a proposal by the Los Angeles Metro Regional Connector Project to build an aboveground light-rail line (Little Tokyo/Arts District Station) right through the neighborhood's main commercial corridor. LTSC, community groups, and residents were able to get the Los Angeles Metro to build an underground light-rail line.

Despite winning the small victory with the Los Angeles Metro, LTSC and neighborhood groups remained concerned that the light-rail station would increase real estate investment, housing costs, and commercial rents, which would ultimately change the character of the neighborhood. The local residents and community leaders were convinced that they needed a bold community-based strategy (de la Pez, 2014). The urban planner from LTSC told the leaders from Calle 24 SF that they had asked themselves an important question: "Can historic and cultural neighborhoods remain true to their roots, or are we on a destructive path to water down these places into trendy interchangeable hotspots?" LTSC eventually decided that in order to achieve equity with respect to transportation, economic growth, and physical development, all efforts at revitalization must consider the impacts on the long-term Japanese residents. LTSC made it a priority to define "sustainability" for itself in order to protect lower-income families and seniors who rely on access to affordable housing (de la Pez, 2014). LTSC teamed up with the Natural Resources Defense Council, Enterprise Community Partners, and the LISC to create a framework for sustainability that focused on several three major areas:

1   sustain a centuries-old local economic base of small businesses;
2   enhance a mature social community fabric; and
3   embrace cutting-edge green technologies to conserve resources and reduce our carbon footprint.

More important, LTSC's efforts were based on cultural and community values passed down from earlier generations. According to an urban planner for LTSC, it focused on community values like "Mottainai" ("what a shame to waste"), "Kodomonotameni" ("for future generations"), and "Banbutsu" ("interconnectedness"). LTSC held community-planning and design charrette meetings with the help of many professionals from architecture, urban planning, engineering, and economics (de la Pez, 2014). This all resulted in the creation of the Little Tokyo EcoDistrict. In June 2014, the Little Tokyo neighborhood was named an EcoDistrict Target Cities site, a Clinton Global Initiative Commitment to Action program focused on district-scale pilot projects emphasizing environmental performance, social equity, and economic growth (EcoDistricts, 2014).

Calle 24 SF found all of this information helpful. The group outlined its next steps for implementing the Latino Cultural District over the next five years. Over the course of the six-month planning period, Calle 24 SF set up four working groups: housing, economic vitality, arts and culture, and governance. These meetings focused on ways residents, businesses, and community leaders could build on the strengths of the community. For example, there were detailed discussions about maintaining and enhancing the cultural diversity within the neighborhood as well as understanding the tangible (murals, art, businesses) and intangible (nonprofits, festivals, community events) assets. In one community meeting in 2014, things got contentious between long-term Latino residents and some newer white residents around the issue of how best to enhance the cultural diversity within the neighborhood while at the same time maintaining and preserving a dominant Latino culture.[3] As an outside consultant, who was hired to facilitate the process, was outlining the language regarding the Latino Cultural District's economic goals of growing the local economy but also maintaining a majority of Latino or at least Latino-oriented businesses, one newer resident raised his hand. He stated he respected the idea of a Latino Cultural District, but suggested that it was also important for Calle 24 SF and the residents to try and be more inclusive of the new people moving into the community, so perhaps maintaining a majority of Latino-owned businesses along lower 24th Street should not be the goal. He received immediate pushback. One Latino resident said, "You don't go to Chinatown and tell the Chinese how to be less Chinese!" Other residents discussed the importance of preserving Latino culture and identity. One even mentioned that it was necessary to create a Latino Culture District so that the neighborhood simply does not become a "museum." This shut down any real response from the newer residents in attendance at the meeting.

This particular exchange highlights the tension that exists between newer, younger technology workers and long-term, older Latino residents. For long-term Latino residents in the Mission District, the increase of "techies" (a term long-term residents commonly use) in the neighborhood is changing the neighborhood's quality of life. They feel the younger people moving into the neighborhood do not respect the Latino community and culture. They also fear that the influx of younger, whiter technology workers is going to create a demand for new types of stores, restaurants, and entertainment venues, all ultimately resulting in displacement.

From the perspective of many of the younger workers, many of whom work in technology-related jobs, they moved to the Mission District for a variety of reasons, such as they liked the neighborhood's character and location, it is affordable compared to other parts of the city, and it has easier access to Silicon Valley. More important, they feel that the Latino residents in the neighborhood should be more inclusive of the new people moving into the neighborhood. These issues were raised in a town hall meeting on February 24, 2015, hosted by the *San Francisco Chronicle* entitled, "A Changing Mission." Erick Arguello from Calle 24 SF and other community and city leaders spoke about the changes happening in the neighborhood and how best to include all Mission District residents.

Calle 24 SF's community meetings were not always contentious. Many of its community-planning meetings resulted in robust discussions about how

Calle 24 SF and its partners could work with the City of San Francisco to develop new land use policies to support cultural assets, create a special-use district, establish a community benefits district, and create loan programs for long-term businesses and renters, as well as create a strong governance structure to manage the Latino Cultural District. Specifically, Calle 24 SF and its allies focused on the following strategies:

- Establish a 501(c)(3) to serve as the Calle 24 Latino Cultural District managing entity.
- Award a "Special Use District (SUD)" designation to help limit unwanted development within the newly designated Calle 24 Latino Cultural District.
- Create a communitywide campaign to establish a Calle 24 Community Benefits District (CBD) Plan and Assessment, which will help to strengthen, preserve, and enhance Latino arts and culture institutions, enterprises, and activities.
- Build an organizing and communications infrastructure to ensure community residents and local businesses have a voice in the decisions that affect their lives (The Battery S.F., 2014).

Calle 24 SF envisions the Latino Cultural District as "an economically vibrant community that is inclusive of diverse income households and businesses that together embrace the unique Latino heritage and culture of 24th Street and celebrate Latino cultural events, foods, businesses, activities, art and music." In addition, Calle 24 SF has stated that it wants to make the Latino Cultural District "a safe, clean and healthy environment for residents, families, artists, and merchants; to foster an empowered, activist community that takes pride in our diversity; to create a beautiful, clearly designated Latino corridor along Calle 24 SF; to ensure stable, genuinely affordable and low-income housing; to establish and manage guidelines for development and economic change that preserve the District's Latino community and culture; and to foster a sustainable local economy that provides vital goods and services."

Ultimately, Calle 24 SF is working to build a formidable social movement around preserving the culture, history, and Latino population living in the Mission District. It would like for its struggle to serve as a model for other communities facing similar struggles around economic justice, development, and displacement. Specifically, Erick Arguello, one of the key leaders of Calle 24 SF, has said that the organization plans "to document processes, outcomes, best practices, and lessons learned so the model can be replicated." Furthermore, the organization wants "to use multimedia technology to document their struggle and to tell their story so they can encourage other communities to organize and protect their neighborhood and culture" (The Battery S.F., 2014).

Conflict over transit-oriented development and urban sustainability: organizing efforts against gentrification and displacement

Since the victory of Supervisor David Campos, Calle 24 SF, and their allies, one of the biggest fights has been over a proposed 345-unit housing development (originally 303 market-rate and 42 affordable housing units) right above the 16th Street BART Station at Mission Street by Maximus Real Estate Partners, LLC. The housing development represents the type of transit-oriented development the City of San Francisco, the Metropolitan Transportation Commission (MTC), and ABAG are promoting in order to reduce greenhouse gas emissions under state law SB 375. From policy makers' perspective, there are many public benefits of transit-oriented development such as reducing household driving; creating walkable communities; increasing transit ridership; improved access to jobs and economic mobility; and the potential for added value created through increased and/or sustained property value where transit investments have occurred, to name just several (Reconnecting America, 2015).

From the neighborhood residents, businesses, and community organizations' perspective, however, transit-oriented development without an explicit focus on "equitable development that creates healthy, vibrant, communities of opportunity," is simply damaging a community. In the case of the proposed large-scale housing development above 16th Street BART Station, many view it as just another step to increasing the population of affluent residents, resulting in higher rents, boutique shops, and expensive new trendy restaurants, ultimately leading to the displacement of less affluent long-term residents, businesses, and nonprofit organizations. This feeling is so strong that many residents in the Mission District neighborhood refer to Maximus Real Estate's development as the "Monster in the Mission."

In an effort reminiscent of community organizing in the 1990s against gentrification and displacement during the first dot-com boom, a coalition of neighborhood residents, businesses, and community organizations from the Mission District have formed the Plaza 16 Coalition to fight the proposed development. The Plaza 16 Coalition is building off of the Mission Anti-Displacement Coalition started in 1999 and argues that the proposed housing development would accelerate gentrification and does not provide enough affordable housing (Plaza 16 Coalition, 2015). In its fliers passed out at community meetings and on the streets within the Mission District, the Plaza 16 Coalition calls for the Planning Commission and the City of San Francisco to reject all market-rate housing and instead follow the guidelines laid out in the "People's Plan" submitted to the city in 2006. Specifically, the Plaza 16 Coalition is demanding the following:

- We demand Maximus Real Estate Partners, LLC abandon their current project at 1979 Mission Street.

- We demand that the Planning Commission and City of San Francisco reject all market rate housing developments in the Mission until housing needs for the poor and working class are fully met. Additionally, we demand that the San Francisco Planning Department abide by the community planning and land-use process outlined in the Plan Popular, specifically the guidelines outlining community planning for "people not profit," for any future developments.
- We demand that the owning partners of 1979 Mission (Maximus Real Estate Partners and the Jang Family Trust) transfer the land to community hands.
- We demand a stop to the harassment and criminalization by the SFPD of low-income people and people of color who use the plaza as public space under the guise of "cleaning up the plaza."

Under pressure from neighborhood residents, community groups, and local businesses, Maximus Real Estate Development, LLC announced on March 4, 2015, a new affordable housing development plan. The developer announced that it would increase the number of affordable units it will construct at 1979 Mission Street. The new plan calls for the development to have 290 rental apartments and 41 for-sale middle-class workforce homes on site. The workforce homes would be priced between $280,000 and $350,000 and households that make between $61,000 and $145,650 would qualify for purchase. The real estate firm says that all of the funds from the sale of the forty-one homes would then be reinvested in the Mission District to build forty-nine additional affordable BMR apartments.

The forty-nine affordable BMR apartments could be rented for between 30–55 percent of average median income (AMI), which means a single-person household making $20,400 a year would qualify for a studio, and a household making $53,400 a year would qualify for a three-bedroom unit. Per the Mayor's Office of Housing's criteria, rent for the studio at 30 percent AMI would be $510/month and rent for the three-bedroom apartment at 55 percent AMI would be $1,335 a month (Maximus Real Estate, 2015). This is a shift from San Francisco's inclusionary housing requirement, which requires all developers of any market-rate development of at least ten units or more to make at least 12 percent of the units affordable or to construct 20 percent of affordable housing units off-site or pay a fee.

In spring 2015, Calle 24 SF and its allies called for San Francisco's Planning Department to temporarily stop issuing approvals for all market-rate housing developments as well as for all high-end restaurants and the merging of retail space. Calle 24 SF called for the moratorium in order for the city and the community to study ways to increase the number of affordable housing units and also allow for time to figure out a strategy to raise or allocate more private and public money for the construction of affordable housing within the neighborhood. San Francisco Board of Supervisor David Campos supported the call for a moratorium on market-rate housing. The feeling among many community activities, Supervisor Campos, nonprofit organizations, and local businesses, is that a moratorium will do two things. First, it will put a "pause" on the construction of market-rate housing and allow the city and community to better understand the overall affordable housing need in the neighborhood. It will also allow for a larger and broader discussion about the ways the city of San Francisco can develop significant levels of affordable housing units in the Mission District.

Second, the broad-based coalition advocating for affordable housing and supporting the Latino Cultural District believes the moratorium on market-rate housing will help protect and preserve Latino culture in the Mission District. Most of the housing being built in the neighborhood is market-rate and there is a feeling that the new development does not fit the neighborhood's architecture, scale, and overall design. This is why Erick Arguello from Calle 24 SF mentioned in an affordable housing town hall meeting that the organization was exploring options to restrict height limits of buildings along 24th Street and is calling for a mural protection zone. He further explained that with the current planned development and renovations within the neighborhood, many murals are set to be demolished. Arguello emphasized that "24th Street is historic, the birthplace of Latin Rock, the mural movement. We want to protect this!" Ultimately, the moratorium failed to get the necessary nine votes from the Board of Supervisors, despite garnering support from the majority of the Board. The moratorium's advocates are working to get it on the November 2015 ballot. In the meantime, the debate over the moratorium increased advocacy for affordable housing within the Mission, reportedly leading to increased collaboration between the mayor's office and Supervisor Campos around strategies to increase building of affordable housing within the Mission.

Shaping the future of San Francisco

San Francisco is in the midst of serious economic, social, and political change. The once progressive city that was celebrated for its uniqueness is now a place of growing income inequality and economic and racial segregation. The increased concentration of wealth generated from knowledge-based industries coupled with an inadequate supply of affordable and market-rate housing has resulted in a situation where the wealthy can pay more for the limited amount of housing available. This pushes up rents, housing prices, and the overall cost of living. In addition, San Francisco is a place where young, educated, and wealthy individuals want to live amongst themselves. This trend was identified by the research of Richard Florida and Charlotta Mellander, who found that "Americans have become increasingly sorted over the past couple of decades by income, education and class. . . . Increasingly, Americans are sorting not just between cities and metro areas, but within them as well" (Florida and Mellander, 2015). The city is at risk of losing its middle class, working class, and communities of color who helped build the city up and made it a beacon of progressive politics and ideals.

Reversing the current trend of outmigration (both voluntary and involuntary) of middle-class and less affluent residents out of San Francisco and removing the many barriers to building an adequate supply of housing for all socioeconomic levels will require government intervention at the state, regional, and local levels. This uneven balance of jobs and housing is destined to create a housing affordability crisis in any major metropolitan area. At the state level, the California Environmental Quality Act has made it relatively easy for residents in wealthier, coastal cities such as San Francisco to object and sue to stop or slow down development projects that they do not support (Taylor, 2015). This has slowed down the production of housing in California. In addition, there is no large amount of money dedicated to the production of affordable housing, especially since the elimination of redevelopment agencies across the state. Finally, state policies to reduce greenhouse gas emissions such as Senate Bill 375 have required regions to development Sustainable Communities Strategies, which are focused on encouraging housing near public transit stations and corridors. This has led to the construction of transit-oriented development within cities, but without a strong focus on equitable development around affordable housing and access to quality jobs for less affluent local residents, neighborhood change and displacement is likely to occur.

The broad-based coalition around affordable housing, economic opportunities, and neighborhood preservation by organizations such as Calle 24 SF has placed greater pressure on San Francisco elected officials, including Mayor Ed Lee. For example, in May 2015, more than 500 protestors shut down City Hall demanding that the mayor and local government officials take the growing housing affordability crisis more seriously. These protests are growing in intensity as residents are calling for equity and justice and demanding a right to the city. These efforts by the broad-based coalition of local residents, businesses, and community-centered organizations is leading to discussions that are resulting in policy and legislation. For example, the City of San Francisco has proposed a number of programs and policies, including:

- *The Affordable Housing Trust Fund.* In 2012, voters in San Francisco passed Proposition C, which established the Affordable Housing Trust Fund. The Affordable Housing Trust Fund is a thirty-year fund that grows over time until it provides $50 million annually for affordable housing. It is estimated that over the thirty-year lifespan of the fund, a total of $1.2 billion will be generated for housing construction and subsidies (S.F. Housing Action Coalition, 2015). The Affordable Housing Trust Fund was an effort to raise money for affordable housing after the state of California eliminated redevelopment agencies, which provided a significant amount of funding for affordable housing. Over time, proponents of the Affordable Housing Trust Fund estimate that the fund will (Center for Community Change, 2013):

- develop more than 9,000 units of permanently affordable housing for residents whose average median income is 60 percent or below.
- create incentives for onsite BMR housing and make housing more accessible for moderate-income families;
- invest at least $15 million over the first five years to expand the city's down payment assistance program (DALP), which provides interest-free loans to moderate-income homebuyers looking to purchase their first home in San Francisco. DALP will also include a new program to assist the city's first responders in the purchase of a home in San Francisco;
- create a Housing Stabilization Program to help distressed low- and moderate-income residents remain in their homes; and
- create a Complete Neighborhoods Infrastructure Grant program to fund public realm improvements such as pocket parks and childcare facilities for growing neighborhoods.

- *Proposition K (passed November 4, 2014)* (City of San Francisco Affordable Housing Policy, 2014). San Francisco voters passed Proposition K by more than 65 percent, which requires the city to construct or rehabilitate at least 30,000 housing units. The legislation requires that more than 50 percent of the housing be affordable for middle-class households, with at least 33 percent of the units affordable for low- and moderate-income households. Any areas in the city that are rezoned for housing construction will ensure that 33 percent of new housing is affordable to low- and moderate-income households. In addition, Proposition K calls for the city to create a funding strategy to build new affordable housing, to purchase land for affordable housing, to preserve existing rental units, and to fund public housing rehabilitation.
- *The Public Land for Housing Program* (S.F. Planning Department Public Land for Housing, 2015). In 2014, Mayor Ed Lee introduced the Public Land for Housing Program, an initiative by the City of San Francisco to build affordable housing on underutilized city-owned land. To get his idea off the ground, Mayor Lee established an interagency working group comprised of numerous departments – the Office of Economic and Workforce Development (OEWD), Planning Department, Municipal Transportation Agency (SFMTA), Public Utilities Commission (SFPUC), Mayor's Office, Mayor's Office of Housing (MOH) and the Real Estate Division, who were charged with "drafting principles to guide potential development of the sites, initial site analysis, development of criteria for site selection, and engagement with stakeholders"

(S.F. Planning Department, 2014). The program will have the following components (S.F. Planning Department, 2014):

1   a set of city-supported principles, based on existing city policy, to guide the process for each selected site;
2   delivery of a comprehensive menu of public benefits the public sites can provide individually and collectively;
3   the use of policy tools and innovative strategies to achieve those benefits; and
4   a rolling review of underutilized properties to establish a portfolio of opportunity sites for which the aforementioned principles and tools will be applied to create approvable and implementable project proposals.

> The Public Land for Housing Program public outreach and community engagement process resulted in several priorities for the city, which include constructing more housing and enhancing the public transportation system. The public outreach and community engagement process also found that residents would like the city to address neighborhood sustainability and resiliency by focusing on green infrastructure and creating and maintaining open space, and by focusing on local economic development and job creation as a community benefit for development projects.
>
> (S.F. Planning Department, 2014)

- *The Small Sites Acquisition Program.* Soon after the announcement of the Public Land for Housing Program, Mayor Lee announced another program focused on keeping low-to-moderate income families from being displaced out of the city. The Small Sites Acquisition Program made $3 million available for the acquisition and rehabilitation financing for multifamily rental buildings of five to twenty-five units. The program's goal is to stabilize buildings occupied by low-to-moderate-income tenants throughout San Francisco who are particularly susceptible to evictions and rising rents. In this case, the program is targeting properties where the AMI of tenants is at or below 80 percent. According to the City of San Francisco, this program is intended to be "a zero displacement program, and no residents, regardless of income, will be displaced due to the building's participation in the Small Sites Program. Small Sites Program buildings will carry long-term affordability restrictions, increasing the City's supply of affordable housing and ensuring that rental units are affordable for future generations of San Francisco residents" (S.F. MOH Small Sites, 2014b).
- *The Proposal for $500 Million towards Affordable Housing.* In January 2015, Mayor Lee announced that the city would be introducing a general obligation bond in November that, if passed, would result in $250 million to be used for new housing construction for the

middle class (approximately $104,000 for a family of three in San Francisco), improvement of public housing, and enhancing afford- able rental housing (Dineen, 2014). This bond proposal is in direct response to the outmigration of middle-class residents out of the city over the past decade. According to some studies, the city has built and entitled only 30 percent of the housing it needs for the middle class (80 percent to 120 percent of AMI), compared to 55 percent for low-income residents and 202 percent for high-income residents (Weinberg, 2015a).

Under mounting public pressure from the community and other elected officials, in May 2015, just a few months after announcing his initial $250 million bond measure, Mayor Lee proposed an additional $250 million for the construction of 3,000 affordable housing units to be built by 2030, bringing the city's contribution to $500 million if voters support it during election time (Evangelista, 2015).

It is too early to determine the impacts of recently passed legislation or how well these programs will even be implemented. What is clear, however, is that the resistance against neighborhood change and dis- placement is growing stronger in San Francisco and the efforts by Calle 24 SF and its allies are a good example of how local residents, businesses, and nonprofit organizations are forming broad-based coalitions to fight against market-rate housing developments by real estate investors and devel- opers. More important, those representing this community are contributing to a definition of sustainable development that goes beyond focusing exclu- sively on energy efficiency and transit-oriented development. Sustainable development is about preserving the history and culture of many ethnic, racial, and working-class neighborhoods. In the Mission District, it is about preserving Latino culture and history while reducing the displacement of long-term, Latino residents. It is about promoting affordable housing devel- opment that meets the needs of all socioeconomic classes in San Francisco and creates jobs and other economic opportunities without solely benefiting the rich. It is about developing an equitable development framework that prepares future generations of healthy residents for jobs, housing, and edu- cational opportunities.

Notes

1 These percentages are higher in certain parts of the Eastern Neighborhoods Plan Area. Project sponsors in certain parts of the Eastern Neighborhoods Plan Area may also apply for the alternative of dedicating land for affordable housing.
2 Resolutions are nonbinding, non-legal statements made by a municipality's legis- lative body. They are often not signed or endorsed by the city executive. Resolu- tions are often used to persuade other legislative bodies (state or federal) to adopt legislation that is beyond the powers of the local body.
3 Meeting, December 20, 2014. Brava Theater in the Mission District Neighborhood.

Bibliography

American Community Survey. 2012. U.S. Census Bureau.

Association of Bay Area Governments (ABAG). 2014. One Bay Area Plan. www. abag.gov.

Association of Bay Area Governments (ABAG). 2015. Regional housing needs assessment 2014–2022 projections report. www.abag.ca.gov.

Beitel, K. 2013. *Local Protest, Global Movements – Capital, Community, and State in San Francisco*. Philadelphia, PA: Temple University Press.

Berube, A. 2014. *All Cities Are Not Created Unequal*. Washington, DC: Brookings Institution. www.brookings.edu/research/papers/2014/02/cities-unequal-berube.

Bort, J. 2013. Twitter's IPO created 1,600 new millionaires and a $2.2 billion tax bill, analyst says. *Business Insider*. November 11. www.businessinsider.com/twitter-ipo-created-1600-millionaires-2013–11.

CA Air Resources Board. 2015. Sustainable communities. California Air Resources Board. May 8. www.arb.ca.gov/cc/sb375/sb375.htm.

CA Department of Justice. 2011. CEQA history. State of California Department of Justice, Office of Attorney General. Retrieved March 28, 2011.

CA Housing and Community Development. 2014. www.hcd.ca.gov/hpd/hrc/rep/state/inc2k14.pdf.

California Housing Partnership Corporation. 2014. *How San Francisco County's Housing Market is Failing to Meet the Needs of Low-Income Families*. California Housing Partnership Corporation. August. Retrieved at: www.chpc.net/dnld/HousingNeedSFFINAL.pdf.

Calle 24 SF. 2015. www.calle24sf.org.

Cantor, M. 2015. SF commuters get Wi-Fi, coffee, pressed juices – on the bus. *Newser*. March 22. www.newser.com/story/204243/sf-commuters-get-wifi-coffee-pressed-juices-on-the-bus.html.

Center for Community Change. 2013. San Francisco announces first investment from new housing trust fund. Center for Community Change. http://housingtrust-fundproject.org/san-francisco-announces-first-investment-from-new-housing-trust-fund/.

Checker, M. 2011. Wiped out by the "Greenwave": Environmental gentrification and the paradoxical politics of urban sustainability. *City & Society*, 23(2), 210–229.

City and County of San Francisco. 2014. Office of the Controller – Office of Economic Analysis. *Review of the Impact of the Central Market Payroll Tax Exclusion*. By Ted Egan and Asim Khan. October 27. http://sfcontroller.org/Modules/ShowDocument.aspx?documentid=5914.

City of San Francisco. 2015. 2014 Housing Element, San Francisco General Plan. www.sf-planning.org.

Day, L. 2014. Interview with Erick Arguello, Calle 24 SF on KALW San Francisco. November 17. Retrieved from http://kalw.org/post/calle-24-official-latino-cultural-district-san-francisco.

de la Pez, R. 2014. Community presentation by Remy de la Pez. Unity Council, Fruitvale District, Oakland, CA. September 24.

Dineen, J. K. 2014. Mayor Lee plans $250 million housing bond for November ballot. *SF Gate*, April 1. www.sfgate.com/politics/article/Mayor-Lee-6173569.php.

Dineen, J. K. 2015. SoMA condos poised to be S.F.'s most expensive ever. *SF Gate*, March 10. www.sfgate.com/bayarea/Record-breaking-condo-project-coming-to-SoMa-6126543.php (accessed March 13, 2015).

EcoDistricts Fact Sheet. 2014. www.ecodistricts.org.

Evangelista, B. 2015. Mayor Lee ups ante with new $500 million affordable housing plan. *San Francisco Chronicle*. May 17. www.sfgate.com/bayarea/article/Mayor-Lee-ups-ante-with-new-500-million-6269570.php.

Families USA. 2014. The voice for health care consumers. *Federal Poverty Guidelines*. February. Retrieved from http://familiesusa.org/product/federal-poverty-guidelines.

Florida, R. and Mellander, C. 2015. *Segregated City: The Geography of Economic Segregation in America's Metro*. Report. February. http://martinprosperity.org/media/Segregated%20City.pdf.

Kelly, D. 2014. San Francisco Health and Human Services Presentation. October 2.

Knight, H. and Tucker, J. 2013. $4 toast prompts housing petition. *SF Gate*, November 7. www.sfgate.com/bayarea/article/4-toast-prompts-housing-petition-4962002.php.

Latino Cultural District Ribbon Cutting Ceremony. 2014. Mission District, San Francisco. May 23.

Mandel, M. 2014. San Francisco and the tech/info boom: Making the transition to a balanced and growing economy. *South Mountain Economics*. April. Retrieved from www.mikebloomberg.com/files/SouthMountainEconomics_SF_TechInfo_Boom.pdf.

Maximus Real Estate, LLC. 2015. www.1979mission.com.

Meronek, T. 2015. Affordable housing in San Francisco affordable only for upwardly mobile. *Al Jazeera America*. http://america.aljeezra.com/articles/2015/2/3/san-francisco-affordable-housing-is-unaffordable.html.

Mirabal, N. Geography of displacement: Latina/os oral history, and the politics of gentrification in San Francisco's Mission District. The Public Historian 31:2 (2009), 7–31.

Moretti, E. 2012. *The New Geography of Jobs*. New York: Houghton Mifflin Harcourt.

O'Brien, D. 2015. San Francisco rent prices continue rapid rise through February. Retrieved from www.zumper.com/blog/2015/03/san-francisco-rent-prices-continue-rapid-rise-february/.

Pearsall, H. 2012. Moving out or moving in? Resilience to environmental gentrification in New York City. *Local Environment: The International Journal of Justice and Sustainability*, 17(9), 1013–1026.

Pender, K. 2014. $1 million city: S.F. median home price hits 7 figures for 1st time. *SF Gate*, July 17. www.sfgate.com/business/networth/article/1-million-city-S-F-median-home-price-hits-7–5626591.php.Reporting findings from DataQuick.

People's Plan. 2006. www.plaza16.files.wordpress.com.

Plaza 16 Coalition. 2015. www.plaza16.org.

Pollack, S., Bluestone, B., and Billingham, C. 2010. *Maintaining Diversity in America's Transit-Rich Neighborhoods: Tools for Equitable Neighborhood Change*. Report. October. www.northeastern.edu/dukakiscenter/wp-content/uploads/2011/12/TRN_Equity_final.pdf.

Reconnecting America. 2015. www.ctod.org.

San Francisco Affordable Housing Policy. 2014. City of San Francisco Additional Affordable Housing Policy, Proposition K. Ballotpedia. http://ballotpedia.org/ City_of_San_Francisco_Additional_Affordable_Housing_Policy,_Proposition_K_ %28November_2014%29.

San Francisco Board of Supervisors, City of San Francisco. Calle 24 Cultural Arts District Resolution. 2014. San Francisco Board of Supervisors, City of San Francisco. www.sfbos.org/ftp/uploadedfiles/bdsupvrs/committees/materials/LU051914_ 140421.pdf.

San Francisco Budget and Legislative Analyst. Fred Brousseau. 2013. Policy Analysis Report: Analysis of Tenant Displacement in San Francisco. October 30.

San Francisco Heritage. 2014. Historic background document. Retrieved from www. sfheritage.org/cultural-heritage/latino-heritage/.

San Francisco Housing Action Coalition. 2015. Affordable Housing Trust Fund. San Francisco Housing Action Coalition. www.sfhac.org/policy-advocacy/affordable-housing-trust-fund/.

San Francisco Latino Historical Society. 2015. Retrieved from http://sflhs.com/.

San Francisco Mayor's Office of Housing. 2014a. Neighborhood Investment Initiative. www.investsf.org.

San Francisco Mayor's Office of Housing. 2014b. Small Sites Acquisition Program. www.sfmayor.org/index.aspx?recordid=653&page=846.

San Francisco Mayor's Office of Housing. 2015a. Neighborhood Investment Initiative. www.investsf.org.

San Francisco Mayor's Office of Housing. 2015b. www.sf-moh.org.

San Francisco Planner. 2015. Interview with S.F. Planner, February 24.

San Francisco Planning Department Housing Inventory. 2013. San Francisco Planning Department. www.sf-planning.org.

San Francisco Planning Department Mission Area Plan. 2008. www.sf-planning.org.

San Francisco Planning Department (Public Land). 2015. Public land for housing (formerly Public Sites Portfolio). City and County of San Francisco Planning Department. March 26. www.sf-planning.org/index.aspx?page=3913#timeline.

San Francisco Planning Department Public Sites. 2014. *San Francisco Planning Department Memo*. December 4. www.sf-planning.org/ftp/files/plans-and-programs/planning-for-the-city/public-sites/PC_12.11.14_HearingMemo_FINAL_ 12.04.14.pdf.

Taylor, M. 2015. California's high housing costs: Causes and consequences. California Legislative Analyst Office. www.lao.ca.gov.

Temkin, K., Theodos, B., and Price, D. 2010. Shared equity homeownership evaluation: Case study of the San Francisco citywide inclusionary affordable housing program. Washington, DC: Urban Institute.

The Battery S.F. 2014. Battery powered. Retrieved from https://thebatterysf.com/ giving/theme/2015Q1/projects/calle_24_sf_latino_cultural_district/.

The Literature Network. 2015. The Beat Generation. www.online-literature.com/ periods/beat.php.

U.S. Census. 2013. www.census.gov.

U.S. Housing and Urban Development (HUD). 2014a. Housing choice vouchers fact sheet. U.S. Department of Housing and Urban Development. http://portal.hud. gov/hudportal/HUD?src=/topics/housing_choice_voucher_program_section_8.

U.S. Housing and Urban Development (HUD). 2014b. Median family income calculation methodology. HUD User. www.huduser.org/portal/datasets/il/il2014/2014MedCalc.odn.; www.hcd.ca.gov/hpd/hrc/rep/state/inc2k14.pdf.

Weinberg, C. 2015a. City needs more housing money, but voters may stand in the way. *San Francisco Business Times*, January 16. www.bizjournals.com/sanfrancisco/blog/real-estate/2015/01/housing-funding-bond-san-francisco-ed-lee-election.html?page=all.

Weinberg, C. 2015b. Mission moratorium proposal progresses, setting up next epic housing fight. *San Francisco Business Times*. February 23. Retrieved from www.bizjournals.com/sanfrancisco/blog/real-estate/2015/02/mission-moratorium-campos-sf-housing-crisis.html.

Weinberg, C. 2015c. Why the Mission is Ground Zero in S.F.'s debate over gentrification. *San Francisco Business Times*. March 13. Retrieved from www.bizjournals.com/sanfrancisco/print-edition/2015/03/13/mission-impassable-the-mission-district-is-ground.html.

6 Washington, DC
"Chocolate city" is changing

"The neighborhood is changing and changing fast. Blacks are leaving and being replaced by young foreigners from all over the world."
(Thirty-eight-year resident of Washington, DC's Shaw Neighborhood)

As word spread on April 4, 1968, that black civil rights leader Reverend Dr. Martin Luther King Jr. had been assassinated in Memphis, Tennessee, anger spread throughout the black communities of Washington, DC. Soon Stokely Carmichael, a former Student Nonviolent Coordinating Committee (SNCC) member and Howard University alum, was walking down U Street asking businesses to close out of respect for Dr. King. A large crowd began to gather near the corner of U and 14th Streets, and the anger and frustration from the crowd erupted. Angry citizens smashed business windows and set buildings ablaze (Muller, 2011). After several days of unrest across the city, ten people lost their lives, more than 1,200 fires burned, the police arrested more than 7,600, and 13,000 federal troops had descended on Washington, DC to control the situation (Muller, 2011).

Standing near the corner of 14th Street and U Street NW, which was at the center of the unrest after Dr. King's assassination, and then riddled with drugs for the decades following, it is almost unbelievable to see the changes that have been happening in Washington, DC over the past decade. On this hot and humid summer day, cranes fill the skyline along 14th Street NW and dot the Shaw neighborhood heading east toward Howard University. Not far from where I am standing is a large luxury housing development being constructed called The Louis. The Louis apartment complex looks enormous and sleek and out of place next to the McDonald's restaurant and other older buildings near the intersection. It is clear that this once traditionally black neighborhood is changing physically and economically based on the number of new stores and restaurants. And this neighborhood's demographics are visibly shifting with more non-black residents living in the area. What happened? How did this change come about so quickly?

The devastation that took place in April 1968 led to a series of events that impacted the demographic, economic, political, and social environment of the nation's capital for decades. Soon after the widespread unrest, the flight of white residents increased as they fled the city for the suburbs. The black middle class soon followed them. In 1950, Washington, DC's white population accounted for just more than 60 percent of the population while the black population accounted for 35 percent. However by 2000, this had completely reversed. Over thirty years the black population had grown to about 60 percent of the city's population and the white population had dropped by half and accounted for only 31 percent (Phillips, Beasley, and Rodgers, 2005). Between 1970 and 2000, Washington, DC may have shifted to a majority-black city and earned the moniker of "Chocolate City," but the city's overall population declined, especially the black population. Between 1970 and 2010, the black population declined at a steady pace, from 538,000 in 1970 to 309,000 in 2010. The white population stabilized in the 1980s and in recent decades Latinos and Asians have been moving to the city (Urban Institute, 2015a).

Washington, DC experienced some challenging times during the four decades between the 1970s and 2010. In the 1970s, the nation's capital experienced disinvestment and its tax base continued to shrink. In the 1980s, violent crime and the crack cocaine epidemic gripped the city. High crime and homicide rates in the 1980s and 1990s placed the city among the most dangerous cities in America and, at one point, the city was known as the "murder capital" (Politic365, 2013). All of this has changed. Washington, DC is now an increasingly diverse city with more affluent, younger residents from multiethnic backgrounds. The city's violent crime and homicide rate has plummeted (Fisher, 2012). The story of Washington, DC's transformation involved the help of Washington, DC's government, access to abundant and cheap capital, and the demographic shift of younger, educated, and affluent people choosing to live in the city.

Transit-oriented development, skyrocketing housing prices, and demographic shifts

The recent economic and demographic changes in Washington, DC were a long time in the making, but after years of planning and trying to attract investment to the city, development and the cost of housing now appears to be in overdrive. In 2000, Washington, DC's population began to grow and the black population began to stabilize. The city's population, however, was still much smaller than it had been in the 1950s, and the city was desperate to increase its tax base and encourage development within the city. The mayor in 2000, Anthony Williams, was the catalyst to move development forward in Washington, DC. Mayor Williams was elected in 1999 and is credited with changing the way government operated in Washington, DC, specifically with having "introduced professional management and dramatically chang[ing] the processes of government, installing performance measurements, compensation systems and program evaluations" (Barras, 2014). Significant to this story: Mayor Williams wanted to grow the population of the city and set a goal of attracting 100,000 new residents.

In an April 2003 presentation to the Brookings Institution entitled "Neighborhood 10: Ten Strategies for a Stronger Washington," he laid out his plans. The mayor said the way he wanted to attract 100,000 new residents to Washington, DC was by building strong and healthy neighborhoods. He mentioned several lofty goals such as empowering and engaging citizens, aligning government action with citizen priorities, and enhancing unity of purpose and democracy. The substance of his presentation was around his plan for citywide neighborhood revitalization, which called for building Strategic Neighborhood Action Plans (SNAP), investing in strategic areas, eliminating blight, enhancing neighborhood commercial centers, and taking advantage of transit by promoting transit-oriented development (Brookings Institution, 2013). If one were not paying attention, the mayor's strategies for a stronger Washington, DC almost sounded like the urban renewal strategies from the 1940s to the 1970s. However, unlike urban renewal programs in the past, Mayor Williams also discussed the city's housing agenda, which called for more affordable housing for people of all incomes, and he also wanted to prevent displacement (Brookings Institution, 2013). In order to jumpstart investment and development, city government provided financial incentives to developers and tried to steer development around transit corridors (Wogan, 2015).

By 2005, investment and development was taking hold all over the city, especially in traditional black and Latino communities. During the crack cocaine epidemic in the 1980s, which tore the city apart, the black middle class continued to leave the city. This left many neighborhoods unsafe with a high level of dilapidated "crack" houses. In an interview with Eric Shaw, the director of Planning for the District of Columbia Office of Planning, he provided his insight on what was happening in the city fifteen years ago when he was living in Logan Circle. "You could buy a townhouse in Logan Circle for $85,000 in 1990." He said it did not take long for private developers to see the potential of the area and that led them to make investments. These investments transformed neighborhoods as construction of higher-end developments began, driven primarily by financial incentives and access to cheap capital. He said,

> One thing we keep on forgetting about is the role of the market and the reality that almost every transaction for community change is a private transaction. . . . I've never seen a neighborhood where we put in new streets or fix the streetlights and the neighborhood changes. That's the public perception of how neighborhoods are redeveloped. The reality is that capital was super, super cheap and loans were plentiful. And it still is and people have now rediscovered the inner-city. . . . Metro [just] made it accessible for people to come to the City.

Recent studies have elaborated on the impacts of transit-oriented development within Washington, DC. In a report entitled "Urban Development: Faster Greener Commutes Key to Sustained City Growth," Cushman and Wakefield found that throughout North America people are moving into downtown areas and that employers are following the same trend (Cushman and Wakefield, 2014). In Washington, DC, the value of real estate within a half mile of a Metro station accounts for 28 percent of the metropolitan area's total value, and within the city itself 70 percent of the city's real estate value is located within a half mile of a Metro station (WMATA, 2011).

The people moving to Washington, DC have been young, educated, and affluent. Many of the people interviewed for this book described the changes happening in the city as "alarming" and "rapid." Mr. Shaw, however, shared that the changes that people see today are a reflection of strategic planning efforts that took place fifteen years ago. He said that there is a lag time between development plans and the time when something actually opens. Many of the changes coming to these neighborhoods involved city-planning efforts and leveraging private capital. Mr. Shaw described how local residents in the Logan Circle area raised money to pay for a market study to lure Whole Foods to the neighborhood, which eventually opened up on P Street between 14th and 15th Streets. "So people who are new [to the City] are seeing this change happen in two or three years or four or five years and they do not realize that it was just a new iteration of what was there already," Mr. Shaw said. It is clear that the people moving to the city have been part of this new change, which in many instances was laid out almost two decades ago. However, the impacts are finally being seen and in a big way, especially within neighborhoods that have been underinvested in for several years.

The points Mr. Shaw raised are worth exploring more deeply. Structural racism can impact residents in a majority-black or ethnic-minority neighborhood in Boston, New York, or San Francisco, but for those in Washington, DC it was especially challenging. Washington, DC, unlike my other strong-market case study cities, has been a majority-black city since the late 1970s, and as a result it has been perceived as a "black city" among those who did not live there. Given the history of racial and ethnic discrimination in the United States, the perception of Washington, DC as a black city has presented major challenges for those who either chose to stay in the city or were stuck living in the city, different from residents in impoverished neighborhoods in my other case cities. For example, there is very little doubt that racial/ethnic discrimination kept private developers from making investments in the city, thus limiting Washington, DC's potential to grow and increase its tax base. The city did not remain stable in terms of maintaining an adequate tax revenue, achieving solid population growth, or experiencing the steady investment that cities need to function on a basic level. Although Boston, New York City, and San Francisco have been through some difficult times, it was nothing compared to what Washington, DC experienced after the 1970s. Those cities were able to attract investment, grow their populations, and steadily increase their tax bases.

In addition, being perceived as an all-black or majority-black city definitely prevented non-black, middle-class, and super affluent families from
buying homes and settling down in the city. Having so few middle-class,
tax-paying residents negatively impacted Washington, DC in a way it never
impacted Boston, New York, or San Francisco. The population of Washington, DC declined and the middle class left the city, including the black middle
class. Those who were left did not have the economic, social, and political
capital to bring in the necessary resources to transform their communities
the way the newcomers did. So if you were a homeowner, especially in the
Logan Circle, Shaw, or Columbia Heights neighborhood, your property did
not gain much equity, if at all. You would have been literally "stuck" in place
and unable to sell preventing you buying a better home in another part of
the city or moving to a different location outside of the city.

As non-blacks began moving to Washington, DC in the late 1990s and early
2000s, this presented an opportunity for the majority-black long-term homeowners to "cash in" on their property as it slowly appreciated in value. Many
older black homeowners were left with a choice that many whites and other
ethnic groups do not have to make. That is, if they decided to sell their homes
once the neighborhoods improved and property values rose, they could finally
get "the financial reward" of staying in the neighborhood all those years. However, once they sold, black homeowners faced the reality of being priced out of
the market and having to leave their neighborhoods. This complicated dynamic
has especially impacted the long-term, black residents of Washington, DC.

Finally, along with whites leaving the city in the 1960s, the black middle
class also left. The black middle class, as William Julius Wilson has shown
in Chicago, can be important in maintaining neighborhood social cohesion
(Wilson, 1996). It is critical in sustaining institutions (i.e., schools) and organizations (nonprofits, volunteer, or faith-based) in underserved communities
of color. It also is necessary to support local businesses and pay taxes that
support the city's infrastructure, schools, and social services. Finally, middle-
class black residents also bring with them some level of social, political, and
economic capital that poorer blacks often do not have. In the case of Washington, DC, neighborhoods were left with high concentrations of poor people and were basically abandoned for several decades. So once middle-class
white residents and other non-black residents began moving into these neighborhoods, they brought their privilege and class connections that enabled
them to transform the neighborhoods in ways that blacks and other people
of color could not have because of the cumulative effects of structural racism.
The perfect case is the Whole Foods example that Mr. Shaw used.

Growth of millennials and neighborhood change

When standing near the corner of 14th Street and U Street in the northwest
section of the city, you see a very different environment than what existed
following the unrest after Dr. King's assassination. Since the early 2000s,

condominium construction, housing renovations, and commercial development has occurred throughout Washington, DC. Neighborhoods such as Adams Morgan, Columbia Heights, Shaw, and Logan Circle have experienced rapid neighborhood investment and change. Areas once home to large populations of working poor and communities of color have quickly gone through economic and physical changes in the built environment or, to put it more bluntly, *intense* gentrification. Row houses once dilapidated or abandoned were being completely gutted and renovated and new condominiums have been rising. New development has been especially noticeable along 14th Street NW from the Logan Circle area all the way up to Columbia Heights and to the east in the Shaw neighborhood. Swanky new restaurants and bars have sprung up everywhere along this transit corridor as they cater to the young, affluent millennials.

In 2000, Washington, DC began growing again for the first time since 1950, when the city had a population of more than 800,000 residents. This trend was significant for several reasons. First, the growth in the city between 2000 and 2010 has been driven largely by millennials between the ages of eighteen and thirty-four. According to the Urban Institute's data analysis, during the 2000s, Washington, DC's population of millennials grew by 37,000 and now accounts for about 35 percent of the total city population (Urban Institute, 2015a). The new arrivals in Washington, DC have been mostly non-black, making Washington, DC by 2012 no longer "Chocolate City" as the black population has dipped below 50 percent for the first time in half a century (Tavernise, 2011). For example, the Urban Institute estimates that about 50,000 whites, 9,700 Asians, and 7,900 Latinos moved into the city during this period (Urban Institute, 2015a). During this same decade, the black population declined by about 11 percent, or roughly 39,000 people (Morello and Keating, 2011).

Another factor contributing to the restaurant, bar, and condominium growth that has been so pronounced in Washington, DC is that unlike much of the nation during the Great Recession, Washington, DC was creating good-paying jobs. Washington, DC was well positioned to survive the recession better than most metropolises because the area experienced an increase in government spending and an increase in federal contractors and consultants. For example, Stephen Fuller from George Mason University estimated that from 2007 until 2012, the local economy expanded by 7.6 percent. Federal contractor spending increased from $12.6 billion in 1990 to $82.5 billion in 2010, with a significant proportion of that money spent on technology goods and services (Schuker Blum and Karmin, 2013). As a result, Washington, DC's metropolitan area median household income has risen above $88,000 (Shah, 2013). This economic growth has attracted many young, educated, and affluent millennials. Between 2010 and 2012, millennials accounted for about half of Washington, DC's population growth (Chang et al., 2013).

These millennials have settled into traditionally black and working-class communities in Washington, DC. For example, "Ward 2 had the biggest growth in population of the decade, adding 13,000 people, particularly in Shaw and Logan Circle" (Urban Institute, 2015a). In these neighborhoods, the demographic changes have been noticeable; young people are everywhere, and it appears that they have disposable income to spend. According to the Urban Institute, the Shaw and Logan Circle neighborhoods were 25 percent white in 2000 and by 2010, those two neighborhoods were 48 percent white (Neighborhood Info DC, 2015b). Walking around the neighborhoods of Shaw and Columbia Heights, young people are shaping the city culturally. It is not uncommon to see young people swarming the latest and hippest condominiums for rooftop pool parties, doing square dancing in the park, or shopping at newly opened boutique stores on 14th Street NW.

As one would expect, the population increase within the nation's capital over the past decade and a half has resulted in higher housing prices as the demand has grown. From 2002 to 2013, the number of apartments renting for less than $800 in the District dropped from almost 60,000 to 33,000 (Walton, 2012). Housing prices have also soared. In 1995, the median sales price for a home in Washington, DC was $186,000, by 2000 it had risen to $209,000, and by 2013 the median sales price for a home in Washington, DC had reached $595,000 (Neighborhood Info DC, 2015a). The median housing prices have also soared in traditionally working-class and minority neighborhoods such as Columbia Heights, Shaw, and Logan Circle.

Residents' response to the change

Some of the sleek condominiums, new restaurants, bars, and cafes have been opening up with trendy names and references to historical black figures and culture.[1] For example, on U Street there are the Ellington Apartments, named after jazz great Duke Ellington. The Ellington development is modern and fits into the landscape of new condominiums built in recent years. The Ellington, like other developments in the area, is also good at marketing and rebranding the neighborhood. It describes the U Street neighborhood in the following way (The Ellington, 2015):

> There's a weight in the rhythm of the living on U. Pulsing beats through open doors of city streets. Jazz. Hip hop. R&B. Blues. Uniting in community. Sharing an affinity for evenings spent savoring food, music, life. Nights alive in the lure of U.

Around the corner from the Ellington Apartments on 14th Street are other condominiums and businesses with names like Langston Lofts (condominiums) and Busboys and Poets (cafe and restaurant), which pay homage to writer Langton Hughes. In the same vicinity, you have Eatonville (restaurant) with a nod to writer Zora Neale Hurston. You also have Blackbyrd (restaurant) acknowledging the great jazz and rhythm and blues trumpeter Donald Byrd, as well as Marvin (restaurant), named after singer

Marvin Gaye. There is no doubt that if Marvin Gaye were alive today, he would be asking "what's going on?" in Washington, DC. All of this has sparked a spirited debate in the local papers, on blog sites, and on social media about this trend and what it all actually means. One local writer even referred to this phenomenon as an example of African American historical "swagger-jacking" (Crockett, 2012). Perhaps a major twist of irony is that neighborhoods that were majority African American and once highly racially segregated now have plaques erected identifying African American sites that are important in local and national history and culture as part of the city's African American Heritage Trail, even though few blacks now live and own homes in many of these areas.

The changes happening in the area have been received with mixed reviews from the long-term residents, small business owners, and workers in the Logan Circle, Shaw, and Columbia Heights neighborhoods. Some residents view the changes as beneficial to the community while others wonder why it took so long for them to happen. For example, when asked about all of the economic and physical changes happening in the neighborhood, a thirty-eight-year black resident named Ms. Johnson (who had grown up in the South before moving to Washington, DC in her twenties) told me, "I like the changes and the area looks nice. I'm just worried I won't be able to afford

Figure 6.1 New housing units in Washington, DC
Source: Malo André Hutson, June 2012.

Figure 6.2 Langston Lofts in Washington, DC
Source: Malo André Hutson, June 2012.

[to live here] anymore" (Johnson, 2012). She went on to tell me that her husband had passed away from cancer a few years earlier and that because she was on a fixed income, she was struggling to take on extra work in order to pay her bills, that she no longer lives in the Shaw neighborhood, but still lives in Washington, DC. She continues to work part time and go to church in the Shaw neighborhood.

Ms. Johnson told me in great detail about the intricate process of how some of these demographic changes were happening in her old Shaw neighborhood, especially how they were playing out for many elderly, longtime homeowners that she knew, as well as for herself. "As soon as someone passes away, real estate agents come asking if you want to sell. The children end up fighting over the house and they eventually sell because they don't live in the area anymore; they haven't for a long time, anyway. This is the story at my church." Ms. Johnson told me that over the years, many of the children who had grown up in the neighborhood had left, some to Maryland suburbs such as Prince George's County and others to faraway places. In any event, many of her friends' children had not lived in the neighborhood for some time and when their parents passed away, they often ended up selling. The point that Ms. Johnson made was an important one. Many of the other residents I spoke to also mentioned that people they had grown up with or

Figure 6.3 Black Heritage Trail, Washington, DC
Source: Malo André Hutson, June 2012.

their friends' children had moved away from Washington, DC. Those who stayed in the neighborhood did so because of personal reasons such as having local ties to faith-based institutions, growing up in the neighborhood and having local ties, or because of financial reasons. This information from the interviews supports the census data that shows that blacks had also left Washington, DC from 1970 up until 2000.

Ms. Johnson also explained that many people eventually sell because they need the money. In her case, once her husband fell ill, money had gotten tight because they had medical-related expenses. As a result, she ended up selling the home that she and her husband had owned. She said, "People end up selling because they can use the money. People offer you a lot of money. Many people are like me and reach a point where they decide to sell." Her observations brought up many key points. First, some residents view the economic and physical changes in the neighborhood as positives. Some like the fact that the neighborhood feels safer and, according to crime statistics, is safer. Others mentioned liking the new restaurants and shops that have come to the area. However, they are concerned about the rising costs of living. In Ms. Johnson's case, she was concerned about rising costs as a result of the changes. Her own personal circumstances led to her selling her home.

Ms. Johnson had many other insights on the changes in the neighborhood, including the changing demographics. She told me, "The neighborhood is changing and changing fast. Blacks are leaving and being replaced by young foreigners from all over the world. People think the people moving in are white people, they just look white. They are international and speak all kinds of languages." She finished by saying that they seemed friendly and they say "hello to her."

Other residents took a slightly different view of the changes. One black male resident who has lived in the Shaw neighborhood his whole life and has worked for a government agency for more than twenty years said he was "frustrated that the [neighborhood] changes took so long. It's as though we didn't exist before. Now suddenly there are bike lanes, new sidewalks, and better overall infrastructure." He questioned whether all of these changes were for him and the overall "black community" or simply for the "new white people moving in." This sentiment was not a unique one. A black barber in the Logan Circle area said the changes happening in the neighborhood are nice, including having a Whole Foods nearby and all the new housing, but he worried about "what this change means for him and his business long-term." He was especially concerned that his "lease would go up as the neighborhood continues to improve" and that his customers would eventually be gone. Right now he says he "is getting by because of loyal customers and because of the black professionals who work in the area that he has built a long-term relationship with."

Other residents were resigned to the fact that the neighborhood was changing and there was not much they could do about it. Several mentioned that this was a "designed plan" by the "powers" that be, in this case the government and private developers, to move the poorer people out of the city. One resident was sad and acknowledged that neighborhoods change. She had lived in the Columbia Heights neighborhood for about twenty-three years and said, "It has been a tough go over the years and I understand that change is inevitable. I just wish many of my neighbors were still around to see all of this [change]."

Community response to gentrification
and neighborhood change

The rapid economic and neighborhood changes happening in Washington, DC have made it nearly impossible for local nonprofit organizations and community residents facing displacement to address these challenges. In the Shaw neighborhood, a traditionally black neighborhood that is in close proximity to Howard University, demographic and economic changes have been rapid. The Shaw neighborhood was named after Colonel Robert Gould Shaw, who led the 54th Massachusetts Volunteer Infantry, one of the first official black units during the Civil War (Sheir, 2011). The area housed many Union Army camps, most of which were black (Sheir, 2011). Shaw is roughly bounded by Massachusetts Avenue NW to the south, New Jersey Avenue, NW to the east, Florida Avenue NW to the north, and 11th Street NW to the west. The area also includes the U Street Corridor, which is the commercial district of the Shaw area. If you have been away from the Shaw neighborhood for at least a decade, you would hardly notice it anymore. The area has become safer, cleaner, and more affluent. New condominiums have sprung up all over the neighborhood and the once dilapidated row houses are being renovated and restored to their former glory.

Over the past twenty-five years, the black population has declined from 89 percent in 1990 to less than 45 percent today. At the same time, the white population has grown from 6 percent to almost 30 percent (Moulden, 2013). In addition, housing prices and rents in the neighborhood have increased precipitously, pricing out long-term residents. There are a number of reasons for this such as the local government's efforts to create tax incentives to attract investment and development into the city since the 2000s. Heavy investment in transit-oriented development around transit stations leads to higher housing costs as young, educated millennials "rediscover" the city and increase demand. All of these issues are no doubt important, but in a traditionally black city such as Washington, DC, one factor contributing to displacement has been the lack of economic opportunity and the restructuring of the labor market.

Struggle for economic opportunity

The city is becoming unaffordable for some of its long-term residents. This housing affordability crisis is similar to that experienced in other major cities. In a comprehensive study on the metropolitan Washington, DC economy conducted by the Commonwealth Institute for Fiscal Analysis, the DC Fiscal Policy Institute, and the Maryland Center on Economic Policy, they found that income inequality is growing. Employment levels for people without a college education are far lower than before the recession. In addition, workers with less than a bachelor's degree have seen their median wages decline since the recession. According to the study, "median wages have dropped by 5 percent since 2007 for workers with only a high school degree and by 13 percent for workers without a high school degree" (DC Fiscal Policy Institute, 2014).

Black workers and young workers have not done as well economically since the recession. Black workers with only a high school degree are less likely to be employed than a white resident with less than a high school degree. The study's authors point out that despite the racial gap in employment being narrower among more highly educated workers, still black workers are more likely to be unemployed than their white counterparts (DC Fiscal Policy Institute, 2014).

> Among workers ages 25–54 – the age range when we would expect most people to be working – Black workers in the national capital region with a bachelor's degree or an advanced degree have higher unemployment rates (6 percent) than White, non-Hispanic workers with only a high school diploma (2 percent).

The income gap and difference in labor market participation between blacks and the growing non-black population in Washington, DC no doubt have made it difficult for black families to compete to afford to purchase or rent a home in the nation's capital. The Economic Policy Institute's family budget calculator estimates that a two-parent, two-child household would need between $81,900 and $89,600 annually just to afford the basic living expenses.

These findings were corroborated by my interviews with six black men in the Columbia Heights neighborhood. We met in the middle of the day during normal working hours in the summer of 2013. I asked them about the changes in the neighborhood and if they saw improvements in the economic opportunities. Several of the men, squarely between twenty-five and forty years of age, mentioned having had worked "odd jobs here and there, but nothing long-term." Some told me that they had been involved with the criminal justice system and that finding work was difficult. As one of the young men told me, "when I got released, I tried to apply for lots of jobs, but nobody called me back. After a while I just gave up looking." He said the only way he can stay in the area is to live with relatives. A couple of others said they lacked the skills or training many employers were looking for. However, one of the older men in his late thirties discussed some of the economic opportunities that had recently come into the area as a result of development. He said that he was glad to see the DCUSA shopping center come to Columbia Heights, a large shopping center not far from where we were standing.[2] "This has provided some people jobs," including him, "but that at the moment he was in between jobs where he worked stocking shelves."[3] The interviews with these men demonstrate the challenges for so many young black men and black communities in general within strong-market cities experiencing rapid economic changes. In many cases jobs are being created, but the best-quality jobs require at least a bachelor's degree or specialized skills. These jobs often pay median wages that are higher and that enable a person to afford the cost of living in Washington, DC. However, as the joint study by the Commonwealth Institute for Fiscal Analysis, the DC Fiscal Policy Institute, and the Maryland Center on Economic Policy found, blacks at all educational levels have lower labor market participation rates.

Because blacks are the ones facing displacement (voluntary or involuntary) out of Washington, DC, it is worth exploring the possible explanations as to how and why their labor market participation may be impacting their economic opportunity. Clearly there is no one explanation, but rather the possible explanations are multifaceted and complex. First, it is important to examine why blacks at all educational levels are still likely to be underemployed compared to whites and other ethnic groups. It could be that blacks still face labor market discrimination at a disproportionate rate compared to other groups. For example, a recent research study examined employment opportunities for white and black graduates of elite top-ranked universities versus highly ranked but less selective institutions. The study found that although a credential from an elite university results in more employer responses for all candidates, black candidates from elite universities only do as well as white candidates from less selective universities. Moreover, the study found that when employers respond to black candidates, "it is for jobs with lower starting salaries and lower prestige than those of white peers. These racial differences suggest that a bachelor's degree cannot fully counteract the importance of race in the labor market. Thus, both discrimination and differences in human capital contribute to racial economic inequality" (Gaddis, 2014).

Second, many black men have been involved with the criminal justice system and this has also negatively impacted young black men and boys of color. There are about 2.2. million people incarcerated in the Unites States, according to The Sentencing Project. More than 60 percent of the people in prison are now racial and ethnic minorities. For black males in their thirties, one in every ten is in prison or jail on any given day (The Sentencing Project, 2014). Black men between the ages of twenty and thirty-four have the highest incarceration rates by race/ethnicity or gender (Pew Charitable Trusts, 2008). The rate is especially high for those blacks who drop out of high school. According to an Urban Institute study released in 2015, among male high school dropouts aged twenty to forty, the incarceration rate is 32.4 percent compared with 6 percent for Latino men and 6.7 percent for white men (Urban Institute, 2015b).

In Washington, DC, the story mirrors national trends. Since the 1980s, violent crime has declined. However, arrests for nonviolent crimes were more than 142,000 between 2009 and 2011, with the majority mostly being blacks (more than eight out of ten arrests) (WashLaw, 2013). Moreover, nine out of ten arrests for drug offenses were black (WashLaw, 2013). These high levels of arrests obviously make it difficult for blacks to find economic opportunities with upward mobility or to find quality housing, especially in an expensive city such as Washington, DC.

In addition to labor market discrimination and the criminal justice system, another possible explanation for blacks' limited economic opportunities has to do with educational attainment and the restructuring of the labor market. Nationally, jobs in the public sector, which many blacks have traditionally worked, have declined considerably. For example, the U.S. Department of Labor reports 500,000 fewer public-sector jobs than before the start of the recession in 2007 (Cohen, 2015). The federal government has eliminated 40,000 clerical jobs, many of which were held by women without college degrees (Khimm, 2014). This has hit residents in the Washington, DC area particularly hard, especially the middle class. It is estimated that more than 45 percent of the area's households make more than $100,000 a year, while one-third make less than $60,000 (Lowrey, 2013). The decline of public-sector jobs that require less formal education appears to be having an impact locally. After much controversy, the city allowed Walmart to open two stores in Washington, DC. The first store opened in October 2013 and received more than 11,000 applications for just 1,800 positions within the first week (Khimm, 2014).

Fighting for equitable development and housing affordability

One organization that has attempted to address these issues in a comprehensive and holistic way has been Organizing Neighborhood Equity DC (ONE DC). ONE DC (formerly Manna Community Development Corporation) was founded in 1997 and is a grassroots membership-based, nonhierarchical organization located in the traditionally black Shaw neighborhood of Washington, DC. The organization's mission is to exercise political strength to create and preserve racial and economic equity in the Shaw neighborhood and in Washington, DC more broadly (ONE DC, 2015a). According to Jessica Gordon Nembhard, a core member of the shared leadership team, ONE DC works closely with residents in the "hardest hit neighborhoods impacted by gentrification and neighborhood change" (Gordon Nembhard, 2015). The organization advocates for the construction of affordable housing, creating quality jobs for local residents, and developing and supporting small businesses. According to Gordon Nembhard, "It's about listening and hearing what residents want and helping them have voices. [Our] focus is on impact and helping people insert their own power and voice [into the planning process]" (Gordon Nembhard, 2015).

In recent years, ONE DC has established itself as an organization deeply rooted in community organizing and has focused its work around several important issues related to mitigating the effects of gentrification and neighborhood change. For example, the organization has developed four key strategies to resist gentrification and neighborhood change: 1) Deep community engagement with local residents to better understand their demands and ways to influence policy; 2) Broad-based coalitions around issues such as local hiring/first source hiring, worker cooperatives, and a black workers' center; 3) Direct action or civil resistance that leads to positive social change related to the areas of affordable housing, local economic development, and small business entrepreneurship; and 4) Conduct research and engage in storytelling. ONE DC has also been advocating for The People's Platform, a set of principles and demands, and is trying to establish a black workers' center (one of only a few nationally). Finally, the organization has also launched a Right to Housing Campaign focused on helping long-time Washington, DC residents fight against displacement and for safe and affordable housing regardless of income or wealth (ONE DC, 2015b).

"The People's Platform Demands" include:

- *Community control over land use*

A major principle for ONE DC is that residents have control over the land use process. The organization is highly critical of the local government subsidizing private developers and selling off city land. ONE DC believes that community residents should be incorporated in the development process, especially over publicly owned land. For example, the organization states that governance should not be based solely on free-market values and that "Community involvement in this process has been severely curtailed. For the most part, these transactions are simply giveaways to private developers. Real community control over land use ends these corrupt giveaways and requires public land be used to meet the community's needs, not political/private interests" (ONE DC, 2015b).

- *Equitable development without displacement*

Building on the national work around equitable development, ONE DC is not opposed to development, but instead it prefers to promote development that meets the needs of long-term residents, especially low- to moderate-income residents. A key strategy of ONE DC's equitable development without displacement is to ensure that all public funds used to support development projects also lead to community benefits such as affordable housing and unionized jobs that pay a living wage. The organization has argued that "much of the development in [Washington, DC] has been geared towards recruiting wealthier 'millennials,' while ignoring the housing and land-use needs of families."

- *Permanent housing affordability*

Given Washington, DC's affordable housing crisis, ONE DC has been a huge advocate for affordable housing. One of the issues it has been tackling has been highlighting the fact that housing is a right and that the city should and can do more to reduce the increasing rents and housing prices. The organization has also highlighted that the federal definition of affordable housing set by the Area Median Income (AMI), which allows the city to claim the creation of affordable housing, often does not meet the needs of longtime, low-income DC residents of color. It has demanded that elected city officials do the following to reduce the affordable housing crisis (ONE DC, 2015b):

1   immediately address the homelessness crisis by investing in both permanent hard stock affordable housing units and long-term subsidies such as the Local Rent Supplement Program;
2   introduce and pass legislation that places a moratorium on rents being raised on tenants as a result of federal or local affordability covenants expiring;
3   introduce and pass legislation to strengthen rent control by eliminating Hardship Petitions; and
4   completely overhaul the Inclusionary Zoning program so that it creates affordable units at increased numbers.

    In addition to the People's Platform, ONE DC has advocated for the ONE Right to Housing campaign. The ONE Right to Housing campaign is focused on preventing displacement of long-term, vulnerable residents by educating and organizing them to fight property owners who try to displace them. The organization also tries to convert buildings into cooperatives or win tenants' right to return after they have been displaced. Moreover, ONE DC seeks to minimize citywide efforts to privatize and demolish affordable housing.

•   *Community and family wealth creation*

    ONE DC is trying to eliminate the disparity in income and wealth in Washington, DC. It has supported raising the minimum wage to $15 an hour. The push for raising the minimum wage gained steam after former Mayor Vincent Gray vetoed a bill that would have required Walmart to pay workers $12.50 an hour. He justified vetoing the bill because he said it would be a "job-killer" and would prevent other larger chain stores from coming to Washington, DC or from expanding their operations (Novack, 2013). ONE DC demands that the city introduce and pass legislation to immediately increase the minimum wage to $15 an hour. It has also been one of the city's biggest proponents of worker cooperative developments. As a result, ONE DC also demands that the city "provide a budget allocation for worker cooperative development, provide tax incentives for worker cooperatives, and change its procurement policies to favor worker cooperatives" (ONE DC, 2015b).
    Finally, ONE DC is working to establish a Black Worker Center. The creation of a Black Worker Center is in direct response to the high black

unemployment rate and underemployment within Washington, DC and nationally. ONE DC hopes the Center will be able to do the following:

- Be a center for finding and creating positive, dignified black work and training.
- Be an incubation space for alternatives to low-wage work, such as workers' cooperatives, collectives, and small businesses created, owned, and operated by black workers.
- Be a place to openly discuss the intersection of race and work, particularly what it means to be "working while black," as well as a place for black workers to positively recognize their blackness.
- Be an environment to challenge bad employers who exploit, cheat, and steal from their workers.
- Be an educational space to talk about ways to work safer and for more money and benefits.

Community Benefits Agreement at Progression Place

In 2004, ONE DC's leadership became interested in ways the organization could promote and implement equitable economic development strategies. As a result, they reached out to several prominent national organizations such as PolicyLink and Good Jobs First, as well as local faith-based institutions and other nonprofits (Juskus and Ella, 2007). PolicyLink, a national research and action institute based in Oakland, California, was particularly helpful because its founder and CEO, Angela Glover Blackwell, has been among one of the national leaders at the forefront of the equitable development movement. Just a few years prior to working with ONE DC, PolicyLink had hosted a series of successful National Equity Summits in various cities across the United States, which was attended by roughly 6,000 people ranging from policy makers to philanthropists to local community nonprofit leaders (PolicyLink, 2014).

Around the same time that ONE DC was exploring ways to develop and implement effective equitable economic development strategies in the Shaw neighborhood and in Washington, DC more broadly, the District of Columbia Office of Planning launched a neighborhood revitalization plan for the Shaw neighborhood. The DUKE Plan, named after Duke Ellington, sought to attract development to the neighborhood by "capitalizing upon the area's historic context and emerging reputation as an arts and entertainment district" (Planning DC, 2011). The DUKE Plan had six guiding principles, two of which were of great significance – to promote transit-oriented development to encourage walking and to promote "cultural tourism initiatives based on the rich history of African-American historical and cultural assets of the area that [would] bring economic development opportunities for local residents and businesses" (Planning DC, 2011).

As part of the DUKE Plan, the District of Columbia Office of Planning specifically targeted redevelopment activities on public-owned properties within the Shaw neighborhood such as the Howard Theatre, Parcels 33 and 42, Metro's Shaw Parcels, and private parcels in the 7th Street/Georgia Avenue and U Street/Florida Avenue commercial corridors (Planning DC, 2005). Parcel 33 was located at the corner of 7th and S Streets NW, above the Washington Metropolitan Area Transit Authority's (WMATA) Shaw-Howard U transit station. The undeveloped site was under the development control of the National Capital Revitalization Corporation (NCRC). NCRC was created in 2001 to serve as an independent entity of the government with the mission of engaging in economic development and revitalization activities for the benefit of the District of Columbia. Specifically, NCRC is tasked with retaining, expanding, and attracting businesses to spur economic development and job creation by providing incentives and assistance "to remove slum and blight" (Adams, 2006).

Soon after the DUKE Plan was conceptualized, NCRC in partnership with private developers – The Jarvis Company, Ellis Enterprises, and Four Points, LLC – started to move forward with plans to redevelop Parcel 33 into a mixed-use development (1.17 acres). The initial plan was supposed to be a $150 million, mixed-use, transit-oriented development, which would include the headquarters for Radio One Corporation and its TV ONE joint venture with Comcast (Cassell, 2013). The project also included 205 units of rental housing as well as more than 100,000 square feet of commercial space and just more than 24,000 square feet of retail space (NDC Academy, 2014).

Because this was a public-private partnership, ONE DC decided it would be a good opportunity to try and implement its equitable economic development principles (Jukus and Ella, 2007). Just about eighteen months before, ONE DC had approached NCRC with some equitable economic development principles it wanted the organization to adopt, but NCRC had declined to do so (NDC Academy, 2014). This time ONE DC, along with its allies, presented NCRC and the private developers with a list of community benefits it demanded as part of the deal in order for the project to move forward. As part of its strategy, ONE DC threatened to organize its constituents and allies to conduct public protests against the proposed development at all city hearings (NDC Academy, 2014). In early 2005, NCRC and the private developers signed the Community Benefits Agreement (CBA), making it the first such agreement in the District of Columbia (NDC Academy, 2014).

As part of the agreement, NCRC and the private developers agreed to provide twenty housing units for families with incomes below 50 percent of AMI and thirty-one housing units were made available to households with incomes between 50–80% percent of AMI (Moulden, 2013). In addition, NCRC and the developers agreed to provide residents with job training and employment opportunities, with a requirement that 51 percent of hires be Washington, DC residents (Moulden, 2012). They also agreed to allocate 2,000 square feet of office space within the new development for local businesses at below-market rates for five years (Moulden, 2012). NCRC and the developers even agreed to provide $750,000 for a local community development fund to provide grants to nonprofits that provide direct health, wellness, cultural, and educational services to the community (Moulden, 2012; Cassell, 2013).

In 2008, when the economy collapsed, the financial backing for the project became questionable and Radio One Corporation backed out of its plans to relocate in Washington, DC. However, the developers secured the United Negro College Fund (UNCF) as the new anchor tenant. In February 2011, a ceremonial groundbreaking was held and key political leaders attended, including Representative Eleanor Holmes Norton, Mayor Vincent Gray, and District of Columbia Council Chair Kwame Brown (Brabham, 2011). The final phase of the development project was completed in July 2013 and received millions of dollars in public subsidies (Cassell, 2013, Sablich, 2013). The financing structure for the Progression Place development included New Market Tax Credits, Housing and Urban Development Federal Housing Administration Mortgage Insurance, and Housing Production Trust Fund, as well as commercial loan and grant funding from the Office of the Deputy Mayor for Planning (NDC Academy, 2014).

DC residents' demand for the enforcement of the First Source Law

In addition to ONE DC's efforts to hold developers and the local government accountable to the needs of less affluent residents via the Progression Place Community Benefits Agreement, the organization was instrumental in getting the "D.C. Citizens' Job Program" passed within the 2009 New Convention Center Hotel Amendments Act. During this effort, ONE DC spent ten years trying to secure living-wage jobs for DC residents. For example, in the mid-2000s ONE DC members sought to strengthen training and hiring agreements for the new Convention Center Hotel by submitting amendments to the funding legislation for job training and community outreach (ONE DC and Kalmanovitz Initiative, 2015). In addition, ONE DC hosted the Jobs Training Community Partnership Forum, with the goal of linking residents to job training organizations (ONE DC and Kalmonvitz Initiative, 2015). Under the 2009 New Convention Center Hotel Amendments Act, $2 million was allocated for the training and hiring of DC residents for permanent positions in the New Convention Center Hotel (District of Columbia, 2009). Specifically the bill called on the future operator of the New Convention Center Hotel (eventually the Marriott Marquis Hotel) to work with "representatives of organized labor, ONE DC, and other community organizations, which have demonstrated experience in providing effective job training and placement in the hospitality industry jobs [and to] participate in the development of the program" (District of Columbia, 2009).

Shortly after the passing of the DC Citizens' Job Program, ONE DC was also active in pressuring the City Council to pass the District's First Source Law, which was originally passed in 1984 and amended by the DC Council in 2011. The District's First Source Law requires that, on any government-assisted project receiving between $300,000 and $5 million, 51 percent of new hires must be District residents. For projects that receive $5 million or more, the law requires that DC residents perform at least 20 percent of journey worker hours, 60 percent of apprentice hours, 51 percent of skilled laborer hours, and 70 percent of common laborer hours (District of Columbia Department of Employment Services, 2011; Neibauer, 2014).

The victories of helping get the DC Citizens' Job Program and the First Source Law passed had members of ONE DC and its partners optimistic that unemployed DC residents would be hired for permanent jobs. They were especially optimistic that the 2009 New Convention Center Hotel Amendments Act would provide long-term unemployed and underemployed residents with the training necessary to be hired at the new hotel within the Convention Center, so much so that ONE DC accepted the task of identifying and recruiting more than 3,000 unemployed DC residents, many of whom were black and Latino, to participate in the Marriott Marquis Jobs Training Program (Gordon Nembhard, 2015).

On May 1, 2014, the Marriott Marquis opened the doors to an estimated $520 million, 1,175-room hotel that called on the city to issue $225 million in bonds to provide $159 million in equity financing (TIF) for the hotel and an additional $24 million from other TIF revenues (O'Connell, 2009; ONE DC, and Kalmanovitz Initiative, 2015). However, despite the fact that 719 DC residents graduated from the Marriott Marquis Jobs Training Program, only 178 were initially hired (ONE DC and Kalmanovitz Initiative, 2015).

Hollow victories

Clearly the impact of the CBA signed between ONE DC and the developers is a positive thing, as are ONE DC's efforts to secure living-wage jobs for DC residents. However, the community benefits are not large enough to be a game changer given the rapid economic and physical transformation happening in the historically black Shaw neighborhood and across Washington, DC. Moreover, hundreds of permanent jobs have not materialized for unemployed and underemployed DC residents, many of them black and Latino. This is precisely why the organization is still deeply committed to establishing a black workers' center. Still, ONE DC's focus on equitable economic development principles and strategies combined with grassroots community organizing and base building helped it score the first CBA in Washington, DC and strengthen its First Source Law. ONE DC's efforts are aimed at holding the government and developers accountable to the community's needs, especially where public subsidies are used to help private developers build projects on publicly owned land. ONE DC, similar to the efforts of BrooklynSpeaks in New York City, is focused on building a grassroots movement with local residents and community organizations to make the community development and land use process more transparent and inclusive of the public in the decision-making process instead of keeping them on the "outside" or having the process bypass them altogether. As Dominic T. Moulden, a resource organizer for ONE DC, wrote in an article coauthored with Gregory Squires about the organization's efforts to promote equitable development, "By engaging in what ONE DC refers to as 'participatory democracy,' this membership-led organization is confronting several powerful private and public entities to protect residents' interests" (Moulden and Squires, 2012).

ONE DC's push to get the developers to agree to make a quarter of the apartments at the Progression Place development affordable for families with low to moderate incomes was significant, especially because the Progression Place project was a mixed-use, transit-oriented development. Neighborhoods with development projects in close proximity to transit stations and corridors have some of the highest housing prices and rents in the city. They are also where some of the fastest demographic and neighborhood change has occurred over the past fifteen years. Therefore, any efforts focused on including more affordable housing through CBAs or by getting local governments to strengthen their inclusionary housing ordinances is important to mitigating the impacts of large-scale development projects on the most vulnerable residents. In 2011, ONE DC reached out to the District of Columbia Council chair, Kwame Brown, in an attempt to increase the amount of funding for affordable housing construction and base the level of affordability on Washington, DC's income levels rather than the AMI (Moulden and Squires, 2012). Mr. Brown proposed the Increase in Housing Affordability Act of 2011, but it failed to pass, and on June 6, 2012, federal prosecutors charged Brown with one count of bank fraud in U.S. District Court. He resigned from office (Wilber and Craig, 2012).

In addition to the organization's demands for affordable housing, ONE DC's equitable development strategy was centered on creating economic opportunities for local residents. It was estimated that the Progression Place development would generate sixty-nine retail jobs and nearly 630 construction jobs (seventeen jobs filled by District of Columbia public housing residents and seven permanent jobs) (NDC Academy, 2014).

Unfortunately, victories are hollow because residents within the Shaw neighborhood and in other neighborhoods experiencing gentrification and neighborhood change are struggling to remain in their residences and have to deal with all the stress and health issues that arise related to this process (Gordon Nembhard, 2015). For example, ONE DC is finding it increasingly challenging to recruit members to the organization. As the key face and voice of ONE DC, Jessica Gordon Nembhard said, "Gentrification has made it harder for outreach because many residents are moving away or are being displaced. Other residents are dealing with wellness issues caused by the stress of trying to just survive. In fact, many are assaulted by wellness issues that increase their levels of stress and negatively impact their health" (2015). When asked about all the demographic and physical change happening within the Shaw neighborhood and U-Street Corridor area, she said, "It's bittersweet. On one level it's good to see black culture recognized [referring to the black-named or themed restaurants, bars, cafes, and housing developments], but on another we (blacks) are not able to enjoy it."

The city's response to demographic, economic, and neighborhood change

In February 2012, former Mayor Vincent Gray announced that he would establish the Comprehensive Housing Strategy Task Force (Task Force). The mayor appointed a multi-sector team of thirty-six housing professionals to serve on the Task Force and they were charged with helping city leaders develop a strategy to create more affordable housing for Washington, DC residents (Flowers and Ladd, 2013). A year later the Task Force released the *Bridges to Opportunity: A New Housing Strategy for D.C.* report. The Task Force proposed some bold strategies and goals for the city to accomplish including preserving and building at least 10,000 housing units by 2020. Specifically, the Task Force called on the city to establish three strategic goals that would address improving the housing continuum from homelessness to building market-rate housing (Flowers and Ladd, 2013):

1   Preserve approximately 8,000 existing affordable housing units with subsidies that will expire by the year 2020.
2   Produce and preserve 10,000 net new affordable housing units by the year 2020 (known as "10 x 20").
3   Support the production of 3,000 market rate housing units annually through 2020.

The Task Force provided a comprehensive list of twenty-four steps for the city to take to address the housing affordability crisis covering policy, administrative, or financial areas. For example, the Task Force recommended that the city fully fund the Housing Production Trust Fund (HPTF); create a new, locally funded Housing Innovation Fund that will finance ready affordable housing developments; support a City Affordable Housing Data and Reporting system that will create a database of locally financed affordable housing units; as well as streamline the permitting process for affordable and market rate housing developments.

Despite the Task Force's bold recommendations, the HPTF had been severely underfunded well below the $100 million annual level that housing advocates had been seeking. The Washington, DC mayoral campaign provided the opportunity for housing advocates to put sustained resources behind the HPTF. One of the leading candidates for mayor was Muriel Bowser, who at the time was a councilmember. In her mayoral campaign, Ms. Bowser ran on a platform that she would work to address homelessness and help build affordable housing in the city. During her campaign,

Councilmember Bowser worked with the Housing For All Campaign to introduce Bill 20–708, the Housing Production Trust Fund Baseline Funding Amendment Act of 2014. The Housing for All Campaign was created by the Coalition for Nonprofit Housing and Economic Development, a membership association that helps nonprofit community development organizations create housing and economic opportunities for the city's most vulnerable residents (CNHED, 2014). Bill 20–708 called for the city to authorize at least $100 million for the HTPF annually. In November 2014, the Washington, DC Council unanimously voted in favor of the bill. Mayor Gray signed it on December 8, 2014, and in March 2015, it officially became the law (DC Municipal Regulations, 2015).

Mayor Bowser appears committed to the construction of affordable housing. In her 2016 budget, she allocated $100 million for housing developments. She also proposed paying for and expanding homeless services and programs through a citywide sales tax increase (Stein, 2015). Within a few months in office, Mayor Bowser went on a tour of the Shaw neighborhood with U.S. Department of Housing and Urban Development Secretary Julian Castro (HUD, 2015). It is likely that she will remain a champion of affordable housing.

Moving forward and key lessons learned

Ever since the social and political unrest of the 1960s, Washington, DC went through a long process of change. The anger local residents displayed after Dr. King's murder was a simply a response to the systematic racial and economic injustice that segregated black residents and other people of color endured. Structural racism created neighborhoods with high levels of poverty and unemployment. Prior to the unrest in 1968, the black population of Washington, DC had grown dramatically while the white population was leaving the city for the suburbs for the better part of the 1960s.

Whites were not the only ones who left the city in large numbers. After the 1960s up until 2000, the black middle class also left the city for the suburbs. Many moved to green, leafy suburbs such as Prince George's County, Maryland, one of the wealthiest predominately black suburbs in the United States. This population decline over four decades had a negative impact on the city, especially many of the poorer residents who stayed in the city. In the 1980s, Washington, DC went through one of the most difficult periods in its storied history. The city suffered through a crack cocaine epidemic that destroyed lives and tore apart communities. The proliferation of crack cocaine and other drugs in the neighborhood was coupled with violent crime. The high level of violent crime and the murder rate made Washington, DC one of the most dangerous cities in America.

The difficult conditions in the city left disinvested neighborhoods scarred. The beautiful housing stock or row houses in certain parts of the city were abandoned or converted to crack houses. Other houses simply burned down and property was left vacant. These conditions resulted in large parts of the city with inexpensive land near transit, which would prove ideal for investors in the late 1990 and early 2000s.

After his election in 1999, Mayor Anthony Williams laid out a vision for Washington, DC that called for 100,000 new residents to move to the city. The city has grown from just more than 572,000 residents in 2000 to more than 658,000 in 2014. This growth has been nothing short of impressive and was facilitated by a local government that provided financial incentives to private developers to make an investment in the city. More important, the Washington, DC metropolitan area fared better than most during the Great Recession while other metropolitan areas were losing jobs and unemployment was rising. This helped Washington, DC attract young, educated people who could find relatively inexpensive housing in some of the city's less affluent areas. The influx of millennials has helped lift up and support the building boom in Washington, DC. In the neighborhoods of Logan Circle, Shaw, and Columbia Heights, young people can be found walking up and down 14th Street NW and the U Street Corridor at night coming to and from the latest bars, restaurants, or boutique retail shops. On the weekend it is not uncommon for young people to be seen atop the latest luxury condominiums having pool parties in the summer.

But the growth in Washington, DC has not benefited everyone. The income gap between the wealthiest residents and the poorest is continuing to widen. For example, the DC Fiscal Policy Institute's study showed that among the top fifty cities in the United States, Washington, DC has the fourth highest income inequality. The richest 5 percent of Washingtonians earn $530,000 while the poorest 20 percent earn $9,900 (Rivers, 2014). Therefore, the way that a long-term resident views these economic and physical changes depends on what side of the fence one sits on. Based on my interviews with residents, small business owners, and those who work in transitioning neighborhoods, the feelings are mixed. For some homeowners who lived in the city through the difficult periods of disinvestment and economic decline (the crack cocaine era as well as the surging crime rates through the 1970s to 1990s), seeing the changes has been good and bad. On one hand, many of them like the changes that have occurred in the neighborhood. In general, they like that the neighborhood is safer and looks nicer because houses have been fixed up or because new mixed-use development has filled vacant lots of abandoned buildings. The negative side to this change has been the fact that many of their neighbors have left the city and the cost of living is rising. This was a common theme that emerged from my interviews.

For those with limited economic opportunities because of a criminal record or being stuck in a low-wage job, the changes happening in Washington, DC are making it hard for them to survive economically and remain in their neighborhoods. The precipitous increase in rents and housing prices are making the city affordable only to those within a certain band of the economic spectrum.

To make strong-market cities such as Washington, DC affordable and accessible to people and families of all income strata requires institutional and systemic change. This means that when public-private partnerships involve public subsidies and/or public land allocations to a development project, it is critical that these development projects provide adequate community benefits to local residents. These community benefits can be in the form of affordable housing, good-quality jobs, environmental improvements (such as parks, open space, recreational facilities), and investments in human capital (through public education, workforce training, and internships).

This is precisely why community-centered groups like ONE DC are essential for bringing about institutional and systemic change. ONE DC's emphasis on equitable development calls for community control over land use. In addition, the organization's focus on affordable housing, especially for the tenants already in subsidized housing, is necessary to balance the amount of market-rate housing being constructed in Washington, DC. Given the economic realities of Washington, DC, perhaps the most critical component of equitable development is creating good jobs for unemployed and underemployed residents, especially for men of color. The national unrest we see is deeply rooted in racial and economic oppression of communities of color. In a city like Washington, DC with a substantial black population, the way to promote the neighborhood diversity and economic opportunity that Mayor Williams advocated for during his first term is for the public, private, and nonprofit sectors to create economic opportunities and develop workforce development strategies that provide people access to good jobs.

Notes

1 Busboys and Poets Cafe is named after poet, social activist, and author Langston Hughes, who once worked as a busboy at the Wardman Park Hotel in Washington, DC; Blackbyrd Bar is named after Donald Byrd's 1972 jazz funk album *Black Byrd*, Blue Note Records' highest-ever selling album; the Marvin restaurant is named after Washington, DC native, singer-songwriter, and musician Marvin Gaye; Eatonville is named after the community in Florida where Zora Neale Hurston, the black folklorist, anthropologist, and author, grew up.
2 DC USA is an 890,000 square foot, three-level shopping complex and is the largest retail development in Washington, DC. The complex is full of typical chain stores found in a suburban community such as Target, Bed, Bath & Beyond, Best Buy, Staples, Marshalls, IHOP, and Petco to name several. DC USA was part of a revitalization plan that placed the shopping center near the Columbia Heights Metro Station stop.
3 Personal communication, June 17, 2012.

Bibliography

Adams, E. 2006. The National Capital Revitalization Corporation ("NCRC") and its subsidiaries. Eugene A. Adams to Anthony A. Williams. December 8. http://oag.dc.gov/sites/default/files/dc/sites/oag/publication/attachments/National%20Capital%20Revitalization%20Corporation.pdf.

Barras, J. R. 2014. Anthony Williams earned the title of D.C.'s "mayor for life." *The Washington Post*, June 26. www.washingtonpost.com/opinions/jonetta-rosa-barras-anthony-williams-earned-the-title-of-dcs-mayor-for-life/2014/06/25/0ba90448-fb1e-11e3-b1f4–8e77c632c07b_story.html.

Brabham, R. 2011. Shaw streets. *Capital Community News*. www.capitalcommunitynews.com/PDF/2011/28–29_MCDC_0311.pdf.

Brookings Institution. 2013. *Neighborhood 10: Ten Strategies for a Stronger Washington*. PDF. Brookings Institution, April 17. Retrieved from www.brookings.edu/es/urban/gwrp/events/20030417_revitalizingdc.pdf.

Cassell, S. C. 2013. Progression place fulfills Duke Plans vision for greater Shaw/U Street. *Pipeline* 20 (August), 13. www.dcbia.org/pipeline/Pipeline_August2013/Pipeline_August13_Final.pdf.

Chang, E., Tucker, N., Goldstein, J., Yates, C., and Davis, M. 2013. March of the millennials. *The Washington Post*, October 18. www.washingtonpost.com/sf/style/2013/10/18/march-of-the-millennials/.

Coalition for Nonprofit Housing and Economic Development CNHED. 2014. What is the Housing for All Campaign? CNHED. www.cnhed.org/housing-for-all-campaign/.

Cohen, P. 2015. Public-sector jobs vanish, hitting blacks hard. *The New York Times*, May 24. www.nytimes.com/2015/05/25/business/public-sector-jobs-vanish-and-blacks-take-blow.html?src=xps.

Crockett, Jr., S. A. 2012. The Brixton: It's new, happening and another example of African-American historical "swagger-jacking." *The Washington Post*. August 3. www.washingtonpost.com/blogs/therootdc/post/the-brixton-its-new-happening-and-another-example-of-african-american-historical-swagger-jacking/2012/08/03/b189b254-dcee-11e1-a894-af35ab98c616_blog.html.

Cushman and Wakefield. 2014. *Urban Development: Faster Greener Commutes Key to Sustained City Growth*. Publication. Fall. www.cushmanwakefield.com/~/media/reports/corporate/Global%20Reports/CW_North%20American%20Transit%20Report%20Fall%202014.pdf.

DC City Council. 2009. New Convention Center Hotel Amendments Act of 2009. http://dcclims1.dccouncil.us/images/00001/20090603141210.pdf.

DC Department of Employment Services. 2011. First Source Agreement for Construction Projects. http://dclibrary.org/sites/default/files/DCPL2015R0011_FirstSourceforConstructionProjects.pdf

DC Fiscal Policy Institute. 2014. *Bursting the Bubble: The Challenges of Working and Living in the National Capital Region*. Report. June 20. www.dcfpi.org/wp-content/uploads/2014/06/6–20–14-bursting_the_bubble_2014_FINAL_web.pdf.

DC Municipal Regulations. 2015. Law 20–208, Housing Production Trust Fund Baseline Funding Amendment Act. DC Municipal Regulations and DC Register. April 10. www.dcregs.dc.gov/Gateway/NoticeHome.aspx?NoticeID=5413296.

DC Planning. 2005. DUKE Framework for a cultural destination for greater Shaw-U Street final report. Office of Planning. June 21. http://planning.dc.gov/publication/duke-framework-cultural-destination-greater-shaw-u-street-final-report.

DC Planning. 2011. *After the Duke Small Area Plan*. August 18. http://planning.dc.gov/sites/default/files/dc/sites/op/release_content/attachments/Duke_ASAP_8–18–11.pdf.

Fisher, D. 2012. How Washington D.C. got off the most dangerous cities list. *Forbes*, October 19. www.forbes.com/sites/danielfisher/2012/10/19/how-washington-d-c-got-off-the-most-dangerous-cities-list/.

Flowers, M. G. and Ladd, A. 2013. *Bridges to Opportunity: A New Housing Strategy for D.C.* Report. March. www.taskforce2012.org/Portals/1/docs/Bridges_to_Opportunity-A_New_Housing_Strategy_for_DC-Official_Report.pdf.

Gaddis, S. M. 2014. Discrimination in the credential society: An audit study of race and college selectivity in the labor market. *Social Forces*, 1–29.

Gordon Nembhard, Jessica. Personal Interview. June 30, 2015.

Johnson, Ms. 2012. Interview June 6. Ms. Johnson is not her real name; a pseudonym is used to protect her identity.

Juskus, R. and Elia, E. 2007. Long time coming. *Shelterforce Online* 150 (Summer). www.nhi.org/online/issues/150/longtimecoming.html.

Khimm, S. 2014. In DC, inequality hits home. MSNBC. January 26. www.msnbc.com/msnbc/dc-inequality-hits-home.

Lowrey, A. 2013. Washington's economic boom, financed by you. *The New York Times Magazine*, January 10. www.nytimes.com/2013/01/13/magazine/washingtons-economic-boom-financed-by-you.html?pagewanted=all&_r=1.

Morello, C. and Keating, D. 2011. Number of black D.C. residents plummets as majority status slips away. *The Washington Post*, March 24. www.washingtonpost.com/local/black-dc-residents-plummet-barely-a-majority/2011/03/24/ABtIgJQB_story.html.

Moulden, D. T. 2013. Equitable development: One example in ONE DC. *Nonprofit Quarterly*. January 29. https://nonprofitquarterly.org/policysocial-context/21705-equitable-development-one-example-in-one-dc.html.

Moulden, D. T. and Squires, G. D. 2012. Equitable development in D.C. *Social Policy*, 42(3) (Fall), 37–39. http://higherlogicdownload.s3.amazonaws.com/EVAL/890fe2db-7161–4acc-96e5–7323d6f9d9bb/UploadedImages/Moulden-Squires.pdf.

Muller, J. 2011. 43 years ago today, DC stopped burning. Greater Greater Washington. April 8. http://greatergreaterwashington.org/post/10005/43-years-ago-today-dc-stopped-burning/.

Neibauer, M. 2014. Lawsuit that could wipe out D.C.'s First Source law allowed to continue. *Washington Business Journal*. July 14. www.bizjournals.com/washington/breaking_ground/2014/07/lawsuit-that-could-wipe-out-d-c-s-first-source-law.html.

Neighborhood Info DC. 2015a. DC city profile – housing. Neighborhood Info DC. April 1. www.neighborhoodinfodc.org/city/Nbr_prof_cityc.html.

Neighborhood Info DC. 2015b. DC neighborhood cluster profile – Population. Neighborhood Info DC. April 1. www.neighborhoodinfodc.org/nclusters/nbr_prof_clus7.html.

Novack, J. 2013. Walmart wins again as Washington D.C. mayor vetoes $12.50 minimum age. *Forbes*, September 12. www.forbes.com/sites/janetnovack/2013/09/12/walmart-wins-again-as-washington-d-c-mayor-vetoes-12–50-minimum-wage/.

O'Connell, J. 2009. DC Oks Convention Center Hotel Financing. *Washington Business Journal*, July 15.

ONE DC. 2015a. About ONE DC. ONE DC. www.onedconline.org/about.

ONE DC. 2015b. People's platform. ONE DC. www.onedconline.org/peoplesplatform.

ONE DC and Kalmanovitz Initiative for Labor and the Working Poor at Georgetown University. 2015. "Trained to Death" and Still Jobless: A Case Study of the Efficacy of DC's First Source Law, Economic Development Policies, and the Marriott Marquis Jobs Training Program. June 19. https://d3n8a8pro7vhmx.cloudfront.

net/onedctrac/pages/332/attachments/original/1434655058/ONE_DC-Marriott Report-1.pdf?1434655058.

NDC Academy. 2014. Progression Place – an anchor for the community. NDC Academy. http://ndcacademy.org/wp-content/uploads/2014/09/Progression-Place.pdf.

Pew Charitable Trusts. 2008. More than one in 100 adults are behind bars, Pew study finds. www.pewtrusts.org/en/about/news-room/press-releases/2008/02/28/more-than-one-in-100-adults-are-behind-bars-pew-study-finds.

Phillips, J., Beasley, R., and Rodgers, A. 2005. *District of Columbia Population and Housing Trends*. Report. Fall. www.neighborhoodinfodc.org/pdfs/demographic_trends05.pdf.

PolicyLink. 2014. About – history and accomplishments. PolicyLink. www.policylink.org/about/history-accomplishments.

Politic365. 2013. Murder rate in Washington DC at lowest point in 52 years. Politic365. January 6. http://politic365.com/2013/01/06/murder-rate-in-washington-dc-at-lowest-point-in-52-years/.

Rivers, W. 2014. DC's income inequality ranks among highest in U.S. DC Fiscal Policy Institute. March 13.

Sablich, L. 2013. Equitable development movement: A progressive response to the urban redevelopment landscape nationwide and in Washington, DC's Shaw community. *Policy Perspectives*, 25–40.

Schuker Blum, L. and Karmin, C. 2013. Washington, DC: The new boomtown. *The Wall Street Journal*, May 23. www.wsj.com/articles/SB10001424127887324767004578489202247919668.

Shah, N. 2013. Millennials flock to Washington after abandoning city in recession. *The Wall Street Journal*, November 14. http://blogs.wsj.com/economics/2013/11/14/millennials-flock-to-washington-after-abandoning-city-in-recession/?mod=e2tw.

Sheir, R. 2011. Shaw's roots: From "heart of Chocolate City" to "little United Nations." WAMU 88.5 American University Radio. May 4.

Stein, P. 2015. Is pricey Shaw a model for retaining affordability amid regentrification? *The Washington Post*, May 21. www.washingtonpost.com/local/dc-politics/is-pricey-shaw-a-model-for-retaining-affordability-amidst-regentrification/2015/05/21/912f3504-ffde-11e4-805c-c3f407e5a9e9_story.html.

Tavernise, S. A. 2011. population changes, uneasily. *The New York Times*, July 17. www.nytimes.com/2011/07/18/us/18dc.html.

The Ellington. 2015. www.ellingtonapartments.com/?utm_source=Yelp&utm_medium=Yelppageurl&utm_campaign=Yelppage.

The Sentencing Project. 2014. Racial Disparity. The Sentencing Project. www.sentencingproject.org/template/page.cfm?id=122.

Urban Institute. 2015a. A history of change. Washington DC: Our changing city. http://datatools.urban.org/features/OurChangingCity/demographics/#history.

Urban Institute. 2015b. www.urban.org/sites/default/files/alfresco/publication-pdfs/2000095-Reducing-Harms-to-Boys-and-Young-Men-of-Color-from-Criminal-Justice-System-Involvement.pdf.

U.S. Housing and Urban Development. 2015. Executive Office of the Mayor. Secretary Julian Castro joins Mayor Muriel Bowser to kick off HUD's 50th anniversary with walking tour of Shaw neighborhood. May 20, 2015. http://mayor.dc.gov/release/secretary-julian-castro-joins-mayor-muriel-bowser-kick-huds-50th-anniversary-walking-tour.

Walton, T. 2012. *Going Going Gone Rent Burden.* www.scribd.com/doc/258486065/ Going-Going-Gone-Rent-Burden-Final-3–6–15format-v2–3–10–15.

Washington Metropolitan Area Transit Authority (WMATA). 2011. *Making the Case for Transit: WMATA Regional Benefits of Transit.* Technical paper. November. www.wmata.com/pdfs/planning/WMATA%20Making%20the%20Case%20 for%20Transit%20Final%20Report%20Jan-2012.pdf.

WashLaw. 2013. *Racial Disparities in Arrests in the District of Columbia, 2009– 2011.* Report. July. www.washlaw.org/pdf/wlc_report_racial_disparities.pdf.

Wilber, D. Q. and Craig, T. 2012. Kwame R. Brown, D.C. Council chairman, resigns after being charged with bank fraud. *The Washington Post,* June 6. www. washingtonpost.com/local/crime/2012/06/06/gJQAUXJqIV_story.html.

Wilson, W. J. 1996. *When Work Disappears: The World of the New Urban Poor.* New York, NY: Alfred A. Knopf.

Wogan, J. B. 2015. Why D.C.'s affordable housing protections are losing a war with economics. *Governing,* February. www.governing.com/topics/urban/gov-washington-affordable-housing-protections-gentrification-series.html.

7 Deepening their roots

The urban struggle for economic, environmental and social justice

For me, conducting these case studies brought all of the statistics, theories, and prior research discussed in Chapter 2 out of the abstract. To start with, reading about the "rediscovery" of the city is one thing, but to walk these neighborhoods analyzed in my case studies and personally witness the dramatic demographic shifts is quite another. Perhaps no city has experienced as dramatic a demographic shift in recent decades as Washington, DC. Neighborhoods such as Columbia Heights, Shaw, and Logan Circle have undergone substantial economic and physical transformations. As detailed in Chapter 6, these neighborhoods, once home to large populations of working poor and communities of color, have seen intensifying condominium construction, housing renovations, and commercial development since the early 2000s. Since the early 2000s, Washington, DC's population of millennials has grown by 37,000 and now accounts for about 35 percent of the total city population (Urban Institute, 2015a). The new arrivals in Washington, DC have been mostly non-black and the black population has dipped below 50 percent for the first time in half a century (Tavernise, 2011). San Francisco's Mission District has also seen rapid demographic changes: between 2000–2010, the Latino population declined from 50 percent to 39 percent (Weinberg, 2015). Having spent considerable time in these neighborhoods in the mid-1990s, I found that the demographic and physical changes *felt* dramatic.

Many of the contributing factors driving the demographic shifts in these neighborhoods are not unique to these neighborhoods, but are endemic to the issue of gentrification in strong-market cities nationwide and follow many of the trends discussed in Chapter 2. For example, these neighborhoods are located in areas where state and local governments have policies and programs that encourage investment in large-scale revitalization projects in the urban core. Local governments have provided private developers with subsidies, tax credits, and access to publicly owned land at low cost, which has resulted in the transformation of many older, industrial parts of cities and historically underinvested neighborhoods. This was best illustrated by the case in Brooklyn with the Atlantic Yards/Pacific Park project. During the bidding process to develop the 8.4-acre Atlantic Yards property owned by the Metropolitan Transportation Authority, Extell Development Company bid $150 million in cash, while Forest City Ratner Companies bid only $50 million, a difference of $100 million. Both bids were well below the Metropolitan Transportation Authority's appraisal of the site at $214.5 million (DDDB, 2005).

Similarly, much of the development coming into these neighborhoods prioritizes transit-oriented development, market-rate housing, and high-end commercial space (Logan and Molotch, 1987). This investment transforms neighborhoods, even some formerly blighted neighborhoods. It also appeals to an educated population concerned about sustainability, climate change, and the environment, but makes it hard for poorer community members to stay in place. To get their projects built with less political conflict, developers make promises to provide local residents with affordable housing, jobs, workforce training, and other community benefits. Unfortunately, without enough community pressure and government oversight, the community benefits developers promise may not materialize as planned. This is what happened in Brooklyn. FCRC and its supporters launched the marketing campaign "jobs, housing, and hoops" (Oder, 2004). Earlier meetings regarding job opportunities with the Atlantic Yards/Pacific Park project drew thousands of people, especially underemployed or unemployed black men (Oder, 2004). Advocates of the project promised local residents that the project would generate at least 1,500 construction jobs and that an additional 1,500–6,400 permanent jobs would be created, as well as 2,250 units of affordable housing (Fainstein, 2009). FCRC estimated that the entire development would generate $5.6 billion in tax revenue over thirty years (Fainstein, 2009). FCRC also entered into a CBA with a group of community, nonprofit, and government entities in order to solidify its support among Brooklyn residents. It promised residents the development would create at least 50 percent affordable housing units; develop a comprehensive job training program that would create 8,500 permanent jobs; and that it would hire at least 35 percent minorities and 10 percent women during construction. Twelve years after this agreement, very few jobs actually materialized. The FCRC development is the perfect example of how private developers try to win favor from local politicians, labor unions, and community residents in order to get their projects approved. It took years of struggle and litigation and the threat of more litigation before the community coalition Brooklyn-Speaks achieved a settlement agreement with the State of New York, the city, and private developers.

This research also vividly illustrated how government efforts to promote environmentally sustainable development policies without incorporating an explicit social justice framework can lead to environmental gentrification, as discussed in Chapter 2. This is what is leading to the battles over development within San Francisco's Mission District. One of the biggest fights in the Mission District has been over a proposed 345-unit housing development (originally 303 market-rate and 42 affordable housing units) right above the

16th Street BART Station at Mission Street by Maximus Real Estate Partners, LLC.

This housing development represents exactly the type of transit-oriented development the City of San Francisco, the Metropolitan Transportation Commission (MTC), and the Association of Bay Area Governments (ABAG) are promoting in order to reduce greenhouse gas emissions under California's 2006 Global Warming Solutions Act and the 2008 Sustainable Communities and Climate Protection Act (referred to locally as AB 32 and SB 375, respectively). This state law drives local and regional policies crafted to create environmentally friendly and sustainable communities that reduce vehicle miles driven, increase walkability and transit ridership, and improve access to jobs and economic mobility. Advocates of transit-oriented development also highlight the potential for added value created through increased and/or sustained property value where transit investments have occurred (Reconnecting America, 2015).

From the perspective of longtime neighborhood residents, businesses, and community organizations, however, transit-oriented development without an explicit focus on equitable development that creates communities of opportunity is inadequate. The San Francisco case highlights this: Mission District residents are against the proposed large-scale housing development above the 16th Street BART Station not because they oppose environmentally friendly policies, but because they do not see how the development will integrate the needs of community members who were already living within the neighborhood. Many longtime community members see this development as one more step to increasing the neighborhood's population of affluent residents, resulting in higher rents, boutique shops, and expensive new trendy restaurants. Residents of the neighborhood and members of Calle 24 SF and their allies think that this development and others like it will ultimately lead to the displacement of less affluent long-term residents, businesses, and nonprofit organizations; pointedly, these residents refer to Maximus Real Estate's development as the "Monster in the Mission."

The impact of the economy's restructuring over the past several decades,[1] and the increased polarization between high-skill, high-wage jobs on one end and low-skill, low-wage jobs on the other, with a significant decline in middle-skill, middle-wage jobs, was equally evident in this work. As discussed in Chapter 2, there has been an increased demand for skilled workers despite a significant slowdown in U.S. educational attainment (Autor, 2010; Moretti, 2012). This storyline suggests that a shift over the past half-century from an industrial and physical manufacturing economy to a postindustrial economy centered around knowledge-based industries (such as the Internet, software, life sciences, and scientific research and development) has resulted in an abundance of high-paying knowledge- and information-based jobs within "innovation hub" metropolitan areas (Moretti, 2012). This demand for skilled labor results in increased income inequality as higher-wage earners earn five times as much as low-wage earners (Brookings Institution, 2010).

Of the four cities that I examined, nowhere was this bifurcated labor market more obvious than in San Francisco.

In San Francisco, billion-dollar technology firms have opened up new offices in the city and these firms have directly created thousands of jobs. The growth of the technology sector has also resulted in the indirect creation of thousands of jobs that support the technology sector and its employees (Moretti, 2012). As mentioned in Chapter 4, since the start of the Great Recession in December 2007, San Francisco has added more private-sector jobs than forty-seven of the fifty states (Mandel, 2014). Over the past four years, the city has added more than 67,000 private-sector jobs (a 15 percent gain), with the tech sector accounting for almost a third of those jobs (Mandel, 2014). In addition, it is estimated that the technology sector has been responsible for the creation of nearly 50,000 private-sector, non-tech jobs over the same period (Mandel, 2014). These jobs consist of construction, manufacturing, health and education, arts and recreation, and restaurants and bars (Mandel, 2014).

Unfortunately, not all residents have benefited from the growth of technology-related jobs, or from the overall economic boom happening in San Francisco, and it is increasingly obvious. The bifurcation in the labor market between higher-skilled, higher-wage jobs and lower-skilled, lower-wage jobs contributes to the growing and extreme income inequality in the city. The median household incomes in San Francisco differ significantly by race and ethnicity and zip code. According to 2012 American Community Survey Data, white San Francisco residents' median household income was nearly $21,000, or 27 percent higher than the median income for all groups. In stark contrast, Latino median household incomes were $20,000 or 25 percent lower than the median income for all groups. Native Hawaiians and Pacific Islanders trailed Latinos, with median household incomes more than $30,000, or 40 percent less than the median income for all groups. Blacks had the lowest median household income, at $44,000 or 59 percent less than the median household income for all groups. At the same time, San Francisco has the highest proportion of very wealthy persons (high net worth $30 million+) than any other city in the nation (ACS, 2012). This extreme disparity fosters extreme differences in lifestyle. On one hand, you have data from the Insight Center for Community Economic Development demonstrating that 38 percent of households with children in San Francisco cannot meet the self-sufficiency standard described in Chapter 2. On the other hand, you have extreme privilege and wealth, reflected in the media's commentary about everything from the high cost of housing, the high rate of private school attendance, and anecdotal evidence of the high cost of living – including the $4 toast featured on the cover of the October 18, 2014, edition of *Edible San Francisco*.

The growing inequality has severely impacted San Francisco's middle-class households. The middle class in San Francisco, defined as middle class by state and national standards, finds itself too wealthy to qualify for many of the city's social benefits programs and too poor to afford to purchase or rent a home and to pay for amenities and services such as childcare, transportation, medical care, and education. Between 1990 and 2012, San Francisco's middle-class households shrank from 45 percent to 34 percent, while the city's high-income population has grown modestly from 30 percent to 32 percent during the same time period. The Insight Center for Community Economic Development reports that 27 percent of households with children in San Francisco cannot meet the self-sufficiency standard but are above the poverty line.

The response of community coalitions: making strides, but still a long way to go

All of these macro-socioeconomic forces have resulted in community coalitions engaging in grassroots organizing to promote equitable economic development, improve environmental conditions, and push for social justice. The strategies these coalitions develop and implement are explicitly focused on helping local residents resist gentrification and neighborhood displacement. In the case of Boston, the Longwood Medical and Academic Area (LMA) anchored by Harvard Medical School and its teaching hospitals is constantly growing and expanding into the surrounding less affluent neighborhoods of color. This has created a contentious relationship between LMA institutions and community residents around gentrification and displacement, traffic congestion, and environmental pollution. My research found that the Jamaica Plain Neighborhood Development Corporation (JPNDC) and its community partners and allies were able to form a public-private partnership with local hospitals, medical facilities, and research institutions, which resulted in a community-focused workforce development program. In addition, JPNDC and its allies managed to work with state and city officials to be sure that residents received community benefits from development projects within the LMA.

Overall, JPNDC succeeded in promoting an equitable economic development agenda. The rapid increase in immigrants and economic changes in the neighborhood encouraged JPNDC to focus more attention on creating economic opportunities for local residents. One strategy was to link residents to good-quality, local jobs that provided opportunities for upward mobility. One obvious target was the growing number of health care jobs located within Boston's LMA.

JPNDC organized local residents and built an effective grassroots movement to demand good-quality jobs. It also started an effective jobs campaign, which highlighted the economic challenges and lack of opportunity for some of Boston's poorest residents. JPNDC succeeded because it was politically savvy and built collaborations across all sectors, with local community organizations, government agencies, elected officials, health care employers, and others in order to better advocate for local residents. These partnerships enabled JPNDC to acquire the necessary resources to make its work sustainable.

JPNDC was particularly successful because it also framed its constituents' needs clearly and concisely. It challenged the city and employers within the LMA to work with it to provide residents with access to good-quality jobs and job support services. JPNDC knew that the demographic trends in the neighborhoods meant that the city's political landscape was changing, therefore it was able to capitalize off this. JPNDC knew that elected officials did not want to ignore the economic and social needs of such an increasingly growing segment of the voting-age population, much of which consisted of Latinos, blacks, and other new Americans. JPNDC successfully got the attention of the mayor and elected officials, who in return placed political pressure on health care employers to hire local residents and also invest in community benefit programs.

Perhaps JPNDC and its partners' most significant accomplishment was the staff's ability to be entrepreneurial. JPNDC led the way in bringing various actors together to form a public-private partnership. It succeeded in forming a broad-based coalition of job training providers, community organizations, health care employers, social service providers, and labor unions, as well as educational and government agencies. JPNDC was not only successful at bringing a disparate group together, but it was a major player in the decision-making process with regard to the Training Institute. It advocated for good-quality jobs, worked with employers to define adequate career ladders, and encouraged hospitals and other health-related employers to focus on investments in community programs such as high school health care academies, community health outreach, and more.

The Boston case study demonstrates how Boston became one of the first cities in the country to tie economic development within the LMA to the level of investments made by LMA institutions (either financially or in kind) and to community-based outcomes for Boston's most disadvantaged and vulnerable residents. This case was particularly significant because the State of Massachusetts began mandatory community benefit reporting by nonprofit hospitals as part of maintaining their 501(c)3 nonprofit status. Massachusetts' health care model helped form the framework for President Obama's Affordable Care Act, which also has a community benefit policy for hospitals (Dokemer, 2011).

In the case of Brooklyn, New York, BrooklynSpeaks and its allies fought to ensure that the Atlantic Yards/Pacific Park development did not negatively impact neighborhood residents. Chapter 4 discussed residents' long-term struggle to hold the state, the city, and private developers accountable for the $4.6 billion Atlantic Yards/Pacific Park development project. More specifically, the BrooklynSpeaks community coalition was one of the leading voices advocating for environmental and social justice around the construction of the Atlantic Yards/Pacific Park development. A diverse group of civic associations, community-based organizations, and advocacy groups sponsored the BrooklynSpeaks effort. One of BrooklynSpeaks' strengths was calling on state and city government officials to be transparent. It was particularly concerned that elected officials were not transparent in their dealings with FCRC around the development of the Atlantic Yards/Pacific Park project. It felt that the community had been bypassed in the planning and development process because local government failed to involve the public in the decision-making process (BrooklynSpeaks, 2015).

BrooklynSpeaks, like JPNDC, was effective at getting its message out into the public. And like JPNDC, it was clear in articulating the community's demands. BrooklynSpeaks signed up thousands of supporters who helped to get its message out. The supporters were especially focused on demanding that the Atlantic Yards/Pacific Park development was integrated into the surrounding neighborhoods. This meant that the residents did not want to see the community's roads and thoroughfares cut off by this development. They also wanted the Atlantic Yards/Pacific Park development to include a transportation plan that benefited local residents. Most important, the leaders of BrooklynSpeaks wanted FCRC and its development partners to follow through on their promise to create 2,250 units of affordable housing.

Despite the long, eleven-year struggle, local residents and the Brooklyn-Speaks community coalition were *persistent* in their demands. Growing tired of waiting for the state and local governments to address their major concerns surrounding the Atlantic Yards/Pacific Park development, Brooklyn-Speaks and local residents began preparing to file a legal challenge against Forest City Ratner Companies and the Empire State Development Corporation under the 1968 Federal Fair Housing Act, which permits a claim for violation if there are discriminatory effects, even absent discriminatory intent. Eventually the coalition succeeded in achieving a settlement agreement with the private developers, the state, and city.

This agreement was not perfect, but considering how the Atlantic Yards/Pacific Park development was stalled because of the economic downturn in the economy, getting something was better than nothing. The settlement agreement sends the message to private developers and government that community residents should not be ignored in the planning and development processes. If public land and public subsidies are used for private development, then it is necessary for the government to ensure that community benefits are allocated to local residents. In addition, the settlement agreement was significant because it created an independent community development corporation charged with monitoring, evaluating, and reporting on the outcomes from the CBA. The Brooklyn case demonstrates that communities can hold government and private developers accountable for their actions and when they do, it is more likely that local residents will benefit.

In the case of San Francisco, the growth of the information technology sector, the lack of housing construction, government environmental policies aimed at encouraging transit-oriented development, and growing income inequality have created conditions that have negatively impacted less affluent residents and the middle class. The San Francisco metropolitan economy has remained exceptionally strong since the Great Recession, with much of this job growth driven by the technology sector. As a result, technology workers have been moving into less affluent neighborhoods such as the Mission District. This has led to a tremendous amount of tension between long-term Latino residents and the "techies." At the same time, middle-class waged jobs have declined over the past two decades and wages have remained stagnant. Therefore, middle-class families or individuals with a median annual household income between $50,000 and $75,000 find it nearly impossible to stay in San Francisco and have been leaving the city.

Although these challenges facing less affluent residents in San Francisco may appear intractable, Calle 24 SF, a community coalition that has successfully organized local residents and nonprofit organizations to advocate for more affordable housing, has also worked in partnership with the City of San Francisco to preserve the history and culture of the predominately Latino neighborhood. Calle 24 SF and its allies have placed pressure on the local city government to develop an affordable housing plan. In addition, city leaders are beginning to broaden the discussion about what exactly "affordable housing" is and who is benefiting from the housing being built in the City. Calle 24 SF and its allies are working with the city to explore policies and programs that could mitigate gentrification's effects and slow down neighborhood displacement. Calle 24 SF and its allies have recently called for a moratorium on market-rate housing in the Mission District until the community, in partnership with the city, can figure out a plan for the neighborhood to grow and also provide an adequate level of affordable housing.

The San Francisco case demonstrates that a broad-based, organized, grassroots community coalition can shape local government policies and push for more equitable economic development policies. Calle 24 SF has been able to enhance its political capital in San Francisco because it has succeeded in creating connections to city government, to the mayor, and to its local San Francisco board of supervisors. It has also mobilized a large Latino constituency, which traditionally has not been the most vocal in city politics. Calle 24 SF's ability to do this is already influencing the decisions made by the Mayor's Office of Housing, the Department of City Planning, and other city departments with regards to how issues related to housing and development are discussed and implemented.

Finally, the case study of Washington, DC highlights how the economic and demographic changes in the city have transformed the Columbia Heights, Logan Circle, and Shaw neighborhoods. This change appears to have happened overnight, but really these changes are in part the result of the city's efforts almost fifteen years ago to attract investment capital. The core part of the city's planning and economic development efforts focused on revitalizing neighborhoods that had experienced severe disinvestment over the past decades. Specifically, former Mayor Williams said he wanted to attract 100,000 new residents to Washington, DC by building strong and healthy neighborhoods. He called for citywide neighborhood revitalization, which led to the creation of Strategic Neighborhood Action Plans (SNAP). He also called on the city to direct investment into strategic neighborhoods, eliminate blight, enhance neighborhood commercial centers, and promote transit-oriented development (Brookings Institution, 2003). For example, the DC Office of Planning launched a neighborhood revitalization plan for the Shaw neighborhood called the "DUKE" Plan, named after the great jazz player Duke Ellington. As I mentioned in Chapter 6, the DUKE plan sought to attract development to the neighborhood by "capitalizing upon the area's historic context and emerging reputation as an arts and entertainment district" (DC Planning, 2011). The DUKE Plan had six guiding principles, two of which were of great significance – to promote transit-oriented development to encourage walking and to promote "cultural tourism initiatives based on the rich history of African-American historical and cultural assets of the area that [would] bring economic development opportunities for local residents and businesses" (DC Planning, 2011).

The local government in Washington, DC developed policies that provided financial incentives for private developers to build large-scale, market-rate, transit-oriented development in hopes that it would result in population growth for the city and increase its dwindling tax base. No one could have predicted how these government policies coupled with a strong regional economy would result in the intense gentrification of less affluent communities of color (Lees, 2003). As a result of these factors, Washington, DC has experienced a dramatic demographic shift resulting in a younger, more educated, and more affluent population. At the same time, housing prices and rents rose and the city is seeing an increase in new investments in infrastructure and local amenities (such as restaurants, parks, and bicycle lanes).

This has led many residents to criticize the outcomes of this development effort. Local writer Stephen Crockett captures the criticism of a city that simultaneously appears to celebrate its black heritage in its design but fails to keep its black residents in place: "all these places are based on some facet of black history, some memory of blackness that feels artificially done and palatable." He went on to ask rhetorically if it matters if the owners of these new developments were not black, or if it matters if these places opened around the time that blacks left the neighborhood. He also says that others may see it another way. "Indeed, some might argue that these hip spots are actually preserving black culture, not stealing it" (Crockett, 2012).

Unquestionably, the government of Washington, DC's planning efforts impacted the local economy and contributed to the demographics changes in the traditionally black neighborhoods in the city. The changes happening in the Logan Circle, Shaw, and Columbia Heights neighborhoods have been received with mixed reviews from the long-term residents, small business owners, and workers. Some residents view the changes as beneficial to the community, while others wonder why it took so long for these changes to happen.

This story of shifting demographics in Washington, DC raises complex issues. As non-blacks began moving to Washington, DC in the late 1990s and early 2000s, the majority-black, long-term homeowners had an opportunity to "cash in" on their property as it slowly appreciated in value. The influx of new residents and new investment presented many older black homeowners the choice of whether to sell their homes once the neighborhoods improved and property values rose. On one hand, selling allowed these longtime residents to finally get "the financial reward" due as a result of staying in the neighborhood all those years. But if they sold their homes, black homeowners faced the reality of being priced out of the market and having to leave their neighborhoods. This complicated dynamic has especially impacted the long-term, black residents of Washington, DC.

Despite this change leading to the gentrification of neighborhoods and to the displacement of long-term residents (voluntary and involuntary), a few organizations and community coalitions have attempted to advocate for the less affluent during this time of change. ONE DC, a membership-based community organization, focuses on promoting equitable development. The organization has developed an equitable economic development framework and is focused on preserving racial and economic equity in the Shaw neighborhood. ONE DC has been challenging the local city government to adopt an equitable development framework in its work and is demanding that community residents have more local control over the land use and community development process. This has resulted in some victories for the membership-based community organization such as negotiating a CBA with private developers around the large-scale, transit-oriented development above the Shaw-Howard U Metro Station. This has resulted in affordable housing, increased access to jobs, and job training programs for some of the neighborhood's most vulnerable residents. They were also instrumental in getting the DC City Council to pass the 2009 New Convention Center Hotel Amendments Act, which allocated $2 million for the recruitment of unemployed DC residents to participate in a job training and hiring program as well as an amendment to the city's First Source Law. Local residents, though, have not been hired for permanent jobs at levels anticipated.

Key lessons learned

This book provides examples of how community coalitions within four strong-market cities are attempting to bring about this type of change. The cases described and analyzed in this book are examples of the first step in neighborhood residents' efforts to fight gentrification and of neighborhood change deepening their roots. These efforts are also deepening the roots of a progressive national movement aimed at addressing racial and ethnic income inequality and advocating for economic, environmental, and social justice.

The case studies in this book show that to achieve these desired outcomes, the process is often messy and imperfect. The current economic, environmental, political, and social conditions within the United States make it difficult for community coalitions to develop a progressive political agenda and social movement around policies, programs, and strategies that benefit metropolitan residents across socioeconomic classes. But difficult is not impossible. To succeed, I observe that the process demands a number of factors at the local, state, and national levels.

1   *Think globally and organize locally: build your base from the ground up.*

The struggle to stay in place exists in numerous cities. It is important to understand the broader economic, market, and political forces impacting local neighborhoods across the country, and to observe the actions of those in government and those organizing on the ground. In all four cities studied in this book, however, community coalitions have had some level of success at reaching their goals **because they focused on organizing their bases, listening to community priorities, and building strong support from the ground up.** In Boston, JPNDC was initially set on helping local residents gain access to affordable housing; however, after holding community meetings and reaching out to residents, the organization realized that jobs were the number one priority. From there, the organization built a strong base comprised of community residents and nonprofit organizations. This enabled it to forge relationships with hospitals, government, and the private sector to help provide low-income individuals, most of whom were women of color with children, gain access to better-quality jobs.

In a world where money and private interests have influence within the democratic process, it is crucial for community coalitions and residents to focus on organizing those affected by the decisions or indecisions of government. Community coalitions' ability to build their bases of supporters can provide them with a louder voice and more political power; both are necessary to help them have more influence over local and state elected officials. It is critical for community coalitions to act locally because it is at the state and local government levels where some key decisions related to land use are made that shape housing and environmental policies. In some instances, this also applies to economic policies; local governments have the ability to enact living wage ordinances, which can provide positive benefits for low-income and working-class residents.

2   *Clearly articulate the community's needs and demands using an environmental and social justice framework.*

Another key lesson learned from analyzing the communities' efforts to resist gentrification and displacement in my case study cities has been their ability to **clearly articulate their needs and demands using an explicit environmental and social justice framework.** For example, in Washington, DC, ONE DC has been clear about its demands and what its community priorities are. It has developed a People's Plan posted on the organization's Web site that clearly lists its priorities. Similarly, in San Francisco, the community coalition, dissatisfied with the lack of community input into the city's planning process, developed *The People's Plan for Housing, Jobs, and Community* and presented it to the city. These similar efforts to articulate the communities' priorities by applying a social justice framework on a traditional governance tool are examples of effective ways to clearly present community priorities.

In addition, these community coalitions have **developed sophisticated communication strategies to get their demands out to the media and into the public.** For example, these community coalitions engaged in a number of actions such as writing letters to government officials describing their needs and demands, holding public protests to attract the media to their causes, and utilizing social media. In San Francisco, the community coalition fighting for affordable housing and other important issues held town hall meetings and staged public protests, including a "town hall" meeting at City Hall, which succeeded in shutting it down.

3   *Be willing to compromise and collaborate to achieve goals.*

There is no denying the importance of community organizations clearly articulating their needs and demands. For them to succeed, however, **they must also be willing to compromise and collaborate to achieve their goals** where appropriate. In every case study, some compromise was made. Compromising has become more difficult in our current hyper-polarized political and social environment; however, this is a necessary step that has to happen in order for the communities' goals to be realized. For example, in Brooklyn, some people have been critical of BrooklynSpeaks' settlement agreement with the state, the city, and private developers. But the settlement agreement actually helps to prioritize and speed up the affordable housing that was promised to residents along with several other community benefits. More important, by reaching a compromise, the community has a seat at the table to help monitor the community benefit process and evaluate the outcomes of the Atlantic Yards/Pacific Park development. The power of government to enact laws and policies that have the potential to benefit and protect the public interest should not be underestimated. Just as much as government can facilitate the gentrification process, it too can hold the private sector accountable for its actions. This does not usually materialize unless one of two situations occurs: 1) there is a charismatic, strong, and progressive mayor or elected official in a position of decision-making power who is willing to bargain hard for neighborhood benefits (the Harold Washington administration in Chicago or the Kucinich administration in Cleveland); or 2) an active community coalition is willing to apply pressure on government officials to adopt an equitable environmental, economic, and social justice agenda.

In some instances, getting some wins (even small ones) is better than getting none, or engaging in expensive protracted litigation that may not resolve the matter in the end. This does not mean that having firm needs and demands is not important; to the contrary, it is. But being willing to compromise in order to meet the majority of your goals, or at the very least to meet the most important goals, can result in significant benefits for the community and provide leverage for the next battle.

The ability to build relationships across sectors and institutions and around issues also creates the possibility for reconciliation over long-held grudges bridging divides. Take, for instance, Calle 24 SF's ability to build relationships with the mayor and other government officials and agencies. This community coalition–governance relationship has enabled the community organization to attract financial support for its cause as well as enhance its social and political capital within City Hall. The mayor and other city agencies helped support Calle 24 SF's efforts to develop a Latino cultural district and move it closer to becoming a designated special-use district. Moreover, examples such as Calle 24 SF show the benefits of community coalitions' building relationships with public institutional actors, nonprofit organizations, and the private sector. As long as these relationships are built on trust, transparency, and respect, they could likely result in bigger wins down the road for neighborhood residents, the city, and even the region.

4   *Public land and public subsidies that support any part of private development should require adequate and fair community benefits.*

Another key lesson learned from my case study analysis is that **in any situation where public land and/or public subsidies are used to support a private development project, the transaction should require adequate and fair community benefits for local residents.** In three of the four cases, there were clear examples of public subsidies and public land used to support public-private development projects. In situations like this, it is in the best interest of community groups to work in partnership with government to support community benefits and vice versa. In cases where the government does not cooperate, like in New York City, community coalitions and residents must pressure government to be transparent and accountable for its actions. History has proven that community residents very rarely benefit, if at all, from these types of projects with no requirements for local community benefits (such as local hiring ordinances and inclusionary housing ordinances). Unfortunately, the cases in this book demonstrate that local government and the private sector must be pressured to "do the right thing."

5   *A national movement that connects environmental activism to economic and social justice activism.*

In all four case studies, environmental policies and sustainable development are contributing to gentrification (or environmental gentrification) and possible displacement. In strong-market cities, local governments are encouraging dense, transit-oriented development and the revitalization of older, industrial parts of the city. From a purely environmental perspective, these policies are positive and can go a long way in reducing greenhouse gas emissions and slowing down the negative effects of climate change. Unfortunately, as mentioned earlier in this book, environmental policies and sustainable development can be problematic in the absence of a social justice framework for several reasons.

First, less affluent residents in neighborhoods undergoing revitalization and gentrification can be adversely impacted by higher rents and housing prices, which forces them to move further from the urban core. Second, as less affluent residents move further from the urban core, it increases their vehicle miles traveled to get to work. For example in the San Francisco metropolitan area, average commute times have increased over the years, placing San Francisco about 30 percent above the United States' average commute time (Taylor, 2015), leaving one to speculate how much of this is related to increased housing costs within San Francisco, and now, in surrounding cities such as Oakland, California (Taylor, 2015). This outcome reduces the whole purpose of transit-oriented development in the first place. For example in California, the state has passed laws requiring regions to reduce their greenhouse gas emissions and to link housing construction near transit stations or along transit corridors. In the San Francisco metropolitan area, this appears to be working well but has also hurt less affluent residents. In 2012, the state also eliminated redevelopment agencies, which provided a substantial amount annually to cities for the construction of affordable housing. Because this pot of money is no longer available, very little affordable housing is being constructed across the state, especially within cities with high land, labor, and construction costs.

Another reason environmental policies and sustainable development can be problematic in the absence of a social justice framework is because this usually results in revitalization that does not benefit local residents economically. Instead, these mixed-use developments tend to build housing and amenities, which meets the needs of the most affluent residents. These types of developments often result in the construction of tall, sleek, glass condominiums or apartments with high-end cafes, restaurants, and entertainment venues, well out of the reach for lower- to middle-class residents.

Therefore, **it is imperative that environmental activists and those advocating for economic and social justice join forces to make a difference in cities nationally.** These two movements have the potential to pack a real political punch and provide financial backing to support local, state, and national efforts aimed at addressing the housing affordability crisis, income inequality, and protection of the earth's natural resources. Having these two movements fragmented over issues related to race, ethnicity, and class only prevents both sides from making progress in addressing the larger external forces contributing to environmental degradation, racial and economic oppression, and income inequality.

National and local policies and strategies that can mitigate the negative consequences of gentrification and displacement

It would be naïve to think that the larger external forces shaping the current development patterns and income inequality within cities can be solved simply through community-organizing efforts at the local and national grassroots levels. A comprehensive set of national and local government policies, programs, and strategies is also necessary to bring about systemic and institutional change that results in substantial economic, environmental, and social justice for the least affluent and people of color in the United States. Also, as these case studies show, increasingly community members are developing strategies to be heard. Government can choose to hear those voices by engaging the community early in the planning process, and prioritizing economic, environmental, and social justice, or it can hear those voices through litigation and protests.

National housing policy and efforts to address income inequality are needed

All across the United States, especially within cities, vulnerable communities of middle-class residents are struggling to afford housing and to live in the city. Housing prices have outpaced wage growth, and cities and states are struggling to find the money to fund affordable housing. Even the notion that "affordable housing" refers primarily to those who live in public housing or who are part of HUD's Section 8 program is completely out of touch with today's realities. What is considered affordable housing today needs to be rethought and the federal government needs to set aside real money to support the construction of housing that supports working- and middle-class families. For some, the mere suggestion that the federal government should support a national housing policy is a nonstarter in today's economic and political climate. The Affordable Care Act, however, was viewed as nearly impossible to pass into law, but it happened and appears to be resulting in positive outcomes for people who had no health insurance before. Thus, those committed to economic, environmental, and social justice must advocate for a progressive national housing policy that declares it is a right for all Americans to have access to adequate, clean, and safe housing and the money behind it to back it up. After all, the right to housing is recognized in Article 25 of the Universal Declaration of Human Rights (UN General Assembly, 1948):

> Everyone has the right to a standard of living adequate for the health and well-being of himself and of his family, including food, clothing,

housing and medical care and necessary social services, and the right to security in the event of . . . circumstances beyond his control.

In addition, the federal government must address the growing income gap and income inequality that is prevalent in our strong-market cities. The government must continue raising the minimum wage so that workers can at least earn a living wage that allows them to support themselves and/or their families. The way things are now, local governments and some states have been taking the lead in advocating for higher living wages, but nationally we cannot afford to ignore how stagnant wages have had an adverse impact on the working poor and middle class. Middle-class families are losing their foothold within strong-market cities and hovering over poverty. At the same time, income inequality continues to grow. There are numerous efforts that can be taken to do this, but are beyond the scope of this book.

Local and state government actions that show promise

State and local governments can take a number of steps to mitigate the effects of gentrification, neighborhood change, and displacement. Policies developed by cities such as New York City and San Francisco have promise. Both cities are focused on building thousands of units of housing, with a significant proportion reserved for affordable housing. For example, San Francisco voters passed Proposition K, supported by Mayor Lee, by more than 65 percent, which requires the city to construct or rehabilitate at least 30,000 housing units. The legislation requires that more than 50 percent of the housing be affordable for middle-class households, with at least 33 percent of the units affordable for low- and moderate-income households. Any areas in the city re-zoned for housing construction will ensure that 33 percent of new housing is affordable to low- and moderate-income residents. In addition, Proposition K calls for the city to create a funding strategy to build new affordable housing, to purchase land for affordable housing, to preserve existing rental units, and to fund public housing rehabilitation. In May 2015, just a few months after announcing his initial $250 million bond measure, Mayor Lee proposed an additional $250 million for the construction of 3,000 affordable housing units to be built by 2030, potentially bringing the city's contribution to $500 million if voters support it during election time (Evangelista, 2015).

Mayor de Blasio's plan to spend roughly $41 billion to build and preserve 200,000 units of housing over the next decade is the most ambitious housing plan in the United States (de Blasio, 2014). Mayor de Blasio's plan aims to create neighborhoods that are diverse, that are affordable across a range of incomes, and that promote homeless, senior, supportive, and accessible housing. The plan calls for refining city financing tools and expanding funding sources for affordable housing. Some of the key specific elements of the plan call for implementing a mandatory Inclusionary Housing Program that will require a portion of the new housing developed to be permanently affordable to low- or moderate-income households in parts of the city that have experienced re-zonings. In addition, as mentioned earlier in this book, the mayor plans to develop affordable housing on underused public and private sites, similar to an initiative in San Francisco.

Mayor de Blasio has also introduced a new mixed-income housing program beyond the traditional affordable/market-rate housing split of "80/20." The mayor's mixed-income program calls for a pilot program that will target 20 percent of a housing project's units to low-income households, 30 percent to moderate-income households, and 50 percent to middle-income households (de Blasio, 2014).

At the state level, the government can increase its support for the construction and preservation of affordable housing. Many states provide direct financial assistance to housing developers for the construction of new housing. States working in partnership with the federal and local governments can use a combination of tax credits, grants, or low-cost loans to encourage the construction of affordable units (de Blasio, 2014). There are many other policies, programs, and strategies that can be deployed by local, state, and federal governments, which require going into great detail about the specific of each. But they are also beyond the scope of this book.

Final Thoughts

Ultimately, if things are going to change in a positive way for less affluent urban residents, they will have to continue building their base from the ground up, strengthening their community coalitions, and pushing ahead with strategies that contribute to programs and policies that enable local residents to resist gentrification and neighborhood change. It is political organizing and the building of strong community coalitions that can often keep other local actors (such as government or private developers) accountable to neighborhood residents. All strategies to advocate for community benefits, or curb gentrification, start with and depend on residents' power to stay organized and build broad multi-sector coalitions.

Note

1 This refers to technological change, decline in real wages, decline in labor union membership, increase in international trade and the offshoring of goods and services, and loss of manufacturing jobs.

Bibliography

American Community Survey. 2012. U.S. Census Bureau. www.census.gov.
Autor, D. 2010. *The Polarization of Job Opportunities in the U.S. Labor Market: Implications for Employment and Earnings*. The Hamilton Project report. Washington, DC: Center for American Progress.

Brookings Institution. 2003. *Neighborhood 10: Ten Strategies for a Stronger Washington.* PDF. Brookings Institution, April 17. Retrieved from www.brookings.edu/es/urban/gwrp/events/20030417_revitalizingdc.pdf.

Brookings Institution. 2010. *The State of Metropolitan America.* Washington, DC: Brookings Institution. Retrieved from www.brookings.edu/metro/StateOfMetroAmerica. aspx.

BrooklynSpeaks. 2015. About BrooklynSpeaks. BrooklynSpeaks. www.brooklynspeaks. net/about.

Crockett, Jr., S. A. 2012. The Brixton: It's new, happening and another example of African-American historical "swagger-jacking." *The Washington Post.* August 3. www.washingtonpost.com/blogs/therootdc/post/the-brixton-its-new-happening-and-another-example-of-african-american-historical-swagger-jacking/2012/08/03/b189b254-dcee-11e1-a894-af35ab98c616_blog.html.

DC Planning. 2011. *After the Duke Small Area Plan.* August 18, 2011. http://planning. dc.gov/sites/default/files/dc/sites/op/release_content/attachments/Duke_ASAP_8–18–11.pdf.

De Blasio, B. 2014. City of New York. Mayor Bill De Blasio. *Housing New York: A Five-Borough, Ten-Year Plan.* May.

Develop Don't Destroy Brooklyn (DDDB). 2005. Extell bids $150 million vs. Ratner's $50 million for the MTA's rail yards in Brooklyn. News release, July 25. www.developdontdestroy.org/bids/release.php.

Dokemer, D. C., et al. 2011. *Hospital Community Benefits after ACA: The Emerging Federal Framework.* The Hilltop Institute. University of Maryland, Baltimore County.

Evangelista, B. 2015. Mayor Lee ups ante with new $500 million affordable housing plan. *San Francisco Chronicle.* May 17. www.sfgate.com/bayarea/article/Mayor-Lee-ups-ante-with-new-500-million-6269570.php.

Fainstein, S. S. 2009. Mega-projects in New York, London and Amsterdam. *International Journal of Urban and Regional Research,* 32(4), 768–785.

Lees, L. 2003. Super-gentrification: The case of Brooklyn Heights, New York City. *Urban Studies,* 12, 2487–2510.

Logan, J. and Molotch, H. 1987. *Urban Fortunes.* Berkeley: University of California Press.

Mandel, M. 2014. San Francisco and the tech/info boom: Making the transition to a balanced and growing economy. *South Mountain Economics.* April. Retrieved from www.mikebloomberg.com/files/SouthMountainEconomics_SF_TechInfo_Boom.pdf.

Moretti, E. 2012. *The New Geography of Jobs.* New York: Houghton Mifflin Harcourt.

Oder, N. 2004. The culture of cheating: The failed promise of union apprenticeships. *Atlantic Yards/Pacific Park Report* (blog), July 10. http://atlanticyardsreport. blogspot.com/p/the-atlantic-yards-cba-promised-path-to.html.

Reconnecting America. 2015. www.ctod.org.

Tavernise, S. 2011. A population changes, uneasily. *The New York Times,* July 17. www.nytimes.com/2011/07/18/us/18dc.html.

Taylor, M. 2015. California's high housing costs: Causes and consequences. California Legislative Analyst Office. www.lao.ca.gov.

United Nations General Assembly. 1948. The Universal Declaration of Human Rights. December 10. www.un.org/en/documents/udhr/index.shtml.

Urban Institute. 2015. *"A History of Change." Washington DC: Our changing city.* Washington, DC: Urban Institute.

Weinberg, C. 2015. Mission moratorium proposal progresses, setting up next epic housing fight. *San Francisco Business Times*. February 23. Retrieved from www. bizjournals.com/sanfrancisco/blog/real-estate/2015/02/mission-moratorium-campos-sf-housing-crisis.html.

Index

Page numbers in *italics* refer to tables.

9; public-private partnerships
11; racial/ethnic discrimination
123; revitalization projects
7–8; sustainable 7; vulnerable
communities and 11, 51
urban growth coalitions 24–5
urban sprawl 16
USC Village 10
U.S. Department of Housing and Urban
Development (HUD) 12, 76
U.S. Department of Labor 28–9, 37
U.S. Department of Transportation
(DOT) 12
U.S. Environmental Protection Agency
(EPA) 12
U-Street Corridor, revitalization of 142,
144

Veconi, Gib 68, 71
very-low-income (VLI)/ extremely low-
income (ELI) households 93
vulnerable communities: affordable
housing 76, 92, 164; displacement of
67, 136; elderly 75; environmental
justice 103; exclusion of 25; health of
34; income inequality 164; large-scale
development and 9, 67; low-income
families 75; middle-income families
75; supportive housing 79

wages: decline in 13, 131–2; minimum
wage 136, 165; stagnant 75, 77;
wage growth 13, 165
Walmart 136
Washington (D.C.): affordable housing
122, 126–32, 134–6, 138, 142–3;
black history/culture in 126–9,
131, 158; black middle-class flight
from 121–2, 124, 130, 143; black
neighborhoods and 120–2, 126–31,
134, 158; Black Worker Center 135–
7; changes in 120–1, 127, 143; crack
cocaine epidemic 121–2, 143; crime
rates 121, 133, 143; demographic
shifts 120–1, 123–6, 128–31, 143,
150, 157, 159; disinvestment 121,
143; displacement 128–31, 133–5,
144, 159; economic growth 125,
128, 131; equitable economic
development 137–41; gentrification

128–31, 134, 158–9; homelessness
136, 142; income inequality 131–2,
144; investment in 122–3, 131;
labor market 133–4, 141, 144;
Latino neighborhoods and 122; local
government 121–2; local hiring 140;
as a majority black community 123–
5; millennials moving to 124–6, 130,
144, 150; mixed-use development
138, 141, 144; property values 124,
159; racial/ethnic discrimination
143; revitalization of 122, 124–5,
139, 144, 150, 158; strategic
planning efforts 123; transit-oriented
development 122–3, 131, 137–8,
141, 158; unemployment 140, 143,
145; unrest 120–1; white resident
flight from 121, 124, 143; workforce
development 138–9, 145 *see also*
Shaw neighborhood
Washington Metropolitan Area Transit
Authority 138
Weld, William 27
welfare reform 26–31, 48–9
welfare-to-work training programs
30–1, 40
Williams, Anthony 121–2, 144–5
Wilson, William Julius 124
workforce development: benefits to the
community 34, 42; Boston 26–7,
30–9, 42–6; career ladders programs
35; federal funding for 30–1; health
care industry 31–9, 42–4, 47–9;
living-wage jobs 139; local hiring 140;
Massachusetts 28–9; New York City
80; public-private partnerships 154–5;
training initiatives 26, 30–1, 40, 43–8;
Washington (D.C.) 138, 145
workforce intermediaries: advocacy 49;
base of support for 49–50; Boston
30–1, 40, 49; characteristics of 49
Workforce Investment Act (WIA)
(1998) 28–31, 36, 38, 48–9
workforce investment boards 28, 30
working-class population: affordable
housing and 56; displacement 1

Yuliang, Zhang 73

zoning codes 79